THE
NEW MIND
OF THE
SOUTH

D1363678

TRACY THOMPSON

FREE PRESS

New York   London   Toronto   Sydney   New Delhi

Free Press
A Division of Simon & Schuster, Inc.
1230 Avenue of the Americas
New York, NY 10020

First Free Press trade paperback edition March 2014

For information about special discounts for bulk purchases,
please contact Simon & Schuster Special Sales at
1-866-506-1949 or business@simonandschuster.com.

The Simon & Schuster Speakers Bureau can bring authors
to your live event. For more information or to book an event
contact the Simon & Schuster Speakers Bureau at
1-866-248-3049 or visit our website at www.simonspeakers.com.

Designed by Renata DiBiase

Manufactured in the United States of America

10 9 8 7 6 5 4 3 2 1

The Library of Congress has cataloged the hardcover edition as follows:

Thompson, Tracy.
    The new mind of the South / Tracy Thompson. — 1st Simon & Schuster
hardcover ed.
        p.   cm.
    Includes bibliographical references and index.
1. Southern States—Civilization—21st century.   2. Group identity—Southern
States.   3. Southern States—Race relations.   I. Title.
    F216.2.T47   2013
    305.800975—dc23   2012021581

ISBN 978-1-4391-5847-0
ISBN 978-1-4391-6013-8 (ebook)

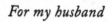

For my husband

CONTENTS

THE

NEW MIND

OF THE

SOUTH

1.

It's Complicated

Being a Southerner is a lot like being a Jew, and every bit as complicated. For starters, this means there is no such thing as "Southern culture"—only "cultures," plural, which range from the equivalent of the militantly Zionist (the neo-Confederate crowd) to the Hassidic (regular attendees of the Ole Miss–Alabama game, perhaps) and all shades in between. Jews and Southerners are both self-anointed chosen people—Jews in a religious sense, Southerners in a cultural sense. Both identities substantially overlap with a specific type of religion (evangelical Protestantanism, in the case of Southerners), though within those parameters there's lots of room for variation. Both identities are voluntary affiliations that can be either adopted or forsworn, even if the natal imprint is tough to erase completely. Jews and Southerners alike know what it is to be a kind of invisible minority in the culture at large, forced to smile politely as they hear themselves referred to in unflattering, one-dimensional stereotypes: I'll see your Jewish American Princess or Shylock, and raise you one Alabama hick plus a Bible-totin', evolution-denyin' school board member from Dogpatch.

1

Jews have Ashkenazi and Sephardic ethnic subgroups; Southerners come in two basic ethnic varieties—African American and Caucasian. Jews have their Diaspora; likewise, millions of Southerners have been forced to hit the road bound for the lettuce fields of California or the steel mills of Chicago. The Jews have their Babylonian captivity; Southerners have—well, slavery. Both groups have ample experience with poverty and deprivation, yet from this poor soil both groups have produced a disproportionate number of authentic and utterly idiosyncratic geniuses. Jewish culture has always placed an extraordinary value on intellectual achievement and scholarly pursuits; Southerners . . .

Well, okay. No analogy is perfect.

I am a Southerner. The Thompson family roots go at least six generations deep in the soil of Georgia, Alabama, and Tennessee (though a few hardy adventurers have made it as far west as Oklahoma). A Southern identity is something I can't imagine myself without, and yet I've spent much of my life trying to come up with a definition of exactly what that is. Southerners are Americans with an extra layer of identity—yet "no Southerner, so far as I know, has yet seen fit to write about the 'twoness' of Southerners," historian Carl Degler wrote a few years back, referring to W. E. B. Du Bois's famous remark about the "double consciousness" of being both black and American.[1] This seems incredible, given the lavish generosity Southerners have shown over the years in sharing their thoughts about their Southern-ness with the world—but it's true. Why? For one thing, because for much of the twentieth century Southerners themselves laid down such strict rules about what was and was not authentically "Southern"—and anyone tempted to tamper or find fault with those rules found that social ostracism was just the start of the punishments awaiting him. For another, it's been hard to lay down the burden of Southern history long enough to get a word in edgewise. Until quite recently, black people whose families had roots in the South as deep as mine were viewed one-dimensionally as just "black," not "Southern"—as if skin color made them magically immune to feeling affection for the place they called home; white Southerners were either racist Confederate flag-wavers, redneck comic relief, or apologetic liberals. If none of those roles appealed, you could try for Resident Southern Genius, but that was a very exclusive club to get into, or you could go into academia. Or you could just shove the whole thing into a mental drawer and get on with your life.

Most of us did just that, saving this subject for idle moments spent in the company of other Southerners when there was nothing better to talk about, a kind of intellectual Rubik's Cube. Then two things happened that made it newly relevant to me.

The first was an interesting story unearthed by a cousin in the course researching a Thompson family history. Among the nuggets of information he came up with was a set of papers on file at the National Archives referring to our common ancestor as a Union sympathizer during the Civil War. Thomas Thompson was a tenant farmer working a piece of land near the Chattahoochee River in what are now the southwest suburbs of Atlanta—in other words, deep in slave country, not in a border state or any well-known Southern pocket of pro-Union sentiment. According to his sworn testimony before a government commission in 1872, he had refused to support the Confederacy despite repeated harassment, imprisonment, and death threats. Toward the end of the war, he had been forced to leave the state in fear for his life, leaving his wife and children behind to make that year's crop, meaning they were on hand to greet General Sherman in August of 1864 when his army arrived to relieve them of their harvest, along with virtually all their other worldly goods.

All these years, this story had been sitting in the files of the National Archives; for all these years, no one in my extended family had ever heard of it—or if anyone had, had never spoken of it. My paternal grandmother, who had been born in Alabama just after the end of Reconstruction and thus had grown up with people who would have been eyewitnesses to these events, had never so much as hinted about any of this. Why would that be? Because nobody in my family wanted to believe it. The consensus was that Thomas Thompson had been trying to pull a fast one, posing as a Union loyalist in an attempt to get reimbursed for his lost property. Intrigued by the realization that most of my relatives would rather be related to a con artist than a Civil War–era Union supporter, I went down to the National Archives and did some more research. With very little effort, I turned up roughly two dozen similar cases just from the small county where these events had taken place. The documents were faded and hard to read, but the contents were vivid—stories of neighbor turned against neighbor, of entire networks of men hiding in the woods and farm wives who secretly fed them, of people who refused to fight for the Confederacy despite social ostracism, beatings, death threats, even being disowned by their relatives. And for what? The basic answer came in my ancestor's own words, carefully noted in a faded handwritten transcript preserved on microfiche: "I always was, am now and expect to be while I live, a Union man."

My family, *anti*-Confederates? I'd always wondered why,

unlike every other Southern family I knew, ours had no Civil War stories. It didn't surprise me that history had not noticed us, but how could we have not noticed history? Now it seemed clear that we had—and the family silence about it actually made sense, too: in the haze of nostalgia that burnished the decades following the war, claiming a connection with relatives who had opposed the sacred Lost Cause would have been claiming kinship with a traitor. Your kids would have been shunned; you might have gotten death threats.

This discovery was both fascinating and unsettling—like learning that some old family keepsake painting you'd had for decades had, in fact, been hanging upside down. These events had happened within a ten-mile radius of where I'd grown up. The people in these stories had stood on their porches in July 1864 and watched as a vast Union army appeared on the horizon—first a trickle of men and wagons, then more, until the landscape was a sea of men and tents and campfires and livestock stretching from one horizon to the other. "The field was plumb full of soldiers picking peas," one said. "The woods was perfectly blue with soldiers," said another.[2] I knew the road they had lived on; I'd passed the sites of those old homesteads hundreds of times. What I hadn't known was what had happened there. My keepsake painting wasn't just hanging upside down; it had been painted over. Now a different and more complicated painting was beginning to emerge.

And here's the interesting thing: when your past changes, your identity changes. People have an instinctive need to reconcile their image of themselves with their image of where they came from, and if necessary they will invent a past to make that happen. But for me, past and present had never quite lined up. I had known for a long time that the history I'd picked up from the adults around me was a confusing jumble of truth and hearsay and propaganda: *Sherman's men came right down this railroad* . . . *The war was about states' rights* . . . *The Yankees took everything we had and then some* . . . *They buried him out under the muscadine vines* . . . *Slavery wasn't all that awful.* I'd figured it didn't really matter; I'd leave the arguments about why the Civil War happened and what it all meant to the historians and the wingnuts who were still mad about it. Now it occurred to me that maybe the reason my identity had never completely made sense was that the history attached to it had never made sense, either.

The second thing that happened was the realization that my past was disappearing. I'd left Georgia for Washington, D.C., in 1989, an ambitious, single, career-minded newspaper reporter eager to start a new job at the *Washington Post*. Now I was middle-aged, married, and living in the Maryland suburbs, a mom who juggled the occasional freelance writing gig with household chores and schlepping kids to play dates and swim meets. Georgia was six hundred miles and two decades away. Yet at some deep level, it was still home. My earliest memories were of the grove of towering red oaks that stood across the cornfield from my bedroom window, right outside my grandparents' farm near Red Oak. My father was buried in Georgia; my sister still lived there; my mother spent her entire life within a twenty-mile radius of East Point. She died of heart failure in December 2005—and by some malign coincidence, about the same time bulldozers came and destroyed those amazing, century-old red oaks. The cornfield had long ago succumbed to pine trees and briars; after the bulldozers came through, it was cleared and paved. The place where I had grown up was now the site of a nondescript warehouse. But the past was still there. Under that asphalt lay the vestiges of my grandfather's muscadine vines and crab apple trees, the tar paper shack where his tenants had lived, the henhouse where my grandmother had tended her chickens. And not far away, an ancestor I'd never heard of had planted his own crops and feuded bitterly with his neighbors over the practical import of a constitutional question that, in one form or another, vexes our political discourse to this day.

I started out, then, with the idea of writing about this mismatch of history and identity that so many Southerners up through my generation have had, this vague sense of cognitive dissonance that comes with growing up in a world where nothing you see around you quite fits with the picture of history made available to you. When we said, "I am a Southerner," what did we mean? Specifically, what did it mean to be a product of a region so largely defined by race in a so-called post-racial era, when the nation had just elected its first African American president? And did it even matter? After all, writers and historians have been lamenting the death of Southern identity for fifty or sixty years now, though nobody can seem to get it to stay in its coffin. Polls consistently show a decline in the number of people who identify themselves as "Southern." But is that the slow death of a regional identity, or just a disinclination to be stereotyped? For something that's supposedly on its last legs—still—again—Southern identity seems remarkably spry: it keeps showing up at political rallies, in films, in literature, at NASCAR races and in music, to name just a few places. The media throws around the terms "Southerners" and "Southern" as if everybody knows what they mean; at the same time, those of us who actually *are* Southerners have made an enduring industry out of the search for a definition. Yes, I decided, it matters.

But the inquiry was an audacious undertaking, to put it mildly. In any generalizations about collective character "the possibilities for embarrassment are numerous," Southern historian C. Vann Woodward once wrote, and this is especially true of the South.[3] Without fully realizing what I was doing, I'd set out on a path littered with the bones of those who had gone before me—many of them famous, many of whom had never reached their destination. And so, to begin with, I started with a simple idea: a box labeled "Southern identity." The existence of this box dates from the earliest days of our nation, when the definition of "American" was still struggling for consensus, and in the beginning its contents were defined in opposition: the South was whatever the rest of the country was not. Some of those early distinctions were true and some were imaginary, but—as happens in families where one child is labeled "the smart one" while another is "the rebellious one"—they soon passed out of the realm of debate into the realm of perception and, to an unquantifiable extent, the realm of reality. Southerners were just different.

Okay, you ask; different how? What *is* in the box? That depends; the contents are always changing. The only constants are two great institutions that have defined the limits of the available contents: evangelical religion and slavery. The history of slavery in the South is like the tracks of an ancient river, clearly visible from a distance long after human habitation has made its outlines hard to discern up close. "The law may abolish slavery," Alexis de Tocqueville wrote in 1832, "[but] God alone can obliterate the traces of its existence."[4] Two hundred years later, God still hasn't gotten around to it. It's in the band of black poverty that curves up through the Deep South from New Orleans through South Carolina; it's in the black and white families united today by genealogical discoveries of century-old acts of rape and forbidden love affairs; it's in urban residential patterns that still bear the traces of decades of laws which sorted out neighborhoods according to the skin color of their residents.

"The South" was a concept born of the increasingly urgent need Southerners had to explain themselves, both to themselves and to everyone else, as the early-nineteenth-century Southern economy became entwined with and heavily dependent on the institution of slavery. In turn, "the South" as a concept birthed the Confederacy and an assertion of separate nationhood. The Civil War that resulted sent hundreds of thousands of farmers marching across disparate regions and transformed a collection of mountaineers, Virginians, Arkansans, and Georgians, among many others, into a group of people who adopted a common regional and political identity. Individually, they fought for a variety of reasons; collectively, they fought to preserve and expand an economic system based on slavery.

The Jim Crow system that arose after the Civil War was an effort to codify the social assumption of white superiority, which was the underpinning of the rationale for slavery. In turn, the civil rights movement was an effort by blacks to break free of the chains imposed on them by the Jim Crow era. The emergence of the Republican South in the 1960s was based on the need of Southern whites to assert the primacy of property rights and freedom from government intervention, which was a reaction to residential integration and school busing, which was born of the civil rights era, which came out of Jim Crow, which emerged from Confederate nationalism, which originated in the South's need to defend . . . slavery. Southerners eat sweet potato pie today because the sweet potato was imported into the South from Africa by slaves. The white columns of traditional Southern residential architecture are a reference to antebellum Southern architecture, which looked to classical Greece for inspiration because identifying with ancient cultures was an important part of the South's explanation and defense of . . . slavery. The line between "history" and "current events" in the South is notoriously hard to draw.

Then there's evangelical religion, which started out as antislavery but over the course of the nineteenth century became entangled in the spider's web of the South's "peculiar institution." Sectional splits among Methodists and Baptists in the 1840s were an omen of the war to come; biblical justifications for slavery helped to cement the image of a region and a people who were special, following a unique (and superior) understanding of God's will. In fact, the South *was* special: evangelical faith would eventually become a source of common ground for the nation's first truly biracial culture and the moral strength behind the movement to break the back of Jim Crow. "The Almighty has His own purposes," Abraham Lincoln said in 1864,[5] but you don't have to be a believer to conclude that mere mortals could not possibly predict the way history has unfolded in our part of the world.

So how to describe the current contents of The Box? Item one: Southerners are conservative people. Everybody knows this is true, but not everybody—including many of my fellow Southerners—understands why it's true, which is that the South is a region that has known more massive, wrenching social change than any other part of the nation. If Southerners place a high value on tradition, it's because tradition in the South is like beachfront property in an era of global warming: as much as you love the view, you live with the knowledge that some morning you will wake up and find it gone. People like the Amish, who actually have held on to many of their customs over the course of several generations, don't seem to feel the need to go on and on about their reverence for the past; Southerners can't shut up about it, which tells you something. As Southern poet John Crowe Ransom once wrote, "nostalgia is the complaint of human nature . . . when it is plucked up by the roots."

This failure to understand the reasons for our conservatism, in turn, means that Southerners are rarely given the credit they are due for sheer adaptability—item two. When Eli Whitney invented the cotton gin in 1793, Southerners took his new-fangled machinery and in just a few decades created the big-plantation model of agriculture, advanced cotton production several thousand years, and became a global economic power. This is a remarkable achievement by any historical standard. Granted, it was built on the backs of forced labor and caused environmental degradation on a staggering scale—but did it take smarts and industry? You bet. Yet to this day, a Southern accent is apt to brand the speaker as stupid and/or lazy. So deeply ingrained is this stereotype that Southerners have been known to apply it to other Southerners—something I realized I was doing one day while listening to a radio stock market analyst who spoke with a Tennessee twang. "What does *he* know?" I thought automatically, before I realized what I was doing.

And that leads me to item three: a lack of historical aware-ness. Popular conceptions of history are always riddled with myths, distortions, and strategic omissions, but the South takes the prize for the way it has assiduously cultivated, refined, and tended these distortions. Take the most obvious example: the Civil War. In the years leading up to the war, Southern leaders were outspoken and quite specific about what was at stake: S-L-A-V-E-R-Y. (You can look it up.[6]) Yet the ink was barely dry on the surrender papers at Appomattox before a new party line was born: actually, folks, slavery had very little to do with it; the issue was *states' rights*. Having settled that little detail, white Southerners then went about constructing a legal edifice of segregation laws that reinstituted slavery in all but name, while at the same time convincing others and themselves that it was *white* Southerners who had suffered most cruelly during the war and Reconstruction. It's interesting to ponder where the United States would be today if Great Britain had been one-tenth as talented at losing the Revolutionary War.

A corollary to the lack of historical awareness is a certain lack of self-awareness. Southern manners frequently come across as phony to outsiders for whom all those "hey y'alls" and "thank *yews*" sound canned and forced. For the most part, this is unfair. The "thank *yew*" that grates on the ear of the outsider is apt to be completely sincere; what the outsider is picking up on are the mixed signals emitted by a culture whose self-image is so fundamentally at odds with its true nature. Southerners are church-going folks with straitlaced morals—but it was a Jesus-loving mama's boy from Mississippi who came up with the radical idea of singing black music to white people, with pelvic gyrations too lewd to be broadcast on TV. People don't think of Southerners as technological envelope pushers, but it was a bunch of dumb Arkansas hicks who invented that sophisticated global retail distribution system we call Walmart. The South is supposed to be a region where conservative politics reign, but once the "conservative" South got through with the Republican Party, it had become a party with some radical ideas about eliminating government. And just when people think they've got a bead on what "the South" is, it changes again. Who would have thought that in 2008 those solidly Republican states of Virginia and North Carolina would ever go for an African American Democrat with an Arabic middle name? *Well, that's different*, the political pundits said; *Virginia and North Carolina aren't really "the South" anymore.* Wrong. They're as Southern as they ever were; they're just doing what the South has always done, which is to morph into something else when everyone—including us—least expects it.

Today the fastest-growing Latino population in the country is in the South—and not in Texas and Florida, but in Mississippi, Arkansas, Alabama, Georgia, Tennessee, and the Carolinas.[7] That exploding Hispanic population, combined with significant Asian immigration, black remigration, and natural population growth, has created a swath of majority-minority counties in the heart of the South's old cotton country, from deep in Mississippi up into South Carolina. After the 2008 presidential race, when many people noticed that the parts of the South that stayed Republican were overwhelmingly white, the prevailing political wisdom chalked it up to the usual suspects—those redneck racists. They didn't notice the fact that white Southerners under thirty voted for Obama at roughly the same rate (40 percent) as white Americans generally (43 percent).[8] And in a region that once led the nation in castrating and hanging black men merely suspected of looking at a white woman, the rate of black-white marriage and/or cohabitation is now comparable to that in the rest of the country. It wasn't so long ago that "Southern" was simply assumed to mean "white." Today, black people who live in the South are more likely than their white neighbors to identify themselves as Southerners.[9]

So: back to the existence of The Box. The reason libraries are full of books by Southerners endlessly explaining the South is that, in truth, we *are* special. Why? Because in the historical experiment we call American democracy, Southerners have been the beta testers. We're the ones who were given the task of working out the practical application of some lofty ideals—concepts such as "all men are created equal," for instance, or the idea that people with dark skin have the same right as anybody else to vote and to choose where to live—in an insular kind of environment where two very different groups of people were forced to live in close proximity. We failed. We failed miserably, in front of the whole world, and we had to deal with the consequences of our failure—and as a result, we learned some things. Southerners who have been paying attention have historical reference points that other Americans lack. It's not a big leap from modern proposals to require voters to produce some government-issued photo identification[10] to literacy tests of the Jim Crow era. The ins and outs of the immigration debate aren't that different from the contortions white Southerners once went through when they needed a minority group around to cook and clean and run a tractor, but didn't really want to think of them as citizens. The Occupy Wall Street Movement borrows its tactics from the civil rights movement, and its rhetoric bears more than a passing resemblance to the outrage of early-twentieth-century Southern populists.

And then, of course, there's race. When Wilbur Cash, from whose classic work *The Mind of the South* I borrowed the idea of a title, wrote that in the Deep South, "Negro entered into white man as profoundly as white man entered into Negro—subtly influencing every gesture, every word, every emotion and idea, every attitude," he was describing the forced mixing of three great streams of culture—one northern European, one African, one Native American—in an agricultural region insulated from the outside world, with results that were both toxic and miraculous. It's hard to imagine how that could have happened anywhere else; it's hard to imagine how it happened where it did. For that reason alone, the South matters to American history in a way matched by no other region of the country, and continues to do so.

So I set out to make sense of the South—and was immediately faced with a basic geographical question: where was it? "I am sitting in a diner in South Carolina," a friend from New Jersey e-mailed me once, "drinking iced tea that is so sweet I could pour it over my fucking pancakes"—and that strikes me as one definition: the South exists wherever people are putting sugar in their iced tea and not in their cornbread. But on second thought, I decided to stick with the eleven states of the Old Confederacy—Alabama, Arkansas, Florida, Georgia, Louisiana, Mississippi, North Carolina, South Carolina, Tennessee, Texas, and Virginia.[11] In recognition of some demographics which have changed drastically in the past century, I narrowed my map further according to some lines set by my friend Joel Garreau in his 1981 book *The Nine Nations of North America*, which shaved off the suburban Washington, D.C., counties of northern Vir-

15

ginia, everything in Florida south of Fort Myers, and everything in Texas west of a line drawn southeast from Dallas–Fort Worth down to Houston.

Then, having defined my territory, I set out to do some traveling. What lay before me was the enigmatic region I called home.

2.

Salsa with Your Grits

T wo dozen high schoolers sat behind tables arranged in a rough U shape in a back room of a strip mall in Asheboro, North Carolina, on a Saturday morning in early November. While their peers were hanging out with friends or sleeping late, these overachievers—with one exception, all children of Hispanic immigrants—had arrived by mid-morning for an all-day high school leadership seminar sponsored by the Randolph County Hispanic Association. As I sat on a folding chair in a corner trying to be inconspicuous, Randolph County High School teacher Yacine Kout led a discussion about the terms used to describe immigrants in political discussions these days: *Freeloaders. Gangbangers. Anchor babies.* These stereotypes aren't just names by which others may define you, he told the students; if you're not careful, they are also ways in which you may start seeing yourself. As an exercise, he asked the students to think of some word that defined them, then to come up with a way in which they did not fit the standard definition of that word. Out of the babble of answers, one voice rose above the rest.

"I am a Mexican," said one of the students. "My parents are from Mexico, but I was born here."

"So how many of you were born here in North Carolina?" I asked, and two-thirds of the group raised their hands. "How many of you consider yourselves Southerners?" There was a moment of dead silence, then a burst of hilarity. Born and raised in the South? Check. Southerners? Not hardly.

In all of the hair-splitting debates about what is and is not "Southern," there's always been one commonsense rule you could count on: a person born and raised in the South was a Southerner, QED. These kids had never heard of that rule. When I told them I was doing some research on the growing Hispanic population in the South, it was news to them that they were *in* "the South"; to them, this was the *north*. Besides, North Carolina did not fit even the few hazy mental images they had of "the South," which to them meant dirt roads and cotton fields, the Confederate flag and oppressed black people sitting in the back of a bus. They'd seen a few Confederate flags, but North Carolina was seriously deficient in dirt roads, cotton fields, and segregation. It was all very perplexing. "Maybe this is borderline South," one student finally suggested.

As the South heads into the second decade of the twenty-first century, the venerable debate about what constitutes "the South" and how to define "Southerner" has run into a complication it hasn't seen in roughly two centuries: an incoming wave of people from Somewhere Else. Between 1990 and 2000, North Carolina had the fastest-growing immigrant population of any state in the country. Georgia came in second, Arkansas fourth, and Tennessee a close sixth. In North Carolina, the number of foreign-born residents increased from a little over 115,000 in 1990 to roughly 614,000 in 2000—a mind-boggling 274 percent.[1] The vast majority of the North Carolina newcomers were people from poverty-stricken rural Mexico who slipped across the border to find work in the hog farms, poultry plants, and furniture factories of the Tar Heel State. Throughout the South, immigrants from Mexico and Central America account for most of the increasing foreign-born populations, but other ethnic groups have contributed as well, especially immigrants from Vietnam, China, Pakistan, and India. The newcomers have shown up wherever the economy has boomed, whether it is cleaning office buildings in suburban Atlanta, beheading chickens in rural Alabama, or working in the dockyards in Gulfport. Post-Katrina New Orleans by itself accounted for a tidal wave of illegal immigrants from Mexico and Central America who arrived to work in construction jobs.

In 1990, the proportion of foreign-born residents in the South as a whole averaged 2 percent, compared to the national average of 8 percent. Today, almost 20 percent[2] of the population of Asheboro, a middling-sized city in the rural north-central part of North Carolina, is Hispanic—the overwhelming majority of them Mexican. And even though the rate of Mexico-to-U.S. immigration appears to have stopped or even reversed in the past year or so,[3] Hispanics make up 8 percent of the total population of North Carolina, a state where for generations the only non-African or non-Caucasian face anybody ever saw was that of the occasional transient farmworker. They make up 8 percent of Georgia's population, too. In fact, Hispanics make up roughly 5 percent of the whole population of the Deep South, not counting Texas and Florida,[4] and Arkansas, Georgia, North Carolina, and Tennessee lead the nation in increases in live births to Hispanic mothers.[5] Southerners need no longer dream of someday taking a vacation in Mexico; Mexico has come to them—and is putting down roots. In the words of Paul Cuadros, a journalism professor at the University of North Carolina who has studied and written about the Hispanic influx into North Carolina, "The second generation is already here. That's what most people don't realize."

All this, of course, means The End of Southern Culture As We Know It. *Bienvenido al siglo 21,* y'all.

Strictly speaking, of course, everybody but Native Americans is from somewhere else—but in the South, the imprint of seventeenth- and eighteenth-century European immigration is clearer than it is anywhere else in the United States. The reason is simple: between then and just a few decades ago, the South was a place where immigrants simply did not go, at least not in any numbers. The traces of two centuries of relative isolation can be seen in the preponderance of old English names in Tidewater Virginia, French in southern Louisiana and coastal South Carolina, Spanish on the Gulf Coast, German in Texas. Settlers who came from the poverty-stricken Celtic fringe—lowland Scots, Irish, and people from the six counties of northern England— settled in the Piedmont South and in Appalachia, where their descendants (including lots of Thompsons) live today. The earliest black Southerners were mostly from Senegambia, Sierra Leone, west-central Africa, and the Gold Coast and became forced labor in the rice and cotton plantations of the coastal and Deep South; today, the legacy of that historical movement survives as the crescent-shaped region called the Black Belt, which starts in the Mississippi Delta and stretches through southern Alabama, Georgia, and to the South Carolina coast.

True, the South has always had its cosmopolitan enclaves—New Orleans, Savannah, Charleston—and there have been trickles of foreigners over the years. After the Civil War, some plantation owners tried importing Italian and Chinese laborers to do the work that African slaves had once done; to this day, you'll find a surprising number of Chinese-owned businesses in the Delta, and an occasional Mississippi good ol' boy named Malvezzi. Part of the wave of Vietnamese immigrants who came here after the end of the Vietnam War in 1975 settled on the Gulf Coast and created a thriving Vietnamese community. But these are exceptions to the rule. Just before the Civil War, only about 5 percent of the population in the South was foreign-born.[6] The great waves of immigration in the nineteenth and early twentieth centuries went north or west, and for good reason: compared to spending all day in 90 degree heat picking cotton with bleeding fingers, eighteen-hour shifts in a textile mill looked pretty good.

For most of the twentieth century, while the American patchwork of skin tones began to feature growing patches of brown and yellow, the South stayed locked into its black-and-white color scheme—and in an era of eugenics and the glorification of certain Aryan ideals, Southerners considered their situation a natural selling point. Businessmen courted Northern investors with flyers advertising their region's "non-unionized, Anglo-Saxon work force" (translation: malnourished crackers who work cheap). If anything, it looked for a time as if the region was trending monochromatic: the biggest internal migration of people in American history involved the hundreds of thousands of black sharecroppers who escaped the South's poverty and the inequities of Jim Crow to look for jobs up north. Up through the 1960s, there were more black people leaving the South than moving into it.

The relative dearth of foreigners in the Deep South in effect encased Southern identity in bubble wrap for much of the twentieth century. If Southerners made a big deal about feeling different from other Americans, somehow set apart, it's because in a very literal sense we were. "Of all the Americans, the Southerner is most at home in the world," wrote James McBride Dabbs. "Or at least in the South, which because of his very at-homeness, he is apt to confuse with the world."[7] What Dabbs was describing in 1964 was the South of my childhood: a binary, white-bread-or-cornbread kind of world in which the human race was divided into black people, Southerners, and the occasional outsider. (The assumption that "Southern" equals "white" still lives, believe it or not: an analysis of the 2008 presidential election in the *New York Times*, for instance, rested on a definition of "Southern" that specifically excluded the Black Belt. It also failed to include the diversity of the so-called suburban South—i.e., North Carolina and Virginia.[8] Evidently, "authentic" Southerners are rural white people. Who knew?) Most of the people I knew growing up even shared the same basic Protestant evangelical religion; to us, a "mixed marriage" meant a Baptist marrying a Methodist or, God forbid, a Catholic. One of my earliest memories is of seeing an Indian woman in a sari walking through the Atlanta airport, a blur of red and purple against a sepia background of people staring at this exotic creature from another land. And this was in Atlanta, which at the time made a big deal about being a cosmopolitan kind of place.

Today, Atlanta really *is* a cosmopolitan place. The Buford Highway corridor on the Northside of the city is home to a thriving polyglot community of Mexicans, Salvadorans, Vietnamese, Thai, Indians, and people from the Caribbean nations; on the Southside of town, where I grew up, a Hindu temple has replaced what used to be a cow pasture on Highway 85 in Riverdale. Tucked away in the pine woods a few miles away is a trailer park of Hispanic residents big enough to qualify as a municipality in itself—just one of dozens like it throughout the country. A sizable Pakistani community has settled in and around Jonesboro, and there's a mosque half a block from the courthouse on the main square in Fayetteville. East of the city, the DeKalb County Farmers Market—founded in 1977 as your basic roadside produce stand—is now 140,000 square feet of produce, coffees, chocolates, grains, and cheeses from all over the world. These scenes are being repeated on varying scales in places like Raleigh-Durham, Charlotte, Nashville, and Little Rock.

Southerners like to portray the South as a region that's resistant to change, but the only tradition here is of change that comes quickly and with stunning force. Immigration is a classic example. While it's too soon to tell for sure, demographers say the incoming wave of economic migrants from Latin America alone is looking similar in size and scope to the Great Migration of blacks from the South in the early twentieth century—and that, as you may remember, has been called the greatest internal migration of people in U.S. history. However, this being the South, this historical event also has some unique features. For one thing, it's made up primarily of people from a single country—Mexico—most of whom are undocumented workers, having either crossed the border illegally or overstayed their visitor visas. (Legal immigration from Mexico to the United States is impossible for all except the well-to-do with a decade or so of time to kill. For a Mexican citizen to gain permanent legal entry to this country, he or she must be a parent, spouse, or sibling—biological or adoptive—of a U.S. citizen who has filed a petition on the applicant's behalf; even then, due to the immense backlog of cases, it can take years for the petition to come up for review, and legal fees run into thousands of dollars.)

In the past, newcomers to this country have tended to head for cities, but much of this immigration is rural-to-rural: small farmers driven out of business by the cheap agricultural imports that have flooded Mexico since the 1995 North American Free Trade Agreement leave home to find jobs in the rural Southeast. A look at a map of Latino population settlement in the South shows that it is about evenly divided among rural, suburban, and urban areas. The dispersal is driven by the fact that Southern cities don't have the long-established ethnic enclaves of, say, Chicago or New York, so the newcomers go anywhere they can find affordable housing. Historian Tom Hanchett has coined the phrase "salad bowl suburbs" to describe these areas, where a Latino grocery, a Korean nail parlor, an African American beauty supply store, and a Vietnamese restaurant may all share the same strip mall.

In recent years, the rate of immigration has slowed as the Great Recession has taken its toll. In North Carolina, the local furniture industry is moribund and the textile mills have had massive layoffs. But the immigrants who came for those jobs in the 1990s have stayed, for the most part, and when the jobs left they set about creating their own—opening the hair salons, car repair shops, restaurants, and *tiendas* that now dot the main roads through Asheboro. I was able to find authentic Mexican pastries fresh from the oven in a roadside *panadería* on the outskirts of Biscoe, North Carolina (population 1,700). And while the newcomers were figuring out ways to make a living, they were also having kids: Hispanic women have, on average, 2.5 children, compared with 2.0 for blacks, and 1.8 for whites and Asians.[9] In Asheboro, the seat of Randolph County, 34 percent of the 4,613 students enrolled in the city school system in the 2010–2011 school year were Latino.[10] Most of their parents are illegal immigrants; most of the children are U.S. citizens.

And totally assimilated—at least to all outward appearances. The Hispanic teenagers I talked to in Asheboro were indistinguishable from their Ugg-shod, skinny-jeaned Anglo counterparts, except for their ability to switch effortlessly between Spanish and English in ordinary conversation. They text, play video games, listen to rap and reggae, and are fluent in hip-hop gestures; their vocabulary is a fascinating mix of English, Spanglish, Spanish, and African American idioms ("I be hungry")—with an occasional "y'all" thrown in. But they definitely don't think of themselves as Southerners—or even completely American, given the fact that extended family in Mexico is only a text message away. And beneath their superficial similarity to native-born North Carolinians, these kids are equipped with very different cultural reference points. Cynthia Martinez, who teaches ESL students at East Montgomery High School in Biscoe, not far from Asheboro, told me that one day she and her Hispanic students were talking about the 1960s-era American involvement in Vietnam, battling the Vietcong. She pointed to a character in the textbook—an obviously non-Caucasian man dressed in black pants and a black tunic, wearing sandals. What nationality would that man be? she asked her class, and one student said "Mexican."

"Oh, come *on*," she prodded.

"It could be," the student insisted. "Mexicans are everywhere."

So. How are Southerners taking it? Not well. In 2011, Alabama passed what is generally considered to be the toughest immigration law in the nation, authorizing police to check the citizenship status of every person they pull over for any traffic violation (the first person pulled over turned out to be a German-born Mercedes-Benz executive) and making it against the law to, among other things, enter into private contracts with illegal immigrants. Georgia and South Carolina quickly adopted similarly stringent laws; all were promptly challenged in court by civil rights groups, who argued that they were legal mandates for racial discrimination. That's an argument you will hear in major urban areas and/or university towns, and farmers say these laws have had a disastrous effect on their labor supply. But overall, the rapid increase in numbers among Hispanics strikes a deep nativist nerve. Outside the Black Belt and urban areas, the South is solidly Republican—and for Republicans, immigration is a subject that begins and ends with the issue of border control. To a lot of Southerners, these Mexicans in their midst are living proof that the federal government is unable to do one of the few things it's actually *supposed* to do, which is to keep people from slipping over or under the national fence.

Supporters of the new immigration laws say they have nothing against Hispanics personally; as one exasperated native North Carolinian put it, "We want people to come to America and better themselves, but you know what? Come through the *front* door." In the next breath, though, they will launch into a litany of complaints that have nothing to do with legal status and everything to do with lifestyle. They leave litter all over the place. They cram three families into one house. They park their beat-up cars on the front lawn. They play soccer on the neighborhood football field and leave it torn up. They make too much noise. Asheboro Police Department major Ralph Norton has been called to more than one exuberant Latino party. "I've had people look at me like I'd grown a third eye," he said. "They say, 'You can get *arrested* for loud music?'" A cashier at a roadside fruit stand in neighboring Montgomery County summed up the prevailing mind-set when she told me sadly that the influx of Mexican immigrants in her area "have taken this place downhill." When I asked how, exactly, she said, "They're a drag on the schools and the social services."

And that's the number two objection, coming in a close second to their legal status—the widespread perception that illegal immigrants all sign up for free medical care via Medicaid the minute they pile out of the coyote's minivan. The free medical care part is not true. At most, illegal immigrants get Medicaid coverage for life-threatening emergencies and for women who are in active labor; in addition, some counties have clinics that provide routine medical care to all comers—Anglo, Mexican, Yankee, or good ol' boy—on a sliding-fee basis. And even illegal immigrants pay taxes, in the form of sales tax. Still, the cashier lady's argument was partly correct. A 2007 Congressional Budget Office analysis showed that state and local governments do indeed end up spending more to provide basic health services and education to immigrant families than those families' incomes generate in taxes.[11] That's especially true in counties like Randolph and Montgomery, which are predominately rural and which have received a disproportionate share of the Hispanic immigration into the state. You can argue that educating children is a good long-term investment, and other studies show that nationally, immigrants generate more in federal taxes than they use in social services. But those dollars go to the federal government, not the counties[12]—and none of this is much consolation to the local property owner who is having to fork over more taxes today to educate the offspring of some person who slipped under a fence to get here.

Then there's the perception that Latinos are the cause of rising crime rates. This is part of the time-honored American tradition of characterizing all newcomers as lowlifes: the incoming Scotch-Irish in the eighteenth century were considered "the scum of all nations"; Irish immigrants of the 1840s were supposedly wife beaters and drunkards; Italian newcomers in the 1920s were supposedly a bunch of thieves; German Jews who came to this country in the nineteenth century were vilified as, well, *Jews*, and they were in turn horrified by the déclassé Eastern European Jews who arrived several decades later. So: *do* illegal aliens cause a spike in crime rates? In particular neighborhoods, maybe; overall, no. Crime rates in the United States actually have been on the decline for the past decade among all groups. A 2009 Pew Hispanic Center report did conclude that Latinos accounted for more than 40 percent of all federally sentenced offenders, more than triple their share of the population. But a lot of those federal offenses were immigration violations, which is hardly a surprise, and there was no data on rates of violent crime, which is usually prosecuted under state law.[13]

With no reliable statistics to go on, I asked a local expert—the aforementioned Major Ralph Norton of the Asheboro Police Department. A native of Randolph County, Norton began with the department in the early 1990s as a patrol officer, then worked in narcotics before being promoted to major. From his experience as a beat cop and a narcotics officer, he concluded that Asheboro's Latinos were no more or less apt to break the law than anybody else—and when they do, their victims are usually other Latinos. Any other perception is due, he thinks, to simple observer bias: with immigration in the news so much, any crime that involves an illegal immigrant gets heavy local news coverage. "People see and hear about that tiny tenth of one percent that's doing something bad. That's what gets the headlines. But 99.9 percent of them are living within the law."

When I was in Asheboro, the local police were not asking for proof of legal residency when they stopped someone for a driving violation, but many of the neighboring municipalities were doing so. For undocumented workers anywhere, any contact with law enforcement could mean the difference between seeing one's children for the next couple of years or not—and fairly or not, rural Southern sheriff departments have a certain reputation for using motor vehicle laws to oppress minorities. This may explain why "profiling" was a subject mentioned by every single Hispanic person I talked to in the first five minutes of our conversation. More than half of the seventy-one state and local law enforcement agencies currently cooperating with federal authorities in an effort to identify illegal immigrants are in the Deep South, and even before the passage of draconian anti-immigrant laws in Alabama, Georgia, and South Carolina, states in the South were quietly enacting a list of statutes designed to make life unpleasant for illegal immigrants. In Georgia, undocumented immigrants are barred from receiving any kind of public benefit and from working for any governmental entity. Mississippi barred them from working, period; in South Carolina, illegal immigrants were prohibited from enrolling in any state university or community college. Even in North Carolina, which has a reputation of being relatively friendly to immigrants, they can be kicked out of a community college class in favor of a U.S. citizen if enrollment exceeds classroom capacity.

The unfriendliness comes even from fellow Latinos who came to this country via legal means. More than once when speaking with a legal immigrant about some issue involving illegal immigrants, the conversation would detour back to the personal details of the legal immigrant's entry into this country—the time and expense it had taken for him to get a U.S. visa, the long family separations he endured. The unmistakable subtext: *Some of us followed the rules.* Juan Rios (Panamanian by birth, a permanent legal resident), a teacher at Asheboro High School and a founding member of the Randolph County Hispanic Association—which is composed mostly of members of the local Mexican community—told me that most of the donations to his group come from Anglos.

Yet even in the midst of so much anti-immigrant sentiment, I still would hear expressions of grudging respect, and sometimes from the most conservative people. Jimmy Walker, the owner of an agricultural equipment manufacturing company in Clarksdale, Mississippi, is a die-hard Republican who listens daily to Rush Limbaugh, but he is in awe of his Latino employees, especially the Mexicans. "The Mexicans come here and they work so hard they by God *create* their jobs. They're just unbelievable, their work ethic," he told me. "They work all the time and send their money home. We've got an ultraconservative radio station here, and they spend a lot of time talking about immigrants. Their main deal is those guys are taking jobs from other people. It's not true. They take a lot of jobs other people here just won't do."

Pro-immigrant or anti-, though, most Southerners I talked to were of the opinion that the influx of Hispanics—and Asians, and Russians, and all the other foreigners—spells the beginning of the end of everything they consider traditionally Southern. Seeing *"Lavandería"* on a storefront instead of "Laundromat," the sound of Spanish conversations in the grocery store, statues of the Virgin of Guadalupe in a neighbor's front yard—it all seems alien, incompatible with the South they are used to. And it is.

"I look at Siler City today—it's 50 percent Hispanic, maybe more. The median age for whites in Siler City is forty-one. The median age for blacks is thirty-five. The median age for Latinos is twenty-five. That's the story right there," said Paul Cuadros, who has written a book about the influx of Latinos into Siler City, North Carolina.[14] "In terms of identity, of what the South is going to be, you look at those demographic trends and you know it's not going to be what it was."

But is The End Of Southern Culture As We Know It the end of the South?

Judging from the past century or so, maybe not. The South

has been disappearing for so long that predicting its demise is an academic and journalistic cottage industry. In the 1960s, we went around this particular barn when Southern historian C. Vann Woodward bemoaned the post–World War II "bulldozer revolution" that was bringing an end to the agrarian South of his youth. In the 1970s, the growing suburban sprawl produced by those bulldozers brought many professional South watchers to the conclusion that "Dixie" had been replaced by something called "the Sunbelt"—a nebulous region with Southern antecedents and a Southern climate, but which in every other way was thoroughly assimilated into mainstream American culture. In his 1974 book *The Americanization of Dixie: The Southernization of America*, journalist and historian John Egerton described a homogenized landscape of chain restaurants and shopping centers, characterized by "an obsession with growth and acquisition and consumption, a headlong rush to the cities and the suburbs, diminution and waste of natural resources . . . increasing depersonalization, and a steady erosion of the sense of place, of community, of belonging."[15] It definitely sounded un-Southern.

And yet, the very existence of Egerton's lament was evidence of *some* kind of continuing difference: nobody was bemoaning the effect of suburban sameness on the character of, say, Des Moines. If anything, the South's presence in the national picture seemed to grow as the 1970s progressed: a Georgia peanut farmer was elected to the White House, country music bypassed pop in national tastes, NASCAR became a national sport, and grits became a standard of haute cuisine. Today, McDonald's sells sweet tea from coast to coast (though it's not very good sweet tea). Thirty-two years after Egerton's gloomy assessment, the author conceded that he'd been wrong. "I have cobbled to-gether a modestly successful career by predicting the imminent demise of the South," Egerton told an academic conference at Emory University in 2006, "and the only thing that's kept me in the game is its refusal to die."[16]

Still, even the Roman Empire eventually did fall, and "the South" really is going to die someday. Will immigration suc-ceed in doing what war, the civil rights movement, and an army of real estate developers have failed to do? Whenever I talked to people who were the most adamant that these immigrants meant the end of all things Southern, I'd ask them what, specifi-cally, seemed to be fading, and how immigration was killing it. The answer usually revealed the Southern genius for living in an imagined past where racial tension was nonexistent, strang-ers would stop to help if you had a flat tire, white people were sweet to black people and black people loved them right back, and everyone went to church on Sunday.[17] "I see a love of family, a respect for parents, dwindling away," one North Carolina lady said. "I see chivalry dying"—as if the rural Mexicans who were now living in her part of the country did not come from a cul-ture that was as conservative as her own, just as family-centric, and with its own cult of honor.

In fact, the really interesting thing about Hispanic immigra-tion into the South is not the spectacle of cultures clashing, but the spectacle of cultures merging. Many of the Mexicans who have moved to North Carolina since the 1990s are country folks—conservative in politics and sexual mores, churchgo-ing, tightly connected in a network of extended family. Self-sufficient but far from rich, they ran small family farms, growing things like beans, corn, and tomatoes in a countryside of green, rolling hills. In North Carolina, what do they find? A surprising amount of the same, and vestiges of a time when the similarities were even greater than they are today. A few years before my visit to Asheboro, Ralph Norton and a group of civic leaders from there traveled to the central Mexican state of Puebla, where many Asheboro's current residents came from and where Norton said he was surprised to find himself feeling right at home. "It was slightly more hilly than Randolph County, but the terrain was very similar," he said. "If you shut your eyes down there, you'd think you were in the same county." In a way, it was like traveling through a time warp, he said; his parents started out as sharecroppers in a small town in rural Randolph County, and the poverty he saw in rural Mexico looked very much like what he saw as a kid in parts of rural North Carolina forty years ago.

Cuadros (Peruvian by birth, longtime U.S. citizen) sees other affinities. "I see a similarity of pride from Mexicans and Southerners, especially Southern males. Mexicans are all about pride—their country, themselves, their manhood. Southerners are like that, too—and they can be just as stubborn." Mexican and Southern cultures share a love of the melodramatic and a fascination with magical realism; when I asked a roomful of Hispanic teenagers in Asheboro if anybody had ever heard of *Gone With the Wind*, I got an enthusiastic yes. "I just love that book," several of the young women said; clearly, it was as much a part of their adolescent reading as it had been to me in 1960s Atlanta—a point of similarity I had not expected. On the highbrow end, William Faulkner is huge in Latin America; writers like Gabriel García Márquez and Isabel Allende, among many others, have acknowledged Faulkner's influence on their own work. In academia, Hispanic immigration into the South is helping to revitalize the field of Latin American studies, as scholars explore similarities between the class- and race-conscious plantation colonialism of the American South and the class- and race-conscious plantation colonialism of, say, Cuba, Haiti, Mexico, or Brazil.

There are political affinities, too: many Latinos who crossed the border as children but who have spent most of their lives in the United States instinctively identify with the disenfranchised black community of the pre–civil rights era South. The nonviolent ethos that Martin Luther King Jr. adapted from Mahatma Gandhi serves today as a template for youthful Hispanic activism on behalf of the DREAM Act—a proposed federal law that would allow immigrants who came to this country illegally before the age of sixteen a chance to earn permanent legal residence and, eventually, American citizenship by completing at least two years of college or serving two years in the military. Support for the DREAM Act is passionately felt among the Hispanic teenagers I talked to in Asheboro, in stark contrast to the prevailing public sentiment in the South. (At last count, Southern senators and congressmen are against the DREAM Act by a margin of about two to one; what support there is comes from those black Southerners in Congress.) At a leadership seminar for high school students sponsored by the Randolph County Hispanic Association, 90 minutes or so was devoted to last-minute lobbying efforts to get support before Congress adjourned in November 2010, via tactics modeled on the Montgomery, Alabama, bus boycott of 1955.

"Rosa Parks's act wasn't spontaneous, but part of a huge strategy," political activist Nayely Perez-Huerta told the stu-

dents, pounding home the theme that nothing in political lobbying matters so much as organization, numbers, and working
the phones. "So how many of you are willing to take action?
Stand up." All but two of the kids in the room stood. In the
babble of voices, I overheard one boy say, "Where *is* Montgomery? Is Montgomery in this county?"

"It's in Georgia," another one assured him. Fuzzy as they
were on geography, these kids were fired up. After breaking up
into small groups to brainstorm, the students reconvened to
discuss their ideas: texting their friends and urging them to call
their congressman, promotional spots on Hispanic radio stations, a Facebook campaign, making announcements in church,
proclaiming a "white shirt day" at school where students could
demonstrate their support. The enthusiasm was contagious; at
that moment, almost anything seemed possible. "If the African
Americans did what they did, we can, too," one young woman
said. When the group dispersed, it was 2:30 in the afternoon,
and the parking lot was full of parents in cars, waiting to take
the students away.

The following week, the DREAM Act failed to reach the
Senate floor, ending its chances for passage anytime soon. But
in that back room of a small North Carolina office park, I saw
a generation of Hispanic youth being schooled in civil rights
activism—and, in the process, acquiring some indelible impressions about the relative merits of the Democratic versus the Republican Party. Who knew what purpose their new knowledge
might be put to in the years to come, what passions it might
ignite? If I were a Republican, especially a Southern Republican,
I would be thinking about that.

• • •

So what does all this mean for Southern identity in the future?

My grandmother had a rueful saying she would trot out when someone inquired after the state of her arthritic knees or how she was recovering from the flu: "I'll live, but I'll never look as well." Southern identity will survive all this, but it'll never look as well—at least not the Confederate flag-waving, "Dixie"-singing school of Southern identity most people today associate with that phrase. Numbers from the Southern Focus Poll, a survey administered yearly by the University of North Carolina between 1992 and 2000, combined with the results of a similar poll conducted in 1971 by sociologists John Shelton Reed and Glen Elder, show that while a hearty majority of around 70 percent of people who live in the South say they identify themselves as Southerners, throughout the last decade of the twentieth century the percentage was slowly but steadily declining. But the rate of decline varied widely among groups. It was steepest among those under thirty-five, among middle-class people who lived in urban areas, and among those who also identified themselves as political liberals; it was barely noticeable among people who lived in rural areas, among lifelong residents of the South, and among members of nonmainstream religious denominations. Among Republicans and the most affluent, it hadn't declined at all. But the prevailing demographic trends in the South point the other way: more people are moving to suburban and urban areas, the baby boom is aging, and the birth rate among minorities is higher than it is for whites. In that sense, immigration may well be the beginning of the end of Southern identity—at least, this particular version of it.

And that might save us from ourselves. For two centuries or so, Southerners have based our identity on *not* being like the rest of our country, and we celebrated our self-imposed internal exile with monuments to the victims of a Lost Cause and the glorification of its generals. But once immigrants enter the picture and the frame on the big picture becomes global, the outsize importance we have placed on that one piece of our identity begins to shrink. We can ditch forever the idea that the Confederate experiment was the crucible of Southern identity; we can finally lose our obsession with being different from other Americans and start seeing our similarities to other peoples of the world—to the Scots or the Irish, in possessing an identity independent of nationality, or to the Québécois, in our stubborn refusal to give up our particular way of talking, or to the Kurds, in being a group of people who belong to a particular subgroup of a major religion.

More important, a Southerner is an American whose history is not the standard triumphalist "we're number one" narrative many foreigners associate with Americans, which could be a huge boon to U.S. foreign policy all by itself. Leaving aside the complex and highly politicized debate over immigration reform, the Latinos now living in the South are here, the vast majority of them are law-abiding, and short of some deportation program that would load them up on boxcars and ship them back to Mexico en masse, they are here for good. Making peace with that fact and learning to think about our common points of reference with other cultures offers a way for today's Southerners to lose the last vestige of the historic defensiveness that is at the bottom of every attempt to minimize the importance of slavery in our past. On the other hand, a past that is fully acknowledged and understood makes Southerners uniquely relatable to people in cultures with tragic pasts of their own. A Southerner, for instance, can empathize with Japan's history of provoking a war out of hubris and for the wrong reasons, and suffering catastrophic defeat as a result. Southerners understand—really, *really* understand—the pain of dealing with the historical legacy of apartheid in South Africa. It's not a huge stretch to see parallels between the political activism of women in Islamic countries today and that of those nice Southern church ladies, black and white, in the early twentieth century who united to oppose lynching.

And just as Hispanics will change the South, the South will change them. "People select the South as a place to live because they think it's a better place," historian Tom Hanchett said. When it comes to the traditional Southern values of "food, faith, and family," he said, "the Latino folks we've talked to say, 'Those are our values, too, and we are pleasantly surprised to find them surrounding us here.' And that's how you create Southerners." The process can take as little as one generation: Nikki Haley, the governor of South Carolina, and Bobby Jindal, governor of Louisiana, are first-generation Americans born to immigrants to the Deep South who came from India. Sooner or later, the DREAM Act will pass, and a new generation of Latino leaders will emerge.

Will they call themselves Southerners? I think a lot of them will, whether they realize it now or not. The students I saw in Asheboro are teenagers, and their identity is still in flux. But looking around, I see subtle signs of infection. Latin influences on country music in the South go back a long way—anybody remember those trumpets in Johnny Cash's "Ring of Fire"?— and nowadays the influence seems to be going the other way: it's hard to find a mariachi band these days that can't do a very respectable version of "The Orange Blossom Special." During a mid-morning break in the Hispanic youth leadership seminar in Asheboro, I noticed several of the students heading for a big jug of good old Southern sweet tea, and one or two had a perceptible North Carolina twang when they spoke English. Can salsa with grits be far behind?

During a break in the seminar, I was talking to Yacine Kout, the Randolph County High School teacher who led the discussion on stereotypes. Kout is a native of France with a toddler-aged son, a beautiful boy with curly black hair Kout and his wife named Odysseus—because, as Kout said to me, "who knows what voyages he will make in his lifetime?" Kout told me about one of his students, a first-generation Mexican American who had recently come back from a trip to New York City. The kid had been disappointed because there wasn't a single place in the Big Apple where he could find what he craved, which was a bottle of Cheerwine. What's Cheerwine? I asked, and learned that it's a cherry-flavored soft drink that for most of the twentieth century has been produced and sold in North Carolina and nowhere else. Kout wasn't surprised I'd never heard of it. Cheerwine is one of those things you wouldn't know about unless you were a native Tar Heel.

3.

The Big Lie

In the course of our conversation, Yacine Kout mentioned something else—an incident that had happened the previous spring at Eastern Randolph High School just outside Asheboro. On Cinco de Mayo, the annual celebration of Mexico's defeat of French forces at the Battle of Puebla in 1862, a lot of Hispanic students brought Mexican flags to school. The next day, Kout said, white students brought Confederate flags to school as a message: *This is* our *heritage.*

The Civil War is like a mountain range that guards all roads into the South: you can't go there without encountering it. Specifically, you can't go there without addressing a question that may seem as if it shouldn't even *be* a question—to wit: what caused the war? One hundred and fifty years after the event, Americans—at least the vast majority who toil outside academia—still can't agree. Evidence of this crops up all the time, often in the form of a legal dispute over a display of the Confederate flag. (As I write, there are two such cases pending—one in Oregon and the other in Florida, making this an average news week.) Another common forum is the classroom. But it's not always about the Stars and Bars. In 2010, for instance, Texas school officials made the news by insisting that Jefferson Davis's inaugural address be given equal prominence with Abraham Lincoln's in that state's social studies curriculum. The following year, Virginia school officials were chagrined to learn that one of their state-adopted textbooks was teaching fourth graders that thousands of loyal slaves took up arms for the Confederacy.[1]

At the bottom of all of these is one basic question: was the Civil War about slavery, or states' rights?

Popular opinion favors the latter theory. In the spring of 2011, in recognition of the 150th anniversary of the start of the Civil War, pollsters at the Pew Research Center asked: "What is your impression of the main cause of the Civil War?" Thirty-eight percent of the respondents said the main cause was the South's defense of an economic system based on slavery, while nearly half—48 percent—said the nation sacrificed some 650,000 of its fathers, sons, and brothers over a difference of interpretation in constitutional law. White non-Southerners believed this in roughly the same proportion as white Southerners, which was interesting; even more fascinating was the fact that 39 percent of the black respondents, many of them presumably the descendants of slaves, did, too.[2]

We pause here to note that wars are complex events whose causes can never be adequately summed up in a phrase, that they can start out as one thing and evolve into another, and that what people think they are fighting for isn't always the cause history will record. Yet, as Lincoln noted in his second inaugural address, there was never any doubt that the billions of dollars in property represented by the South's roughly four million slaves was somehow at the root of everything, and on this point scholars who don't agree about much of anything else have long found common ground. "No respected historian has argued for decades that the Civil War was fought over tariffs, that abolitionists were mere hypocrites, or that only constitutional concerns drove secessionists," writes University of Virginia historian Edward Ayers.[3] Yet there's a vast chasm between this long-established scholarly consensus and the views of millions of presumably educated Americans, who hold to a theory that relegates slavery to, at best, incidental status. How did this happen?

One reason boils down to simple convenience—for white people, that is. In his 2002 book *Race and Reunion*, Yale historian David Blight describes a national fervor for "reconciliation" that began in the 1880s and lasted through the end of World War I, fueled in large part by the South's desire to attract industry, Northern investors' desire to make money, and the desire of white people everywhere to push "the Negro question" aside. In the process, the real causes of the war were swept under the rug, the better to facilitate economic partnerships and sentimental reunions of Civil War veterans.

But an equally important reason was a vigorous, sustained effort by Southerners to literally rewrite history—and among the most ardent revisionists were a group of respectable white Southern matrons known as the United Daughters of the Confederacy.

The UDC sounds like one of those genteel ladies' organizations that would have quietly passed into oblivion about the time women ditched their girdles and entered the labor market, but they are still around—a group of about twenty thousand ladies dedicated to various educational and historical preservation causes. Since 1955, the UDC has recruited next-generation members through a young persons' auxiliary called the Children of the Confederacy,[4] which does similar kinds of work. Blight was surprised when I told him in an e-mail that as part of my research I planned to visit the 2008 C of C convention in Fredericksburg, Virginia. "I knew there used to be such an [auxiliary] organization decades ago but did not know that it still exists," he replied. "Amazing. How I would like to be a fly on the wall there."

The significance of the UDC lies not in its present-day clout, which is negligible, but in its lasting contributions to history—both for good and for ill. From its inception in 1894 up through the 1960s, the UDC was the South's premier social and philanthropic organization, an exclusive social club where the wives, sisters, and daughters of the South's ruling white elite gathered to "revere the memory of those heroes in gray and to honor that unswerving devotion to principle which has made the Confederate soldier the most majestic in history," as cofounder Caroline Meriwether Goodlett grandly put it.[5] At first, the UDC provided financial assistance and housing to veterans and their widows, offering a vital public service at a time when for all practical purposes most local and state governments in the South were nonfunctional and/or broke. Later, as the veteran population aged, the UDC built homes that allowed indigent veterans and their widows to live out their days with some measure of dignity. Long before there was such a thing as the National Park Service, the UDC played a crucial role in preserving priceless historic sites, war cemeteries, and battlefields across the South. At the same time, it embarked on a spree of monument building: most of those Confederate monuments you can still find in hundreds of courthouse squares in small towns across the South were put there by the local UDC chapter during the early 1900s. In its way, the UDC groomed a generation of Southern women for participation in the political process: presidents attended its national convocations, and its voice was heard in the corridors of the U.S. Capitol.

But the UDC's most important and lasting contribution was in shaping the public perceptions of the war, an effort that was begun shortly after the war by a Confederate veterans' group called the United Confederate Veterans (which later became the Sons of Confederate Veterans—also still around, and thirty thousand members strong). The central article of faith in this effort was that the South had *not* fought to preserve slavery, and that this false accusation was an effort to smear the reputation of the South's gallant leaders. In the early years of the twentieth century the main spokesperson for this point of view was a formidable Athens, Georgia, school principal named Mildred Lewis Rutherford (or Miss Milly, as she is known to UDC members), who traveled the South speaking, organizing essay contests, and soliciting oral histories of the war from veterans, seeking the vindication of the Lost Cause "with a political fervor that would rival the ministry of propaganda in any 20th century dictatorship," Blight writes.[6]

Miss Milly's burning passion was ensuring that Southern youngsters learned the "correct" version of what the war was all about and why it had happened—a version carefully vetted to exclude "lies" and "distortions" perpetrated by anti-Southern textbook authors. To that end, in 1920 she wrote a book entitled *The Truths of History*—a compendium of cherry-picked facts, friendly opinions, and quotes taken out of context, sprinkled with nuggets of information history books have often found convenient to ignore. Among other things, *The Truths of History* asserts that Abraham Lincoln was a mediocre intellect, that the South's interest in expanding slavery to Western states was its benevolent desire to acquire territory for the slaves it planned to free, and that the Ku Klux Klan was a peaceful group whose only goal was maintaining public order. One of Rutherford's "authorities" on slavery was British writer William Makepeace Thackeray, who visited Richmond on a tour of the Southern states during the 1850s and sent home a buoyant description of the slaves who attended him: "So free, so happy! I saw them dressed on Sunday in their Sunday best—far better dressed than English tenants of the working class are in their holiday attire."

But presenting the "correct" version of history was only half the battle; the other half was preventing "incorrect" versions from ever infiltrating Southern schools. Before the Civil War, education was strictly a private and/or local affair. After the Civil War, it became a subject of federal interest. The first federal agency devoted to education was authorized by President Ulysses S. Grant in 1867, and Congress passed several laws in the 1870s aimed at establishing a national education system. White Southerners reacted to all this with a renewed determination to prevent outsiders from maligning the reputation of their gallant fighting men by writing textbooks especially for Southern students. One postwar author was none other than Alexander Stephens, former vice president of the Confederacy, whose portrayal of the war sounds remarkably like the version you hear from many Southerners and political conservatives today: it was a noble but doomed effort on the part of the South to preserve self-government against federal intrusion, and it had little to do with slavery. (This was the same Alexander Stephens who had proclaimed in 1861 that slavery was the "cornerstone" of Southern society and "the immediate cause of the late rupture and present revolution.")

As the UDC gained in political clout, its members lobbied legislatures in Texas, Mississippi, North and South Carolina, and Florida to ban the purchase of textbooks that portrayed the South in anything less than heroic terms, or that contradicted any of the Lost Cause's basic assertions. Its reach extended not just to public schools but to tenured academia—a little-known chapter of its propaganda effort is detailed by James Cobb in his 2005 book *Away Down South: A History of Southern Identity*. Cobb recounts how in 1911, for instance, University of Florida history professor Enoch Banks wrote an essay for the *New York Independent* suggesting that slavery was the cause of secession; Banks was forced by the ensuing public outcry to resign. Perhaps Banks should have seen that coming: seven years earlier, William E. Dodd, a history professor at Virginia's Randolph-Macon College, had complained that to merely suggest the Confederacy might not have been a noble enterprise led by lofty-minded statesmen "is to invite not only criticism but enforced resignation." Dodd himself would later migrate to the University of Chicago, where he established a Northern outpost for Southerners who were interested in a serious examination of Southern history. Such scholarship was not encouraged back home: the first postwar society of Southern historians was created in 1869 for the explicit purpose of vindicating the Confederate cause.[7]

The fear of losing one's job worked to keep most dissenters in line, but if that failed, self-appointed censors in the community were always on the lookout. In 1913, for instance, the Sons of Confederate Veterans succeeded in banning from the University of Texas history curriculum a book that they felt offered an excessively New England slant on recent history. The UDC industriously compiled lists of textbooks used in schools across the South, sorting them into one of three categories: texts written by Northerners and blatantly unfair to the South; texts that were "apparently fair" but were still suspect because they were written by Northerners; and works by Southern writers. Outside academia, the New South creed, popularized by Atlanta newspaper editor Henry Grady in an effort to spur economic development, also reinforced this new orthodoxy. A big part of Grady's canny public relations was to pay extravagant homage to the imagined splendor of the antebellum South, and to portray the New South as a revival of that genius instead of what it really was: the rise of a whole new class of plutocrats.

If all of this wasn't enough to stifle all public debate and intellectual inquiry in the decades after the war, other prevailing conditions might have finished the job: the widespread poverty of those decades, the rise of Jim Crow and the need to maintain the belief in white supremacy, a pervasive religious mind-set that put a higher value on faith than on reason. There were more thoughtful voices, of course—in Atlanta, W. E. B. Du Bois was writing brilliantly about the black experience and Reconstruction. But the racism of his day postponed his wider influence to a later era. For all but the rich and/or socially elite this was the South that H. L. Mencken lampooned as "a stupendous region of worn-out farms, shoddy cities and paralyzed cerebrums"—far more concerned with the next meal than with intellectual inquiry. Among white Southerners, rich or poor, the universally accepted history was the version that would later find fame in Margaret Mitchell's 1936 novel *Gone With the Wind*—a book that sold millions, was translated into twenty-seven languages, and has probably had a more lasting influence on public perceptions about the South to this day than any other single work. It's no wonder that the so-called Southern Renaissance of the 1930s happened outside academia, in the field of fiction; as Cobb points out, the people least interested in understanding Southern history at that time were Southern historians, and Blight agrees. "It would have been impossible to grow up in the South from 1890 to World War I and not have heard or read [the Lost Cause version of history] many times over as the common sense of white Southern self-understanding."[8]

I would quibble with that last part; the era when this was "the common sense of white Southern self-understanding" lasted at *least* until 1960, very conservatively speaking, and its legacy thrives to this day. In an era when any assertion of "fact" is met by noisy counterassertions of competing "facts," it's hard to grasp how completely this warped version of history was accepted as gospel in the South, as silly to dispute as the law of gravity. Former *New York Times* correspondent John Herbers is an old man now, living in retirement in Bethesda, Maryland, with his wife, Betty. But when he was growing up in Mississippi in the 1930s and 1940s, "the Lost Cause was one of the main themes my grandmother used to talk about: 'Slavery was nothing to do with the Civil War—we had a cotton economy and [the North] wanted to dominate us.' It was an undisputed topic." At the time, he accepted this version, as children do;

today, he is struck by the vigilance with which adults in his world implanted this story in the minds of their children. "They pushed themselves to believe that," he said. "If [the war] had anything to do with slavery, they had no ground to stand on."[9]

Claude Sitton, another Southerner who covered the civil rights movement for the *New York Times*, remembers participating in a yearly essay contest sponsored by the UDC when he was a high school student in Rockdale County, Georgia, in the early 1950s. I did not encounter the UDC essay contests when I was a student in public schools in the 1960s, but the things I heard from my mother could have come straight from Miss Milly's approved textbooks. History books were unfair to the South, she told me, so I was not to believe anti-Southern things I might read in them, and she was vigilant about correcting me if she heard me use the term "the Civil War" in conversation. To call it a civil war was to concede that secession was impossible and/or unconstitutional—something no self-respecting Southerner should ever do. "The proper name," she would say, "is The War *Between the States*." Her reminder to me was nothing out of the ordinary; millions of Southern schoolchildren of my generation had absorbed such messages, as had several generations before us. "As late as the 1970s, neither textbooks nor curricula veered far from Lost Cause interpretations, especially in the Deep South," writes historian Karen L. Cox[10]—and in his book on the Civil Rights era in Mississippi,[11] historian John Dittmer concluded that the Lost Cause version of post-Civil War Reconstruction in the South still held sway among the vast majority of whites in that state as recently as the early 1990s.

Die-hard defenders of some version of the Lost Cause today say that the South has always been the victim of "political correctness" in school textbooks, and that this continues to this day. The truth is just the opposite: for decades, publishers of school textbooks went out of their way not to offend delicate Southern sensibilities in their treatment of the Civil War. One longtime publishing executive told me that when he got into the business in the 1960s, it was common to see two different versions of school history textbooks—one for in the Deep South and one for everywhere else, "and the difference was how you treated the Civil War." By the mid-twentieth century, even textbooks that did not repeat the UDC party line still tiptoed carefully through the minefield. Take this passage, for example, from a widely used 1943 high school history textbook, which depicts a slave-holding South of stately mansions and benevolent slave owners: "The Confederates . . . believed they were fighting for the democratic principle of freedom to manage their own affairs, just as the thirteen colonies had fought in the Revolutionary War."The same textbook describes the Ku Klux Klan as a group that "sometimes" resorted to violence in its effort to retake local governments from the hands of incompetent former slaves.[12] A 1965 textbook used in Alabama public schools taught another key point of the Lost Cause creed—that slavery was a benign institution: "In one respect, the slave was almost always better off than free laborers, white or black, of the same period [because] the slave received the best medical care which the times could offer."[13]

Publishers don't offer a special "Southern" version of history anymore; these days, they cater to individual state educational standards, though some states—like California and Texas—have a disproportionate national influence on what those standards are. The problem today, the former publishing executive told me, is that "with so many state standards, the books have become in the last ten years longer, blander, more visual, certainly—and more inclusive. There's so much to cover." The result is like light beer: better tasting, less filling. With no space to truth-squad a 150-year-old public relations campaign, today's texts simply strive not to offend; they don't perpetrate the Lost Cause myth, but they don't do much to correct it, either. Take this passage from a text widely used in public high schools today, which neatly splits the difference between the "states' rights" and the "slavery" camps: "For the South, the primary aim of the war was to win recognition as an independent nation. Independence would allow Southerners to preserve their traditional way of life—a way of life that included slavery."[14] That's a way of putting it even Miss Milly might have been able to live with.

"I grew up in a cocoon," Herbers says today, recalling his childhood and the version of history he absorbed. It's an apt metaphor for what happened to any Southerner born before about 1970, and to a good many of those born since. Although the field of Southern history underwent a revolution at the university level in the 1940s and 1950s, the version ordinary Southerners knew in 1970 and even later had not changed appreciably since 1900. Perhaps 1970 sounds like a long time ago, but in educational terms it's not: 1970 was when a lot of people who are still teaching today learned what they know, and what they've passed on to their students. James Loewen, a sociologist and author of *Lies My Teacher Told Me*, has said that when he speaks to public school educators across the country today, somewhere between 60 and 75 percent say that the Civil War was fought over the issue of states' rights. Whether the group he's speaking to is predominately white, predominately black, or racially diverse, the percentage stays roughly the same.[15]

The Southern version of history also prevailed for decades at Civil War battle sites, thanks to the fact that Congress appropriated money for the National Park Service, and Southerners in Congress had their hands on the purse strings. It wasn't until the 1990s that the Park Service—under pressure from the academic community and a few members of Congress—made it a priority to revamp its exhibits to "interpret [the Civil War] and the causes of the war based on current scholarship," said Dwight Pitcaithley, a professor of history at New Mexico State University who was chief historian of the Park Service from 1995 to 2005. In December 2008, Pitcaithley gave a talk to public school educators in Mississippi, and used as part of his presentation this quote from the Mississippi Declaration of Secession: "Our cause is thoroughly identified with the institution of slavery, the greatest material interest of the world." That sentence is now prominently displayed on the wall of the National Park Service visitors' center in Corinth, Mississippi, near the site of the Battle of Shiloh. Pitcaithley took a picture of the display and used it in his presentation. After his talk, he was chatting with a thirty-four-year-old black school principal who had grown up in Mississippi, attended its public schools, and received his university education there. "I asked him if he'd ever seen that [quote] and he said no—he'd never even heard of that."[16]

All of which explains both how that dubious assertion that thousands of slaves fought in defense of the Confederacy[17] came to be included in that Virginia textbook back in 2010, and how the error came to light. As it turns out, the textbook's author took her information from the Sons of Confederate Veterans' website; the error was discovered when a history professor at the College of William and Mary happened to come across it while browsing through a copy of one of her fourth grade daughter's schoolbooks. Had that not happened, who knows how long the book would have been in use? To this day, it's possible to stir up a hornet's nest among ordinary Southerners by asserting that slavery was a primary cause of the Civil War; at the least, it will earn a native Southerner the accusation of having signed over his brain to those Ivy League intellectual snobs who despise all things Southern. The conviction that the South went to war primarily to defend the concept of states' rights "is in [Southerners'] families, in their churches, in their schools, in their political structure," Pitcaithley said. "They've been taught that over generations. It so embedded that—as you have found—if you suggest otherwise they look at you like you've put your pants on your head."

"I'm not taking up all the room, am I?" a friendly voice whispered off to my right. "If I am, just squeeze me."

I turned to see a middle-aged lady with black hair and a magnolia-blossom complexion settling herself two seats away—which was a good thing, since hoopskirts take up a lot of space. Hers was red satin, trimmed with black lace. On the other side of her sat a little blond boy of about two, sucking on a sippy cup and wearing a tiny pair of neatly creased Confederate gray flannel trousers, suspenders, and a Rebel kepi hat. Before I could ask her where on earth a person went to find a Confederate Army private's uniform in size 2T, the program started: an invocation, followed by a salute to the Christian flag, a hymn, the Pledge of Allegiance, "The Star-Spangled Banner," and—of course— "Dixie."

"Oh, I wish I was in the land of cotton/Old times there are not forgotten," we all sang, and it occurred to me that though I'd known the words to "Dixie" all my life, I'd never sung it in public before. At the end, a couple of people in back let out a Rebel whoop or two, and then came the recitation of the Children of the Confederacy Creed: "We, therefore, pledge ourselves to preserve pure ideals; to honor the memory of our beloved Veterans; to study and teach the truths of history (one of the most important of which is that the War Between the States was not a rebellion, nor was its underlying cause to sustain slavery); and always to act in a manner that will reflect honor upon our noble and patriotic ancestors."

It was July 2008, and I was at the Children of the Confederacy convention I had mentioned to David Blight. As national conventions go, this one was tiny. Only about three hundred people had shown up at the Fredericksburg Convention Center, but that only made it seem more like the kind of Homecoming Day church gatherings I remember from childhood. Young men in suits said "yes, sir" and "yes, ma'am" and leaped to open doors; teenage girls glided through in strapless prom gowns that revealed their tan lines. Little girls darted in and out of the crowd in demure dresses of white eyelet or lace, often adorned with red sashes in honor of the colors of the Confederacy. In a conference room, vendors had set up their wares: gold earrings bearing the Great Seal of the Confederacy, coffee mugs with the likenesses of its generals, dolls in antebellum outfits, books on Southern history, Confederate key chains, an assortment of trinkets.

A highlight of the four-day event was a Saturday night Confederate Ball where the girls could break out their hoopskirts, which I would love to have seen, but the event I was looking forward to the most was the Saturday morning "catechism quizzes"—an interesting description that perhaps unintentionally betrayed the fact that we had passed out of the realm of facts and into the realm of faith. The first contestants were a group of about eight children six and under, who were asked to identify a picture of Robert E. Lee and answer a few other easy questions. Then it was time for the junior division, where the questions got a little harder. Did slavery at one time exist in all thirteen colonies? (Yes.) Where did Confederate generals receive most of their training? (West Point and Virginia Military Institute.) Who was the commander in chief of the Confederate forces? ("Robert E. Lee," said one girl, but she was wrong; the correct answer is Jefferson Davis.) How long was Jefferson Davis imprisoned at Fort Monroe? (I thought this would be a stumper, but to my surprise half a dozen youngsters leaped to their feet with the answer: two years, from 1865 to 1867.)

And so on. If a question did not immediately elicit an answer, the twenty or so contestants were allowed to consult their catechism pamphlets. Looking at the row of heads bent low over their books in a furious race to be the first with the answer, I was reminded of the Sunday School Bible drills of my childhood. Finally, I heard the question I'd been waiting for: "What did the South fight for?" But the youngster who answered spoke so softly I couldn't hear. I was forced to consult my own copy of the Junior Catechism pamphlet for the approved answer, which was: "The South fought to repel invasion and for the right of self-government, just as the fathers of the American Revolution did." Both the Junior and Senior catechism pamphlets bore a 1954 copyright, and the information in them did not seem to have been revised since then. At question 22, I found this: "How were the slaves treated by their owners?" Answer: "The slaves were treated, in most cases, with kindness and care. Many claims of cruelty and abuse were found to be the results of the behavior of plantation overseers, rather than the slaves' owners." Then question 23: "What was the feeling of the slaves toward their masters?" Answer: "Slaves, for the most part, were faithful and devoted. Most slaves were usually ready and willing to serve their masters."

By now it was almost lunch, and the seniors' round hadn't started yet. Pressed for time, the organizers stepped up the pace. In what order did the states secede? Who was called the Plumed Knight? And then, finally, a more sophisticated version of the "What did the South fight for?" query: "What were the causes of the War Between the States?"

One of the last three contestants, a young boy, leaped to his feet. "The Union started taking rights away from the South and tried to tell them what to do and keep them from doing what they wanted to do," he said confidently.

The emcee smiled broadly. "Absolutely right!" he said.

So why does all this matter? What difference does it make if a bunch of nice white ladies want to dress up in hoopskirts and relive *Gone With the Wind*? It matters because history matters. The stories we believe about our past have a huge role in determining how we live in the present. If Southerners of 1890

believed that slavery was not really a crime, then poll taxes and
literacy tests and other means of keeping black people from voting hardly qualified as misdemeanors; Southerners of the 1950s
who believed the South fought for "states' rights" found it easy
to use the same argument for resisting school integration; today,
the venerable "states' rights" argument is a convenient rationale
for punitive state immigration laws. Most important, if slavery
is relegated to an incidental role in what is arguably the most
important period of American history, then all of the history associated with those slaves and their descendants is relegated to
incidental status, too—or wiped out of public memory entirely.
And that, as we will see, is exactly what happened in the South
for most of the twentieth century. Though today, finally, things
are changing.

4.

Shadow History

bout 9 P.M. on an October evening in 1994, a hysterical young white woman pounded at the door of a house just outside Union, South Carolina, sobbing that a black man had hijacked her car and taken off with her two little boys. Within hours, pictures of Susan Smith and her two dark-eyed little boys were on television screens across the country, along with a police artist's sketch of the carjacker. In Union County, a rural area near the North Carolina border, any black man driving a red car—the color of Susan Smith's car—became an instant suspect. The mere sight of one black man walking along a state highway sent sheriff's deputies swarming to shut down the road. The drone of police helicopters filled the air; citizen volunteers came from other states to comb the woods on horseback, loaded shotguns slung across their saddles. For nine excruciating days the searches went on before Smith told the truth: she had rolled her car into a lake with the boys inside, in despair over an affair with a man who didn't want "a ready-made family."

During those nine days, there was talk of little else among

the young black men who gathered at Modest Keenan's barbershop in Union. Bitter about being made the target of suspicion, they ridiculed Smith's story in biting, just-us humor: why would some brother take off with a white lady's kids when black men don't even mess with their *own* children? Keenan, a seventy-five-year-old man who has spent most of his life in Union, listened to the jokes and worried that these young men did not understand the extreme dangers they were facing. These were kids born in the 1970s, who had no idea of how cheap a black man's life had once been in the South—and, on occasion, still was. "Sometimes when I'd leave at the end of the day, I'd tell them, 'You better be careful out there, because there are people who are looking for an excuse to shoot somebody.'"

White people in Union would have found that insulting. To them, the case offered a sad but heartwarming lesson of blacks and whites united in their concern for the little boys, united in their grief at the story's tragic end, united in their outrage that a mother had done this to her own children. If there was any good thing to come from this whole dark story, their thinking went, it was that it had shown the world how completely people in the South had gotten over race. Outsiders might speak of "racial profiling" and try to stir up trouble, one middle-aged white woman told television talk show host Phil Donahue at the time, "but this is not a racial thing." Around her, white people murmured in agreement.

Historian Barbara Tuchman once described the past as "a distant mirror." In the South, it's more like a journey through the looking glass. Few black people in Union today know the details about Dan Jenkins, a black man who in 1930 was arrested for trying to rape a white woman and whose body was shot into ribbons of flesh by a mob of whites from Union as the sheriff stood by.[1] Even fewer would be conversant with the details of the murder of Mose Hughes, a black man who in 1906 was shot and thrown into the nearby Tiger River by two white men from Union who had accused him of arson, who were later freed for "lack of evidence."[2] Nobody alive today remembers the 1871 incident in which ten black members of the state militia were executed en masse by members of the Ku Klux Klan just outside town,[3] or the many stories of the way the Klan once roamed Union County at night, murdering those blacks who dared to try to vote and terrorizing others to the point that they abandoned their crops and fled.[4] Such details fade, especially when they involve questionable doings of people in authority, and especially when the descendants of those people may still be around.

Fear, however, gets burned into the brain. That much was evident in the instant success of Susan Smith's desperate cover story. It lived on in the community's uncritical readiness to see black men as criminals, in the resentment bred by that suspicion, in the tension people felt but tried to explain away—and that, in turn, barred any discussion of how all these things came to be. That was something nobody wanted to talk about.

And then, something surprising happened—something that, even though it happened in 1995, is indicative of some deep changes happening in the twenty-first-century South: a few people in Union did start talking. In the comparative lull between Smith's first appearance in court and her trial, several pastors in the Union Ministerial Association began to discuss the deluge of media attention they knew would be coming, and how best to handle it. Church is a huge part of the social fabric in Union. The town's ministers knew some of the secrets that were going to come out once the life story of a troubled young woman was laid bare in court; they knew the simmering resentment created in the black community by her false accusation.

"This could have divided the town—divided it racially," said Thomas Currie, who at the time was pastor at Union's First Presbyterian Church. But somehow, the ministers' discussion evolved into a plan for an interfaith, interracial worship service, to be held on Monday nights in a different church each week. And suddenly, black and white people in Union who worked together and attended school together but who during the other sixteen hours of the day lived separate existences were now worshipping together. A line was crossed—several lines, in fact, because small-town life in the South on any given Sunday morning is as divided along denominational nuances as by race. Some of the Baptists had never seen a Roman Catholic priest up close; most of the white people had never been in a black church, and vice versa. In those weekly sessions, Southerners did what they do most naturally, which is to sing and pray and sit in pews listening to a preacher—only this time, it was a preacher of a different race or faith. The meetings lasted only about six weeks, but people in Union still remember the intangible effect they had—a centering, somehow, and a calming of passions. Personal resentments abated; big issues seemed to get clearer.

And then the meetings ended, and the trial came, the media descended, and Smith went to prison on a life sentence. Ordinary life in Union resumed; the case passed out of the realm of public discourse and into the realm of psychology dissertations. Today, when Modest Keenan is asked about those interfaith, interracial meetings, he doesn't remember that they happened at all. All he remembers is a group of four ministers, two white and two black, standing on the courthouse steps one day to pray that Susan Smith would not get the death penalty. "I don't remember no community meetings," Keenan said, "and I got no reason to tell no lie about it . . . After they passed the sentence on her they didn't meet anymore—and *that's* when they should have started praying, to try to bring this community back together."

Currie is retired now, raising goats on a farm in North Carolina. When I called him later to ask him about the discrepancy between his recollection and Keenan's, he sighed deeply. "I think you're talking about the difference between the white perspective and the black perspective," he said.[5]

So there was no Kumbaya ending to the Susan Smith story;[6] those interracial meetings not only failed to bridge the gap between two different versions of the town's past, they actually seemed to create one more. But in some subtle way, it was a start. A few years after the Susan Smith case had faded out of the public consciousness, the Union County Historical Society put on an exhibit about the town's eighteenth-century-era jail, designed by American-born architect Robert Mills. The museum is in an old store on Main Street, and one of the items put on display was the jail's old gallows—the wooden frame jailers once used to hang convicted felons—complete with a noose. When Modest Keenan saw that noose, he went straight to the president of the Union County Chamber of Commerce and complained. The rope was gone the next day; museum curator Ola Jean Kelly saw to that. There was no uproar, no discussion— just a new realization by the town's white historians that what to them was a simple historical artifact was to many of their black neighbors a gut-wrenching reminder of an era of violence and terror. The day had not yet come when white and black residents of Union could look at that noose and openly acknowledge who did what to whom in a racially violent era of their community's history, but at least bland denial was no longer an option; maybe exposing the old wounds laid bare by Susan Smith's decision to play the race card been a good thing. Ola Jean Kelly, who attended those interfaith meetings fifteen years ago, put it this way: "We *want* to get along. We have to *live* together."

Union is unusual only in having once played unwilling host to a sensational crime. In every other way, it is a typical small Southern town—typical in its history of racial violence, its decades-long refusal to acknowledge that violence, and its residents' instinctive realization that the time has come for something different. Mrs. Kelly's heartfelt sentiment is increasingly being felt these days across the South, brought to life by a confluence of disparate trends: the advent of a generation of youth who have never experienced overt racial discrimination and for whom race has never been a political issue; the Internet, which has made serious genealogical research possible for millions of African Americans whose hunger to know their family history has been thwarted by the logistical problems of tracing records of slavery—and, most important, the aging of the civil rights generation and its need to come to some kind of reckoning of its place in history. Bit by bit, the dead are beginning to rise; in family reunions and conference rooms and museum exhibits across the South, black and white people are beginning to confront the past. Up to now, the South has been where white America first confronted the task of reconciling its noble democratic ideals with the realities of race, and the scene of its most public and ugly failures. The twenty-first-century South promises to be the region where Americans of different races learn, at last, how to honestly discuss both the present and the past with each other.

To understand why this is so significant, you have to understand how Southerners' ignorance of their own past helped to create a vast culture of silence. The Lost Cause myth plays a huge role, as does the systematic bowdlerizing of history in Southern textbooks. But another problem is that it's impossible to learn what you think you already know—and in the South, history is a passionate hobby for a whole lot of people. It's hard to walk a block in Savannah or Charleston without bumping into a self-taught expert on antebellum architecture. A U.S. senator has written a book on the subject of his own Scotch-Irish heritage and its influence on Appalachia. The Mississippi Delta is swarming with authorities on blues music. Grannies on the Sea Islands can speak knowledgeably about the history of Gullah speech. In my career as a newspaper reporter, I once mischaracterized one of the fine points of Lincoln's Emancipation Proclamation. I got irate corrections in the mail for weeks, all from Virginia or points farther south.

But the big picture it's not—and when it comes to the period from 1865 to World War II, most Americans are working with just a handful of faded snapshots: Depression breadlines, the Model T, World War I doughboys. With the benefit of hindsight, it's possible to see the seeds of a lot of hopeful social change being planted during this period. White and black church women, working on parallel tracks that would eventually converge, were beginning to establish public-political roles for themselves by working in the temperance movement or establishing settlement houses for the indigent.[7] A. Philip Randolph was organizing the Brotherhood of Sleeping Car Porters, a black labor union whose victories would eventually propel thousands of black families into the ranks of the solidly middle class. At the same time, there were violent uprising targeted at blacks in places like Tulsa, Oklahoma; Wilmington, North Carolina; Atlanta, Georgia; and Rosewood, Florida; and the threat of similar violence in other places forced thousands—tens of thousands, a number we will never know—of black families to abandon their homes and property. And across the nation, but mostly in the South, somewhere between four thousand and five thousand black people were tortured and lynched at the hands of whites.

The historical record is there to be found, and it makes for vivid reading. When Congress held hearings on Ku Klux Klan terrorism in the South in 1871, it collected volumes of testimony from white and black Southerners about the Klan's formidable arsenal of intimidation tactics: the whippings, the mutilations, the gagged and bound bodies thrown into rivers, the houses burned down. The testimonies were detailed; in many instances, victims could state the date of their attack and the names of their attackers (masks and bedsheets may hide faces, but it's hard not to recognize the voice of a neighbor you've known for years). None of this mattered to Democrats, whose minority report characterized the victims of Klan violence either as black persons of low intelligence or as contemptible Southern scalawags—both, obviously, born liars. Racist attitudes like these found a natural ally in the Southern gift for fabulous storytelling. One Alabama congressman of the 1870s went so far as to assert that no such thing as the Klan had ever existed in the South, period, "except in the disordered fantasies" of people who had never lived there. What these people were describing, he explained, were just exaggerated tales of silly personal feuds.[8] Five years later, in the political fistfight that was the 1876 presidential election, Northern Republicans and Southern Democrats reached an agreement in which Republican Rutherford B. Hayes got the White House in exchange for a tacit agreement that Democrats could run things in the South pretty much as they liked—and *that*, boys and girls, was the reason Klan violence abated: they won—at least for a while.

Until maybe twenty years ago—since very few school systems these days keep old textbooks, it's hard to tell exactly when things changed—standard public school curriculums didn't breathe a word about this unlovely period of American history. This wasn't a case of forgetting, but of active censorship: when historian James Loewen and coauthor Charles Sallis wrote a textbook for Mississippi schools in 1975 that included passages on that state's history of lynching, the state textbook commission rejected it for being too controversial.[9] More recent textbooks have ventured to bring up the subject, but only in the most milquetoast kind of way. Here's a typical example, from a widely used 2000 high school history text: "To test his newfound freedom, in 1865 Henry Adams left the plantation where he had been a slave. A group of white men stopped Adams on the road, demanding to know who owned him. When Adams replied that he was a free man, the strangers beat him. Such violent attacks were not unusual in the South in the years following the Civil War."[10] But the textbook reassures students that after Congress passed some laws against this kind of thing, "within a few years the Klan was no longer an organized threat." Whew! What a relief.

Such whopping omissions of history affect everybody, but since the vast majority of this early Klan violence took place in the South, it's fair to say that Southerners have lost more of their history than anyone else. The South is home to 55 percent of the nation's blacks, and roughly 23 percent of those live in poverty. Exactly how much of that is the direct result of generations in which blacks were systematically denied a chance at decent jobs, land ownership, or a quality education is impossible to say, but it was access to those kinds of things that allowed millions of poor white families like my own—and black families, too, when they were given the chance—to work their way up the economic ladder. Through such omissions, denial, and willful ignorance, generations of white people were able to convince themselves of their inherent racial superiority. It's hard to confront the legacy of history when you don't know what the history is.

We've paid in other ways, too. Gigantic omissions of history require face-saving measures—and so we've invented that educational plague we call Black History Month, a kind of retroactive "separate but equal" approach that segregates black historical figures in a way nobody would tolerate in real life. They have also deprived generations of students of stories about individual acts of heroism—the occasional sheriff who defied a lynch mob, the examples of black officeholders during Reconstruction who were both educated and eloquent. Instead, generations of black students have gotten the subtle but devastating message that these events were not of great importance for the very reason that they *did* involve black people. That, at least, is how it seemed to Patricia Moncure Thomas, a sixty-three-year-old

black school principal from Washington state who went to public schools in Grand Rapids, Michigan, in the late the 1950s and
early 1960s. "We got up to the Civil War, and then suddenly it
was World War II," she said, and she was pained by the fact that
she never saw anyone who looked like her in any of her schoolbooks.[11] She did not know then, though she would later find
out, that this violent chapter was part of her own family history:
after her grandfather and an uncle were murdered by whites in
a small Mississippi town in the 1920s, her father left the state,
never to return. "There's nothing good in Mississippi," he would
tell her when she was a child—beyond which, he had nothing
to say.

And here we get to the most basic reason why Southerners know so little about these years: *we all agreed not to talk
about it.*

I grew up in a house that faced the Atlanta–West Point Railroad just southwest of Atlanta, on a stretch that runs between
the towns of East Point and Red Oak. Every schoolchild in the
Atlanta suburbs of the 1960s knew about that railroad; it was
prominently mentioned in all those stories about the Battle of
Atlanta that we heard when we took the obligatory pilgrimage
to the Cyclorama (an enormous circular painting of the battle
on display in Atlanta's Grant Park). As a child, I heard from
my grandmother that during the battle, soldiers commanded by
Union General William T. Sherman tore up our railroad, built
bonfires from the ties, and heated the rails until they could be
bent into what were called "Sherman's neckties." My grandmother had heard the story from *her* mother, who as a little
girl had seen it happen, *right in front of our house.* I wasn't sure
I believed her—but decades later, reading Sherman's *Memoirs,* I

happened on a description of that exact event described in precise geographic detail, as well as the date: August 29, 1864.

Four decades later, another bonfire was built about twenty
miles down the road, in Newnan. This was the one in which a
twenty-one-year-old black man named Sam Hose, accused of
killing his white employer and, later—on hearsay evidence—
of raping his employer's wife, was slowly roasted alive. Before
the fire was lit, however, members of the crowd cut off both
of Hose's ears, all ten of his fingers, and finally his genitals.
The body pieces were distributed as souvenirs to people in the
crowd. The mutilated man was then doused with kerosene and
set ablaze as he screamed "Sweet Jesus!" in agony. This horrify-
ing event was national news in its day; contemporary accounts
estimated the crowd at roughly two thousand—many of whom
got there via specially chartered trains that came down from
Atlanta on the same railroad tracks that passed right outside my
bedroom window. The Hose lynching forever altered the career
of W. E. B. Du Bois, then a young professor at Atlanta University. Du Bois was on his way to the office of *Atlanta Constitution*
editor Joel Chandler Harris to discuss the paper's sensational
and one-sided coverage of the case when he learned that Hose's
knuckles were being offered for sale in a grocer's window just up
the street. The shocking sight, he later wrote, "pulled me off my
feet."[12]

When I first came across an account of the Sam Hose lynching, I had to throw the book down—and that was just *reading*
about it. But part of my shock had to do with the fact that this
was news to me. I had never heard of Sam Hose. I also never
heard about any of the six other recorded lynchings that happened around the same time in the vicinity of what are now

south Fulton, Fayette, and Coweta counties, which roughly encompass the borders of my childhood universe. In fact, none of the books I read mentioned *any* violence against black people in the area where I grew up. Southerners rightly have a reputation for being obsessed with the past, and there was no shortage of people in my childhood who were happy to regale me with stories about the Yankee soldier buried under the muscadine vines, the privations their families endured during Reconstruction, or the damage sharp ends of cotton bolls could do to a person's hands. Every once in a while, somebody would mention the Klan (who were not, of course, anybody we knew). But lynchings? What lynchings?

In fact, lynchings used to happen practically every week somewhere in the South. The black press of the time reported them extensively in coverage pioneered by a former Mississippi slave named Ida B. Wells, whose stories are the primary source for much of what we know about lynching today. There were 4,742 documented instances of lynchings in thirty states between the end of the Civil War and the murder of Emmett Till in Mississippi in 1955 (though hundreds were never reported), but if you marked a map with pushpins for the location of every known lynching, three-fourths of those pushpins would be in the Deep South. There were clusters—Mississippi had more than any other state, with a total of 538; Georgia was a close second, with 491[13]—but it would be tough to find any community in the South that was not home to, or near to, some act of racial violence during that period. Because lynching was, technically, a crime even in the Jim Crow–era South, a strict veil of silence quickly surrounded anybody remotely connected with the deed. Yet publicity was an essential ingredient of the terror. As the photography collected in the 2000 book entitled *Without Sanctuary* has so compellingly shown, pictures of these events were often made into postcards, some of which have survived with incongruously casual notes on the back: "All OK and would love to get a post from you"—as if the writer had just attended a county fair.[14]

Respectable middle-class white Southerners didn't send such postcards. They disapproved of lynchings, but their attitude was often driven less by moral outrage than by their awareness of how poorly such incidents reflected on the South as a magnet for business investors. If people just didn't talk about lynchings, the thinking went, we can keep investors from fixating on the subject; if we don't talk about lynching, eventually the poor white trash (who were always blamed for these things) will quit doing it. Black Southerners kept their lips sealed, too—in public, for obvious reasons, and at home, too. They walked a tightrope between the need to tell their children enough to keep them out of danger and the desire to shield them from knowing that such horrors existed. Fear taught them to be harsh in their discipline; a child who ran around too freely might be a child who one day would never come home. "We weren't allowed to go nowhere. We went to Sunday School—you *had* to go to church—and we went to school," recalled Robert Howard, a black resident of Walton County, Georgia, describing his childhood there in the 1950s and 1960s. If he or his siblings wandered off alone, or went on an errand without another family member, his parents "would give you a whupping."[15]

These unspoken rules held sway for most of the twentieth century—through the lynching period itself, through two world wars, through the civil rights era (which brought a resurgence of vigilante violence). After the civil rights movement, if anything the silence intensified; many leaders in the black community were concentrating on more immediate concerns, and believed that publicly dwelling on incidents of racial violence would distract from the fragile progress they had just made. As the twentieth century headed into its final decades, the emphasis was on tales of survival and triumph, not humiliation and oppression. Elders in the community, white and black, who had seen these horrors with their own eyes found that sometimes the best way to cope was not to speak of what they had seen—the same survival strategy used by some Jewish survivors of the Holocaust. The perpetrators didn't have much to say, either. Some were tortured by guilt; others, serenely confident that they were on the side of God's angels, nevertheless understood that there is no statute of limitations on murder.

I think it was this vast silence that first made me realize I was confused. What I saw being played out before me when I was a child—John Lewis felled by a state trooper's blow at the Edmund Pettus Bridge, Lester Maddox standing at his restaurant door with an ax handle in his hands—did not make sense. What was this terrible thing that had happened, to make black people so resolute, so angry? "We shall overcome sooomeda-a-a-y"—the drawn-out syllables of the last word implied a long history—but of what, exactly? Generations of white children in the South had accepted segregation without a thought, but by the time I came along it was pretty hard not to notice gaping holes in the logic. What writer Lillian Smith wrote of her Southern childhood was also true of mine: "Even its children knew that the South was in trouble."[16] I just wasn't sure what the trouble had been.

My parents personified these contradictions. My father grew up in Gadsden, Alabama, and was in every way a conservative white Southerner of his time. But he had also served in India with the Army Air Corps during World War II, and perhaps seeing another brand of racism in a distant part of the world did something to broaden, and soften, the attitudes typical of his race and class. He was among the first managers at Delta Air Lines to hire a person of color, even though I never actually heard him utter a single sentiment that might be called "liberal" or "progressive." My mother considered the Klan a bunch of poor white trash. Yet I also once heard her remark, "Say what you want about the Klan, they sure took care of any man who beat his wife." I was five or six when I met an honest-to-God Grand Dragon in a Woolworth's one day. I was terrified—yet after hearing my mother's remark it occurred to me that there might be certain situations in which knowing a few scary goons like that might come in handy. It was exactly the same conclusion a lot of "moderate" white Southerners had come to over the years.

Life was a mosaic of a thousand such contradictions, large and small. By the time I was old enough to notice things around me, the segregated South that had endured for so long was like a piece of crazed glass, one instant away from shattering into a million pieces. And one more contradiction, on top of all the others, was the fact that most people were aware of this mosaic—and yet nobody talked about *that*, either. So, for example, most of us knew of, but did not talk about, at least one place where (it was said) there had once been a sign posted at some city limit or county line that read: "Nigger, don't let the sun set on you in _____," referring to whatever place it was. But the link between such things and events happening before our eyes was not a connection many of us made. On a day-to-day basis, black and white Southerners dealt with each other as if all of these stories—the lynchings, the night riders, the tales we heard about the Klan—were legends with only a tenuous connection to actual history, in the same way that the story of Robin Hood or King Arthur may have been based on actual persons. If F. Scott Fitzgerald was right—if the test of a first-rate intelligence is the ability to hold two opposed ideas in the mind at the same time and still retain the ability to function—then the South in those years was doing a phenomenal job of raising the national IQ.

In researching this book, I developed a habit of asking all the native-born white Southerners I talked to whether they recalled hearing any mention of incidents of racial violence in their hometowns. With three exceptions,[17] they all said no. John Herbers, the former *New York Times* reporter, recalls that one of the towns he lived in growing up, Brownsville, Tennessee, had been the site of a lynching.[18] "But in all the time I lived there, I never heard a word about it. It was blacked out. They didn't want you to know about it." Elizabeth Spiers, a New York–based writer and media entrepreneur best known for being the founder of Gawker.com, is five decades younger than Herbers. She grew up in the small central Alabama town of Wetumpka. When I asked her if she had ever come across any disturbing stories about lynchings when she was growing up there, she said no, Wetumpka had such a large black community she seriously doubted that white people would have had much success at pushing them around. After we talked, I found references to three lynchings known to have occurred in Wetumpka between 1898 and 1912, involving a total of eight victims—one of whom, interestingly, was named Spiers.

I made sure to include in my pool several well-known authorities on Southern culture, on the chance that their early inclinations had made them pay closer attention in childhood than the rest of us, but the answers there were the same. Sociologist John Shelton Reed was born in 1942 and grew up in east Tennessee. When I asked him what memories he had of hearing about any racial violence in Kingsport, his hometown, his e-mailed answer was the same as Spiers's: but with an inverse rationale: "Black folks were (and are) not much of a presence, so perhaps it's not surprising that I don't recall any stories of racial violence at all."

One of the exceptions in my straw poll grew up in Johnson City, Tennessee, about twenty-five miles southeast of Reed's hometown of Kingsport. Journalist Bill Kovach, who was once executive editor at the *Atlanta Journal-Constitution* and who went on to run Harvard University's Neiman Program, remembers hearing in his youth about a 1918 incident in Erwin, a town in neighboring Unicoi County. A black man accused of trying to abduct a young white girl was summarily shot, Kovach wrote to me in an e-mail, and "the town rounded up all blacks in the area, some said as many as 60, and [took them] to the [rail]yard where a pyre of railroad cross ties had been built on which the black man's body was burned. The blacks were then put aboard a train and taken out of town and told never to come back." Kovach also remembered hearing about a sign warning, "Nigger! Don't let the sun set on your ass in Unicoi County."

Though he never saw the sign himself, Kovach said, "when I was growing up there were no blacks in Unicoi County, and the ones I knew [in Johnson City] were as familiar with the story and the wording of the sign as I was."[19]

The difference between Reed's memories and Kovach's is partly explained by the ten-year gap in their ages, but what's probably more germane is skin pigmentation. Reed is a standard-issue white hill country Southerner of Scotch-Irish extraction; Kovach is the son of Albanian immigrants. When he was growing up in the Johnson City of the 1940s, recent immigrants from Albania weren't considered truly "white"—a fact of life Kovach remembers being explained to him in blunt terms by the father of a girl he once asked out on a date.

In her research into lynchings on Maryland's Eastern Shore, scholar Sherrilyn Ifill found a similar pattern. If longtime white residents knew about the area's history of lynching at all, they had only vague impressions of what had happened, and they insisted that whoever perpetrated the violence had come from "out of town." The memories of black residents were not necessarily more historically accurate, but they were emotionally vivid and personal—stories of a relative who had known the victim, of overheard conversations, of glimpses of a mutilated body; remembrances of other incidents nobody had ever bothered to record. I remembered that when Mattie Savage, an elderly black resident of Union, South Carolina, told me about what she remembered of the 1930 lynching of Dan Jenkins in her town, she also remembered hearing her father describe squeezing into the hollow of a large oak tree while members of the Klan combed the woods in their neighborhood looking for somebody. Were they looking for Dan Jenkins, or somebody else, or looking for her father? Mrs. Savage did not remember, but after seventy-five years she could still vividly recall the fear.

My first encounter with the South's shadow history happened on February 16, 1982, in a courtroom in Walton County, Georgia. I was a new reporter for the *Atlanta Constitution*, and I was covering an inquest into the death of a twenty-three-year-old army private named Lynn McKinley Jackson. A native of Monroe, the county seat, Jackson had been seen in town the previous August by several people the night before he was due to report back to Fort Bragg in North Carolina. Nobody knew he was missing until a few weeks later, when the army reported him AWOL. On December 8, his decomposing body was found hanging from a pine tree in the woods just outside Social Circle, Georgia. The county coroner saw no signs of foul play, and ruled the death a suicide—but if so, it was a strange one. Jackson had left no note, and had given no sign of emotional turmoil or depression. To reach the branch from which his body was found hanging, he would have had to shimmy twenty feet straight up a pine tree with no intervening branches, wearing ordinary tennis shoes.

Among black residents of Walton County there were plenty of rumors. One I heard at the time was that there had been a fire the previous August in the section of woods where the body had been found; another rumor, which did not see print then and which I did not hear until fifteen years later, was that Jackson had angered some locals with his predilection for dating white girls. At the time, when the inquest was announced, it was seen as an attempt to calm things down. Instead, it had the opposite effect. A local Klan leader announced his intention to attend, seizing the event as a recruiting opportunity; civil rights leaders drove out from Atlanta. But nine hours of testimony only deepened my confusion. Army psychiatrists described an emotionally unstable young man who had used drugs and had expressed suicidal thoughts; friends and family described a well-adjusted young man with many friends. That left the forensic evidence, which was basically nonexistent, due to the weeks in which the body had been exposed to the elements. When the jury of three whites and three blacks came back with a verdict of suicide after deliberating for only forty-five minutes, the black spectators crammed into the courtroom erupted with a spontaneous, angry "NO!"

It was like a wave of electricity had passed through the room. For a split second, it seemed to me that the sound was coming from all around us, as if the past were literally speaking—which, in a way, it was. Before that day, I had never heard of a 1946 incident in which two black ex-servicemen and their wives, one of whom was seven months' pregnant, were dragged from their car at a bridge in Walton County and shot to death by perhaps a dozen white men. The true cause of the lynching may never be fully known; the proximate cause was the stabbing of a white farmer by one of the black men when the farmer intervened in a domestic dispute. No one was ever charged in what came to be known as the Moore's Ford lynching. I was a twenty-six-year-old reporter with exactly six months' experience at a major metropolitan daily, so maybe my ignorance of an event that had happened thirty-five years earlier was somewhat excusable—but my editors (who were all white) were hardly better informed. Decades later, rereading my own story from that inquest and comparing it with contemporaneous coverage of the case by reporters from the black-owned and -staffed *Atlanta Daily World*, it was clear to me that we had all been living in parallel universes—and that the universe my black colleagues lived in had been a lot closer to reality than my own. My ignorance of the past had blinded me to the present, and in that I had plenty of company.

"Is it possible for white America to really understand blacks' distrust of the legal system, their fears of racial profiling and the police, without understanding how cheap a black life was for so long a time in our nation's history?"[20] asks writer Philip Dray. The answer is obvious; what's not obvious is how, given this long, frozen silence, whites and blacks in this country ever managed to communicate at all. Today, we're like partners in a marriage that has suffered a profound trauma, and who have decided to just pick up and go on without ever grieving or speaking out loud about the terrible thing that happened. But the terrible thing won't go away. Once in a while, some news event—an O. J. Simpson verdict, a fiery speech from a Reverend Jeremiah Wright—will stab us with a reminder. It's a symptom of our disconnect that at such moments blacks and whites tend to be so bewildered by the idea that there might be another point of view, so angry that other people can be so clueless. And then our attention shifts, and we go back to not talking.

In the South, though, this seems to be changing. The region that once proclaimed "Segregation today, segregation tomorrow, segregation forever" is discovering that the quickest route to the future is to finally deal honestly with the past; at a time when cities like Atlanta, Charlotte, and Nashville are becoming authentic multiethnic urban melting pots, our old black-white distinctions are dissolving. I caught my first glimpse of this new reality at, of all places, a United Daughters of the Confederacy convention.

It was Richmond in November 2008, just a few days after the election of the nation's first black president and a few months after that Children of the Confederacy convention I had attended. Still in the beginning stages of researching this book, I had come to the annual UDC convention with the idea that this would be a good place to find people who would talk about what being Southern meant to them. I wasn't having much luck. Most of the conventioneers I cornered looked baffled; the rest immediately veered off onto the subject of cooking, as if they could explain the whole concept of Southern-ness that way— and maybe they could, but that wasn't the book I was writing. After a while, I wandered off and sat down in the lobby next to a lady whose bosom was draped with gold pins attesting to the number of her ancestors who had fought for the Lost Cause. Since UDC materials frequently allude to the legions of loyal slaves who took up arms on behalf of their masters, I decided to ask her why there were no black people at this convention. She assured me that the UDC *did* have black members.

"In fact," she added, as if this clinched her argument, "my granddaughter is married to a black man."

I don't just believe in interracial marriage, I've *seen it done*, to paraphrase an old Southern joke about infant baptism, but her words stopped me in my tracks. Here I was in a city where Southern tradition was a civic religion, with a group of white ladies for whom history had basically stopped in 1865. When the *UDC* crowd gets comfortable with the idea of interracial marriage, it's clear that a profound, top-to-bottom cultural change has quietly taken root. "What did you think of that?" I asked cautiously. She said that at first the family had been upset, but in the nine years her granddaughter had been married she had grown quite fond of her grandson-in-law. "He provides for her very well," she said, with obvious satisfaction—an old-fashioned compliment, I thought, but a compliment all the same.

Some readers may find this little story anachronistic or condescending, but consider the distance we have traveled here. In his book on Mississippi, *The Most Southern Place on Earth*, James Cobb recounts an old story about two Mississippi planters in the 1930s who take their teenage sons to New York to initiate them into the ways of the world. They check into a suite at a luxury hotel and order room service from the kitchen—steak dinners for eight—and another kind of room service from the concierge: send up four hookers, please. The dinner arrives, but when the hookers get there the men discover that the women are black. One of the planters berates the concierge. "Son, what were you *thinking*?" he says. "We can't eat with these girls!"[21]

Amazing though it may seem now, real social equality between whites and blacks, one symbol of which is the simple act of sharing a meal, is a fairly recent invention in this country. In 1967, when the U.S. Supreme Court struck down Virginia's antimiscegenation law, marriage between persons of different races was a *felony* everywhere in the South,[22] and Alabama didn't get around to wiping its defunct antimiscegenation law off the books until 2000. White people's fear about miscegenation was the ugly underside of much opposition to school integration: put boys and girls of different races together in the same classroom, segregationists warned, and sooner or later you will get "mongrel" babies. The segregationists seemed to think the mongrel babies would start arriving exactly nine months after the National Guard escorted the first black students into Little Rock High School, when in fact it took a couple of generations. But in the end, the racists got this one point right, sort of.

Between 1980 and 2010, the last year for which figures are available, the percentage of new marriages between persons of different races more than doubled in the United States, from 6.7 to 15 percent, according to the Pew Center for Research into Social Change.[23] In the South, the number was 10 percent, which looks like the South is once again lagging behind national trends—but a closer look at the statistics shows that there are more new marriages between blacks and whites in the South these days than the national average[24]—with Virginia, the state that once prosecuted an interracial married couple all the way to the U.S. Supreme Court—leading the pack. Nationally, roughly 5.7 percent of all existing marriages are interracial;[25] in the South, it's 4.1 percent—again, not a big difference.

Of course, all these numbers are rough guides at best, since we are talking about marriage rates in an era when cohabitation is increasingly the norm.[26] While these statistics don't prove that the post-racial society has officially arrived, they reflect a powerful change in social attitudes. In 1987, only 48 percent of Americans thought interracial dating was okay; by 2010, that number had risen to 83 percent;[27] among people born since 1980, you'd be hard put to find anybody who thought it *wasn't* okay. Put another way, in my own lifetime we have gone from a time when the sight of an interracial couple would have prompted shouts of "Nigger lover!" to a point when an interracial couple trolling the aisles of Toys R Us in, say, Fayetteville, Georgia, is a total nonevent.

Clearly, twentieth-century notions about the overwhelming importance of skin color are breaking down. But that doesn't mean race is becoming irrelevant; it's just becoming relevant in more complex ways. In an era when legal distinctions based on race have been abolished completely in theory and almost completely in practice, race has morphed from a political issue into a matter of personal identity—and discoveries about the human genome have revealed what a nuanced and plastic identity that is. The person probably more responsible than anybody else for bringing these ideas into the realm of popular discourse is Henry Louis Gates Jr., head of Harvard's African American Studies department. The host of three PBS series on African American genealogy and the mixed origins of American cultural identity, Gates is also the founder of AfricanDNA.com, a popular website devoted to helping African Americans trace their roots. The 1976 publication of Alex Haley's *Roots* is usually credited with sparking modern interest among blacks in charting their family tree, but a quick look at some scholarly title links on AfricanDNA.com—"Rates of Evolution in the Coding and Control Regions of African mtDNAs" is a typical example, and by no means the most complicated—shows how far we have come from the Kunta Kinte era, when for most African Americans, genealogical research consisted of poring through dusty courthouse records and probing the uncertain memories of elderly relatives.

Today, anybody with access to a computer can dive into a deep pool of online databases and original sources—things like Freedmen's Bureau records, slave narratives, and individual family histories. In the past, things like that were available only to scholars and professional researchers, all of whom had to travel to where the records were. Today, the "wall" of slavery, when so many black-skinned people were tallied like livestock, can often be pierced by an amateur with some basic research skills, a home computer, and access to the Internet. Secrets are coming to light.

One of those secrets is the legacy of the venerable Southern tradition of miscegenation. The irony is exquisite: for generations, middle-class white Southerners defended themselves against the suspicion of bigotry by insisting that "their" black people—the people who cleaned their houses, the people who were childhood playmates, the people who raised their children—were so highly regarded that they were "just like family." Now, as it turns out, sometimes they *were* family—third and fourth cousins descended from some locally prominent white landowner from pre–Civil War days, who after Emancipation simply stayed on in a place that they, too, called home. Considering that in the federal census of 1860 more than half a million persons in the slave states were listed as "mulattos,"[28] the only thing surprising about these discoveries is that we so often find them so surprising. The real revelation here is the history of our rigid notions of what constitutes race and what a deeply guarded secret interracial relationships used to be. But we're learning.

One of the first signs of change was the 1998 publication of Edward Ball's book *Slaves in the Family,* in which Ball meticulously traced the rise and fall of his aristocratic South Carolina ancestors and the slaves whose toil created their rice plantation empire. Two years later, the publication of Henry Wiencek's *The Hairstons: An American Family in Black and White* did the same on a far broader scale for a wealthy North Carolina white family and its black descendants, who stayed on in the land of slavery even after Emancipation because its soil was the only place they had ever called home. More recently, New York–based film critic Godfrey Cheshire's 2008 film, *Moving Midway*, set out to tell the history of the North Carolina plantation built on land granted to his mother's family by the British crown decades before the American Revolution—but, in the process, Cheshire discovered an African American branch of his family, one descendant of which was a professor of African American Studies at New York University who lived only a few blocks away.

There are plenty of less famous examples. Coming to the Table, a nonprofit group based at Eastern Mennonite University in Virginia, was founded in 2006 with the sole purpose of helping the descendants of slave owners and the descendants of slaves reconnect and acknowledge their shared history; at last count, the center was working with twenty far-flung families and regularly fields new inquiries. And in recent years, Tony Burroughs, president of the African-American Genealogical and Historical Society of Chicago, says that he's noticed that "there's quite a few people who come up to me who are white and who say they traced their family tree back and discovered having black ancestors. Some try to deny it; some are fascinated."

I told Burroughs that I grew up hearing that the Thompson family tree included a Cherokee woman. My father's complexion might have fit that theory—he was dark-skinned for a Caucasian—but his hair did not: it was black and so tightly curled that it would be safe to call it kinky. I inherited the hair gene; years later, when one of my cousins had a baby whose hair was so tightly kinked none of us knew how to comb it, the silence in the room was so loud you could almost hear what everybody was thinking. But the Cherokee woman was our story, and we were sticking with it.[29] Burroughs laughed when I told him this—because, as it turns out, the Indian in the family tree story is popular among black families, too. "When I talk to black audiences and ask if anybody has white ancestors, very few people raise their hands," he said. "When I ask how many people had Indian ancestors, about 90 percent of the room will raise their hands." It's certainly possible to have Indian heritage, as many Americans proudly claim, and there was plenty of intermarriage between blacks and Native Americans in the nineteenth century. Still, Burroughs noted, 90 percent is an extremely high number, especially considering the U.S. government's forced expulsion of Native American tribes from the Southeast in the 1830s.

There were no Cherokee grandmother stories in Patricia Moncure Thomas's family lore. She grew up knowing that her great-grandfather had white blood, though his parentage was referred to only in vague terms as "that black woman who had all those children by a white man." For years, she made a habit of talking to older relatives and collecting stories, birth dates, and nicknames. It wasn't until the late 1990s that she collected all those pieces of the puzzle and made the trip back down to Mississippi, the state her father had left decades earlier. Her search took her to the little towns of Edwards, Utica, Terry, and Crystal Springs, where her father's family was from. She started with courthouse records, and then did the tedious shoe-leather work of tracking down older residents in the area who could fill in the blanks.

What she discovered was a slave woman named Charlotte

Shakespeare, who in the late 1860s was listed as living next door to a local cotton planter named John E. D. Moncure. Mrs. Thomas isn't certain, but the proximity suggests to her that Charlotte was one of John Moncure's former slaves. Charlotte had thirteen children, seven of whom were fathered either by John E. D. Moncure's brother, William Augustus Moncure, or by John's son, Robert; some records say William while others say Robert. Family stories had cast the relationship as a story of a forbidden love affair, but Mrs. Thomas thinks the truth was more painful: her great-grandmother was simply one of the perquisites of ownership slave owners took for granted in those days—and though slavery was legally over by the time the first of Charlotte's children was born, in 1868, it was a long time in many parts of the South before anybody could tell much difference. "Stories don't always have the ending people want them to have," she said.

But Charlotte Shakespeare turned out to be a crucial link—because John E. D. Moncure was the grandson of "Reverend John" Moncure, a Scottish emigrant whose arrival in Virginia in 1733 made the Moncures one of the famous "first families" of Virginia. Among the white Moncures, the existence of black Moncures had been known for generations, at least among family members who bothered to do any genealogical research. Years ago, Thomas said, an aunt of hers in Chicago had gotten a letter from a member of the white Moncures in Virginia, asking if she was kin. "She wrote back to them and she said, 'I am black,' and they never wrote back again." For the Virginia Moncures, the branch on the family tree that bore the names of John E. D. Moncure and William Augustus Moncure said "moved to Mississippi"—and nothing else. The existence of

Charlotte Shakespeare and her progeny had been deliberately omitted.

It was an interesting moment, therefore, when Patricia Thomas, this black school principal from Washington state, showed up at the all-white Virginia Moncures' 2002 family reunion in Fredericksburg. By then, she had been in touch with several distant cousins among the Virginia Moncures, and had accepted the invitation of a distant cousin to stay at her home during her visit. That cousin and her two sisters expressed their welcome by attending the first night of the reunion in identical black-and-white dresses they had bought to celebrate the joining of the Moncures' black and white branches. But the welcome was not unconditional. "Some people were dead agin' it, some were enthusiastically for it, and most were in the middle," said Tom Moncure, one of the Virginia Moncures and provost of George Mason University, in describing the gamut of reaction. One elderly kinsman made his displeasure known by boycotting the event and, after it was over, circulating an e-mail blasting his kinfolk for opening their doors to people whose skin color made it so obvious that they could not possibly be related. (Patricia Thomas has had her own DNA tested, and that of her father, "and it goes right to Scotland," she said. "Skin color means nothing.")

Tom Moncure also noted an interesting phenomenon: most of the Moncures who were unhappy about welcoming Patricia Thomas's people were elderly women. His theory is that they were expressing a kind of "pent-up, inherited resentment"—not just at Thomas herself, but at what she represented: here was a visible reminder of those long-dead white husbands and sons whose sexual wanderings had created her lineage in the first place. It was a resentment Thomas herself had encountered during her trip to Mississippi, when a white woman who headed a local historical society told her point-blank that she would not help her, and that furthermore all these questions were "upsetting" to the Virginia Moncures. The woman had not disputed Thomas's kinship, only her right to assert it. This was the unseen side of the infamous "all black men lust after white women" myth: the fact that *white* men had sometimes lusted after *black* women, and in doing so had dealt a profound sexual rejection to the wives whose beds they so casually deserted. Generations later, it seemed, that pain was still alive.

Tom Moncure and Patricia Thomas have gotten to know each other over the past few years, and they like each other; they can talk without pussyfooting around difficult topics. But on a deeper level, the conversation between the black and white branches of this very old American family is just beginning. When Tom Moncure refers to his "poor" childhood growing up in Stafford County during World War II, Patricia Thomas says, she finds herself wanting to blurt, "Yeah, but you were never *black*." But even that doesn't really get at what she wants to say; "black" does not equal "oppressed" and her life has not been a life of oppression. Nor does she think he is inventing or exaggerating his past. But there is money, and there are intangible assets—"social capital," as sociologists call it: family connections, friendships with people of means, memories of old favors done and returned for people in positions of power. All those her cousin and his branch of the family inherited, along with the security of living in a place where their familial roots have grown for generations—while her family inherited nothing, and was forced into exile from home by the threat of violence and the lack of decent jobs. Those nineteenth-century ideas about race that Tom Moncure can discuss so knowledgeably still have personal meaning to someone like Patricia Thomas. Sometimes she wonders if Tom really gets that, if he truly understands how different their lives have been.

I asked Tom Moncure if meeting Patricia Thomas and her branch of the family had altered any of his views about race. "Oh, no," he said immediately. "I've always had black kinfolk." But now that Patricia Thomas's branch has come to meet your branch, I pressed, are you going to pay a visit to hers?

"I don't leave Virginia, madam," Moncure said, in a mock-formal tone that made me laugh. He paused, enjoying his own joke, but then assured me that he was only partly joking. "Intellectually," he said, "I reside in the eighteenth century." For him and his family, Virginia is home and there they will stay—though the Mississippi Moncures are welcome anytime: "We are always delighted to see kinfolk at home, but I have no intention in my lifetime of setting foot in Washington state."

"That is sooo-oo Tom," Patricia Thomas wrote me in an e-mail when I reported this conversation to her, but she was not irritated about this failure to meet halfway. The Virginia Moncures are friends, "but not bosom buddies," she said. "My black family is still my closest family." And yet, there is this pushing, nagging impulse she has. She wants the Virginia Moncures to hear—to really *hear*—the story of the Mississippi Moncures, to reflect about the social forces that ripped her family apart, the immense courage that kept them going in the face of obstacles that are hard to imagine today, the successes they have achieved despite having few of the advantages their cousins had. That story, she thinks, is every bit as heroic, and quintessentially

American, as any Founding Fathers story or colonial mansion or three-hundred-year-old family church. On one of her last visits, after sitting through another one of Tom Moncure's mini-lectures about the history of the Virginia Moncures, she seized a pause in the conversation.

"Tom," she said, looking directly at him, "I'm going to ask you to do one thing. I'm going to ask you to be totally silent, and just listen, and I'd like you to *hear* me." And then, she said, "I just talked." And he listened.

When history becomes personal, it confers ownership of the past. History becomes less an abstract list of dates and trends, and more a story of people more or less like ourselves who lived in a certain way and did things that now seem mundane or courageous or, sometimes, unfathomable. It's the personal quality of the photographs in *Without Sanctuary* that makes those pictures so deeply disturbing: the amateurishly framed shot, the pitiful corpse, the banal surroundings, the faces of the observers. These are the ordinary people you see in family scrapbooks; maybe one is in *your* family scrapbook. Before historian and collector James Allen found them, the pictures had been hidden away for years in old rolltop desks, in attics, in piles of brittle, yellowed newspapers. Brought into the light of day, those ordinary faces were transformed into witnesses from the past. History, they remind us, is *what we did*.

A traveling exhibit of the pictures in *Without Sanctuary* opened in New York in 2000 and then toured the country. When it came to Atlanta in 2002 it happened to coincide with the end of a three-year visiting professorship at Emory

University by South African archbishop Desmond Tutu, the former chairman of the South African Truth and Reconciliation Commission. In his farewell speech, Tutu admonished his audience at Emory that the effort they were putting into their analyses of the South African experience might be put to better use at home. In effect, he said: *Go downtown and look at these pictures. This is your history, not ours. You have work of your own to do.*

Tutu's words could not have come at a more crucial moment. Interest in genealogy and rising rates of interracial marriage are like foam on a wave: evidence of bigger forces at work. In this case, the force is the simple passage of time. The civil rights generation is old. Pioneers like Dorothy Height, Rosa Parks, and James Forman have passed on; Julian Bond, who I used to watch back in the 1960s on Atlanta's WSB-TV as he announced another march or sit-in, looking like a precocious high schooler out past curfew, is now a venerable white-haired professor at the University of Virginia. The field of African American Studies has matured as an academic discipline; a new generation of scholars has begun to offer fresh perspectives on chapters of black history we already know and to uncover new ones. Not coincidentally, there has emerged an unspoken consensus that a summing-up is in order, an assessment of the civil rights generation's place in history somewhat like the spate of books and films that extolled the achievements of the World War II "greatest generation" a few years ago. But there's also a big difference: the greatest generation gets to look back on a "good war" that ended in unequivocal victory, while the civil rights generation looks back on years of struggle, some resounding victories, a few equivocal ones (see: affirmative action)—and a whole lot of loose ends. Before any final reckoning, there are accounts to be settled.

Hollywood, exquisitely attuned as ever to marketing and demographic trends, may have been the first to pick up on the emergence of this historical moment. The 1988 movie *Mississippi Burning* came out almost exactly a quarter of a century after the events it supposedly portrayed, the infamous "long, hot summer" of 1964—and though the film played fast and loose with a couple of historical realities (Gene Hackman played a courageous white liberal Mississippi sheriff, about as common back then as six-foot-tall albino rabbits), the movie did at least introduce a new generation to an era they knew little about. One person who saw the movie was Jerry Mitchell, who was then and still is a reporter at the Jackson, Mississippi, *Clarion-Ledger.* Mitchell was not a native Mississippian, but he was pretty close: he grew up on the Texas side of Texarkana, near where Texas, Arkansas, and Louisiana meet. Mitchell and I are roughly the same age, which means that we are too young to have witnessed the worst of the violence that accompanied the civil rights era—"when I was growing up it was almost like the civil rights movement was taking place in an alternate universe," he said—but old enough to have been imprinted at an early age with its psychic fallout. When Mitchell saw *Mississippi Burning,* he had two reactions. The first was basic: "The way we treated people as a society was wrong. What happened was *wrong.*" The second was to wonder: can we really let all those guys get away with it?

Over the next two decades, Mitchell's dogged investigative reporting led to the reopening of criminal prosecutions and eventual convictions of four defendants in some of the most notorious cases of that era: Byron De La Beckwith, who was behind the 1963 assassination of NAACP leader Medgar Evers; Sam Bowers, the Klan leader who ordered the fatal firebombing of NAACP leader Vernon Dahmer in 1966; Bobby Cherry, who masterminded the infamous 1963 bombing of a Birmingham church that killed four little girls; and Edgar Ray Killen, who helped organize the 1964 killings of civil rights workers Andrew Goodman, Michael Schwerner, and James Chaney. Mitchell's journalistic work was largely responsible for the 2007 creation by the U.S. Justice Department of the Civil Rights Cold Case Initiative, which has since drawn criticism for failing to actually issue any new indictments. But indictments may not be the only yardstick by which to measure its impact; the Justice Department's interest, as well as the handful of successful prosecutions of cold cases on the state level, has educated a new generation about the civil rights era and created a resurgence of interest in finding other ways of coming to terms with this chapter of the South's past.

"Blacks were like, 'Yeah, they'll bring him to court, but nothing will ever happen,'" said the Reverend Dolphus Weary, a longtime community activist who lives in Jackson, Mississippi, speaking of the 1994 conviction of Byron De La Beckwith. "And when they saw something did happen, it gave them hope."

And, on rare occasions, a chance for reconciliation. A crucial prosecution witness against Sam Bowers was a man named Billy Roy Pitts, a former Klan member and confederate of Bowers who over the years had undergone a change of heart and a religious conversion. After one court hearing in the Bowers case, Pitts approached Ellie Dahmer, the elderly widow of Vernon Dahmer, a Hattiesburg, Mississippi, civil rights activist who died in 1966 of third-degree burns he suffered when the Klan firebombed his home. With tears on his face, Pitts apologized for his role in Dahmer's death. Mrs. Dahmer wept, too. So did Jerry Mitchell, who was standing nearby and witnessed the encounter. After Mitchell told me this, I called Mrs. Dahmer, who is now in her eighties. After all these days, I asked, did that moment help her and her family?

"It helped us with Billy Roy Pitts," she said, "but the state of Mississippi was behind all this, and they are still pretending they had nothing to do with it—when they created the environment that the Klan could thrive in, and be so successful."

And here we arrive at the limits of the criminal justice system: it deals only with specific wrongdoing, not with broad societal inequities or fundamental failures of government. For that, an entirely new system is required—which, as it happened, is exactly what happened in South Africa in the mid-1990s, when then-President Nelson Mandela ordered the creation of a national Truth and Reconciliation Commission to help his nation come to terms with its long history of apartheid.

The TRC, as it came to be known, became a template for an emerging legal field known as "restorative justice"—which, strictly speaking, is actually an old idea currently undergoing a revival in legal and human rights circles. In traditional criminal law, the state acts as proxy for the victim; in restorative justice, victim and wrongdoer confront each other directly, but collateral victims are also recognized by including members of the community where the crime took place. The aim is not punishment or deterrence, but healing—a process that requires the perpetrator to do the hard work of making amends and the victim to do the hard work of forgiveness. "Hard work" in this context specifically means a full examination of what happened, undertaken on the belief that there is no way to bury painful chapters of the past without holding an inquest.

That's the theory, anyway, and the theory has its limits: restorative justice forums don't enforce any laws, and the efficacy of the process is dependent on the good faith of the participants. But when it comes to dealing with historical wrongs, especially in the South, restorative justice theory is a natural fit with the region's "come-to-Jesus" religious culture. It is no coincidence that before there was ever a South African TRC, a group of Christian businessmen in Jackson, Mississippi, had already founded a group called Mission Mississippi, based on the concept that racial reconciliation was fundamentally a spiritual issue, and that the most pressing need of the church was not, as one member said, "a crusade to make more Christians, but [to make] people who call themselves Christian start living it out." Founded in 1991, the group is now active in nineteen communities across the state, helping facilitate daylong community meetings where whites and blacks sit in the same room to actually talk frankly about the dangerous topic of race, usually in the context of some current event or pressing community problem. Mission Mississippi is an overtly Christian group, but in a state where the vast majority of people go to church that's not a limitation.

"We think if racial reconciliation is going to change things in Mississippi, the church is going to lead the way," says the Reverend Neddie Winters, executive director of Mission Mississippi. His group has no agenda besides fostering racial cooperation. He thinks of what they do as akin to a farmer amending the soil; after that, who knows what plants may grow? In 2008, the interracial cooperation born in Mission Mississippi meetings bore fruit in the form of a group that calls itself the Mississippi Truth Project. The group is collecting oral histories with the aim of creating a new Truth and Reconciliation Commission, one that will focus on racially motivated crimes and injustices that happened in Mississippi between 1945 and 1975.

The Mississippi effort would be the second commission in the South in recent years built on the South African model. In 2002, citizens of Greensboro, North Carolina, formed a TRC to examine the causes and long-term results of a 1979 incident in which Greensboro police failed to monitor a Communist Workers Party "Death to the Klan" rally in a local housing project. In the absence of a police presence, the communist demonstrators were attacked by local members of the Ku Klux Klan and the Nazi Party; in the ensuing gun battle, five CWP demonstrators were killed and ten others wounded. Klan and Nazi members were twice acquitted by all-white juries, though a jury in a later civil trial held the Greensboro Police Department jointly liable with the Klan and the Nazi Party for the wrongful death of one of the victims. The lack of police at the 1979 rally grew to symbolize what many blacks and Latinos in Greensboro saw as white city officials' basic indifference to their welfare.

The results of the Greensboro experiment were, at best, a qualified success. The city refused to participate in the commission; one city official told the panel he found it "distasteful" to dredge up unhappy chapters of the city's past, and another remarked that the whole thing was "a big yawn." In contrast, the final TRC report said that the panel encountered one witness after another who feared economic or social retaliation for testifying about an event which by then had happened fifteen years earlier.

Yet these efforts in Mississippi and North Carolina are part of a broader and much more hopeful picture. In the past fifteen years or so, a loosely affiliated network of roughly two dozen groups has sprung up across the South, each devoted in one way or another to the cause of racial reconciliation. Their specific agendas vary: in Georgia, the Moore's Ford Memorial Committee has reopened a criminal investigation into the infamous 1946 Walton County lynching whose legacy I encountered that day in 1982; in Wilmington, North Carolina, a group called the 1898 Foundation held community meetings to talk about the causes and lasting damage inflicted on that city by an 1898 coup, in which a white mob seized control of city government from its democratically elected biracial officials, burned down the city's black newspaper, and drove most of the city's black residents from their homes. In East Texas, a group is lobbying the state legislature for laws that would prevent private property owners from blocking public access to historic black cemeteries.

A significant proportion of the membership of these groups tend to be "adopted" Southerners—people who have moved to the region from other places—but it is no coincidence that most of the groups are led or mentored by veterans of the civil rights movement. In the view of Southern historian Melton McLaurin, who served on the board of Wilmington's 1898 Foundation, the effort to integrate the South's history is the natural coda to a movement that sought to integrate its schools and restaurants.

"The schools are integrated," McLaurin said. "So are public

accommodations. You can be employed anywhere and you can buy a house anywhere.... The legal barriers are all gone, and frankly nobody gives much of a thought to them anymore." But when it comes to how the past is remembered—or not remembered, as the case may be—"the myths are still up. Barriers are still held. I think you had a group of people who had thought to do away with those earlier barriers saying, this is what's remaining."

Just as in the civil rights days, grassroots efforts are now beginning to coalesce into something more organized, and have begun to draw on the energy and logistical support a university setting can provide. The William Winter Institute for Racial Reconciliation, founded in 1999 on the campus of Ole Miss in Oxford, Mississippi, is one example; another is Southern Truth and Reconciliation (STAR), based on the campus of Atlanta's Emory University. At a 2006 conference at Ole Miss sponsored by the William Winter Institute, STAR, and the Birmingham Pledge, an educational group devoted to teaching cultural diversity and the history of racial oppression, twenty-four reconciliation groups agreed to form the Regional Alliance for Truth and Racial Reconciliation. Its mission: "To promote truth-seeking and reconciliation on issues of racial violence by deepening our understanding of history and its continuing effects and by working for justice."

Atlanta, the self-proclaimed Capital of the New South and center of the civil rights movement, promises to become a nexus for the racial reconciliation movement, thanks to the planned opening in 2014 of the National Center for Civil and Human Rights on two and a half acres of land near Five Points donated by the Coca-Cola Company. The $100 million project will house the papers of Martin Luther King and serve as the permanent home of collector James Allen's *Without Sanctuary* exhibit of lynching pictures and postcards. In addition, it will host a variety of historical exhibits on the civil rights movement, linking that history to contemporary issues in human rights around the world.

But the ultimate test of racial reconciliation efforts is not just educating people in history or convincing them that it's a worthy idea; the real challenge is showing it can create tangible results. Fifty years ago, Atlanta's reputation as "the city too busy to hate" helped to ignite its explosive economic growth—demonstrating, in the process, that racial enlightenment could actually be a highly effective marketing tool. So why didn't cities all over the South immediately try to copy the Atlanta experience? Because it's not that simple. An understanding of racial history has to connect to money, and money has to be on speaking terms with people in political power. These are conditions that just happened to prevail in Atlanta of the 1960s. But how could that kind of social change happen in a more tradition-conscious place—a city like, say, Richmond?

That question, or something like it, was what faced Rob Corcoran in 1980, when he and his wife moved to an inner-city neighborhood in the former capital of the Confederacy. The son of a Scottish trade unionist, Corcoran had worked abroad as a community organizer for twenty years for an organization called Moral Re-Armament (since renamed Initiatives of Change). Richmond presented its own challenges to a community organizer, especially a newcomer. The city had just elected its first black mayor, and local politics was tense. Black inner-city residents were outraged at an annexation plan of a mostly white area of surrounding Henrico County, seeing it as a blatant attempt by the city's white power structure to dilute the impact of the black vote. Whites were fleeing the city for the suburbs, in large part to escape court-ordered desegregation of city schools; the city's old-line white power structure viewed the new black administration with suspicion and contempt; class distinctions among both blacks and whites in this very conservative and traditional city created even more barriers to communication.

Corcoran spent the next ten years trying to understand and bridge the enormous racial divide that seemed to stifle all kinds of things—community projects, business ideas, political compromise. In 1990, he founded an organization called Hope in the Cities, which is in some ways the grandfather of the racial reconciliation movement in the South. HITC programs offer a variety of templates for community groups dealing with the issue of racial reconciliation. It's a little like a cross between marriage counseling on a civic scale and an Alcoholics Anonymous meeting: participants are asked to begin with an individual moral inventory, in which they try to honestly come to terms with the ways race has affected their lives—how it has influenced their choice of where to live, how it may have embittered them, how they may have benefited from its legacy. The rest involves people sharing stories and, eventually, forming friendships that become a social framework for working on community projects.

That's a simplistic summary, of course, but the bottom line, Corcoran said, is that "you have to make the linkage between history and what is now. . . . In Richmond, we simply could not progress as a community in all kinds of ways, whether we're talking about economic development, housing, or education—

we simply could not progress as a community and as a region if we continued to ignore and avoid our racial history. It just kept popping up."

As it did, for example, when in 2003 local businessman H. Alexander Wise proposed creating a Civil War museum at the Tredegar Iron Works, a nineteenth-century gun foundry on the banks of the James River where slaves had once helped forge cannons for the Confederacy. Black residents of Richmond rolled their eyes: *another* museum? Would these white people never shut up about their late, lamented Lost Cause? But what Wise had in mind was different—a museum that would tell the story of the war from three perspectives: North, South, and African American. Had this idea surfaced in the malignant racial atmosphere of Richmond in the early 1980s, Corcoran thinks, it would have been a nonstarter. As it is, the American Civil War Center at Historic Tredegar today is a thriving tourist attraction in the heart of downtown.

Every year, Hope in the Cities holds a Metropolitan Richmond Day breakfast and invites community leaders from the private and public sectors. Back when I was a newspaper reporter, I sat through my share of these events, but the 2010 Metropolitan Richmond Day breakfast differed from the standard-issue civic ceremony I was once sentenced to cover. The usual cadre of middle-aged white men was there, but so were an equal number of corporate-looking middle-aged black men, representatives of a generation that has not always had a seat at the main table. I saw older white ladies wearing suits and pearls, Muslim women wearing hijabs, black ladies in their church hats; I saw men with dreadlocks and men in yarmulkes. It was a study in ethnic diversity, with presentations made in teams chosen for their "opposite" value: a Muslim paired with a Jew; a black person paired with an Asian. There was a goodwill vibe in the room. At the same time, the whole thing felt incredibly awkward.

Eventually I struck up a conversation with one of the ladies at my table—Ceona Johnson, a neighborhood activist from Gilpin Court, the last major public housing complex in Richmond. Why are you here? I asked her, and she began telling me about how she and her fellow residents had to mail their rent checks each month to a bank in New York City. The mail took at least a day and sometimes two, meaning that in order not to incur a late fee everybody had to pay a day or two early—a significant hardship for people on fixed incomes, whose cash reserves were always their lowest at the end of the month. There was only one resident representative on the seven-member tenants' council that heard resident complaints; all the others were people from government or the banks. On top of that, the city was now considering a proposal to tear down Gilpin Court and redevelop it into a neighborhood of mixed-income housing—a proposal that, even if it happened exactly as planned, would inevitably force the poor and elderly to move.

In the old days, a person like Ceona Johnson might have led a march on city hall and yelled through a bullhorn; talking to someone like me might have been one of her few options for being heard. On this morning, however, she and the decision makers were all in the same room, and she knew who to buttonhole. "Excuse me," she said the minute she finished her breakfast. "I got to go talk to some people."

Racial reconciliation can be incredibly simple, like being able to talk to the head of the city housing agency at breakfast. It can also utterly confound even the best of intentions. Theophus

Smith, a professor at the Candler School of Religion at Emory University, works as a consultant with groups in the South who are trying to establish some kind of truth and reconciliation process, or memorials to lynching victims, or both. Among his goals is some kind of marker on the spot where Sam Hose was lynched—but there's a problem: to this day, there is a "black" version of the Sam Hose story, and a "white" version. In one, Hose is a farm laborer who killed his employer in self-defense and never raped his employer's wife; in the other, he is a criminal who gratuitously murdered his employer, raped his wife, and maimed one of their infant children.

In 2007, Smith and others convened a community meeting in Newnan to discuss the idea of creating some kind of commemoration of the Sam Hose lynching, and ignited a whole new uproar. "I am amazed there are plans to have a memorial service to show respect and honor for Sam Hose, the man who murdered and raped in our county many years ago," one Newnan resident wrote to the local newspaper. "There are numerous descendants of the victims still living here, and it was their grandparents who were the children involved in this horrendous crime." It's true; everybody in Newnan knows who the Cranfords are; the family includes a socially prominent local judge as well as a local doctor. Between these realities and the competing versions of the crime, efforts to come up with a meaningful way of marking the place of Hose's death have so far run aground.

Yet the question, having been raised, now refuses to go away. As William Faulkner said, the past is never over. It's not even past.

5.

Jesusland

There's a bumper sticker and/or T-shirt slogan you will see if you hang out long enough in the South: "American by birth, Southern by the grace of God." The key word is "grace." Southern identity is really just an exaggerated form of American exceptionalism: God shed his grace on America, the thinking goes, then threw in some extra by making some Americans Southerners. The proof is in reams of polling data that clearly show that Southerners go to church more than other Americans, that more of us consider religion to be a "very important" part of our daily lives, that we pray more often than other Americans, and that we see evidence of divine intercession in our daily affairs more frequently than people elsewhere.

The way Southerners express this love for Jesus is, for the most part, in evangelical Protestant terms—meaning, among other things, that they believe in the Bible as the ultimate authority, that history is heading toward a cataclysmic conclusion that will arrive with the Second Coming of Christ, and, most important, in the necessity of an intensely personal "born again" experience. Numbers on evangelicals are fuzzy, since the mean-

106

ing of the term differs according to who is doing the polling, but the best estimates are that between one-fourth and one-third of all Americans identify themselves as this way. In the South, where the most important Mainline Protestant denominations all share a solidly evangelical lineage, you can come up with a good seat-of-the-pants estimate by simply deducting all the Jews, Catholics, atheists, Muslims, Hindus, and pagans. That yields a ballpark estimate of 75 percent of the population[1]—and the deeper South you go, the higher that percentage gets. In Mississippi, it comes to 81 percent, which probably explains the existence of an online support group called Mississippi Atheists. They must feel like they are on Mars.

The result of this religious saturation is a certain amount of spiritual hubris. While Southerners don't go around saying "Jesus loves me, but he can't stand you,"[2] there's an unmistakable if unspoken assumption that God loves us *better*. This is a strand of Southern exceptionalism that's has been around since before the Civil War, when Southern ministers were hotly reacting to abolitionist attacks on the morality of slave ownership. Sometime in the 1970s, however, this Southern exceptionalism fused with a peculiarly white middle-class Southern sense of grievance in a way that sent vast numbers of evangelicals into the arms of the Republican Party. The result was nothing less than momentous: a religious mind-set that once united Southerners across denominational, political, and even racial lines has become a tool of division and a badge of ideological purity.

And this huge change has been happening at the same time as other social, demographic, and technological changes have been sweeping the region. Hispanic immigration has introduced Catholicism into parts of the rural South where it was once rare;

meanwhile, as native-born rural populations dwindle, small rural Protestant churches are dying off. (In the Mississippi Delta, the number of abandoned church buildings rivals the number of abandoned gas stations and stores.) The hymns and worship services I knew as a child are still around, but an increasing number of churches have glammed up with a menu of worship options designed to appeal to the broadest demographic possible, an effort to make up for aging congregations and declining interest among eighteen- to twenty-nine-year-olds.[3] The church I grew up in is an example of both trends: its congregation had become so small that it celebrated its hundred-year anniversary in 2011 by going out of business. Today it's a remote campus of a suburban congregation forty miles away, where congregants can opt for worship services in traditional or "contemporary" style—or, if that doesn't appeal, a late-morning coffee bar. Dedicated deer hunters can get live streaming on their mobile phones. Once all you needed for a music service was an organist or a pianist—and in a pinch, some a cappella singing would do; today, you need a sound system, a five-piece band, an opening act, and a Jumbo-Tron so everybody can see the stage. The line between church and marketplace, between religious service and entertainment, gets harder to draw every day.

The one thing that hasn't changed is the uniquely emotional intensity Southerners bring to their religion. You can't drive anywhere in the South without meeting Jesus, so to speak: the name pops up on road signs, bumper stickers, and T-shirts everywhere. In DeKalb County, Georgia: "Obama Spends, Jesus Saves." On a car bumper on I-85: "Jesus: a Friend for Life." On the back of a teenager's T-shirt in Asheboro, North Carolina: "My peace I leave with you, not as the world giveth..." On a towing company sign: "Jesus Never Fails." A sign welcomes me to a small town with "Jesus Is Lord" (in big letters) "Over Grays Chapel." Newcomers to the South often marvel at the sheer number of churches—"more per square inch than anything I'd ever seen," reported one of my husband's Marin County, California, relatives when she moved to Knoxville, Tennessee. Clearly, there is still something distinctly Southern going on here.

What is it? To answer that question, we have to go back to the very beginnings of the "South" as we now know it—a time when Southerners were not exactly known for their piety.

"The Sabbath is but seldom observed," Anglican minister Charles Woodmason complained in 1768, speaking of the settlers on the Congaree River in what is now central South Carolina. A former Charleston planter, Woodmason had become a priest in his forties, volunteering to establish Anglican parishes and administer proper church rites in the pre–Revolutionary War backcountry. He was an educated man of high culture and strong opinions—I imagine him as a kind of eighteenth-century Frasier Crane—and the things he saw among the South's Scotch-Irish proto-rednecks struck him as outrageous. The swearing! Those women with the wads of snuff in their lower lips, brown drool trickling down their chins! The knee-walking drunks!—nine out of ten of whom had the clap, not that anybody seemed to care. "They are very poor, owing to their extreme indolence. . . . They delight in their present low, lazy, sluttish, heathenish, hellish life, and seem not desirous of changing it."[4]

Clearly, these lost sheep needed what Woodmason was selling. Yet he couldn't seem to pry their attention away from the itinerant "New Baptist" missionaries who had beaten him to the backcountry. They were converting sinners right and left. Their popularity mystified him, their lack of education appalled him, and their church services looked like a hootenanny. "Here, one fellow mounted on a bench with the bread, and bawling *See the Body of Christ*, another with the cup running around and bellowing, *Who cleanses his soul with the blood of Christ*, and a thousand other extravagancies—one on his knees in a posture of prayer—others singing—some howling—these ranting—those crying—others dancing, skipping, laughing and rejoicing." When Woodmason chastised one Baptist group for improperly observing the Sabbath, the members sent back a message "that if I offered to come into their parts for to preach, they would give me corporal punishment.... To such heights of insolence are these Sectaries grown."[5] Two and a half centuries later, you can practically hear the reverend's blood vessels pop.

From the get-go, then, the South was fertile soil for religious innovation. This was on the eve of the American Revolution, which made the Church of England the only legally authorized religious establishment—and yet in the minds of these up-country settlers, it was no match for a worship style that interposed no human authority figure between the believer and his God. While the Anglican Church retained its influence among the planter class and in long-settled parts of the region, and other churches—the Quakers, the Presbyterians, the Catholics—made an imprint in a few places, evangelical religion began to make steady inroads among the yeoman farmers and herdsmen who pushed into the Appalachians and the Indian lands of the interior. Within the next fifty to seventy-five years, it had become the faith of the masses, and by the end of the Civil War, it had reached what religious historian Samuel Hill calls a "virtual saturation" point in Southern society.[6]

Having saturated, it proceeded to steep: in an agrarian region with a minimal transportation infrastructure and very little outside influence from immigration, evangelical religion became the only kind of religion many Southerners ever knew. In that sense, the South had become something unique in American history: a biracial culture bound together by one religion. In 1906, 96.6 percent of the population of the United States east of the Mississippi and south of the Potomac identified themselves as churchgoing Protestants—"the most solidly Protestant population of its size in the Western Hemisphere,"[7] as Southern historian C. Vann Woodward called it. It was the original, often imitated but never duplicated, Bible Belt.

The Civil War fused evangelical religion with the interests of Confederate nationalism. Southern churches were a major conduit for war news, and eve-of-battle revivals in the Confederate ranks were common occurrences. The war itself was cast as a religious crusade, the South's defense of its traditional morality and agrarian values against the increasingly industrial and atheistic North. Confederate heroes were painted in Christian colors: Robert E. Lee was a saintly knight, Jefferson Davis was a Christian martyr, Stonewall Jackson and Nathan Bedford Forrest filled the roles of stern Old Testament prophet-warriors. Southern women—white Southern women, anyway—were cast in the role of the Virgin Mother: brave, morally pure, and self-sacrificing. The Confederacy's motto—*Deo vindice*—was Latin for "God will vindicate us."

It might seem that losing a war would strike a fatal blow to that argument, and in fact most white Southerners saw the Confederacy's defeat in apocalyptic terms. In his study of Lost Cause theology, historian Charles Reagan Wilson quotes the diary of a Georgia woman who wrote in 1865, "Clouds and darkness are round about us; the hand of the Almighty is laid in sore judgment upon us; we are a deserted and smitten people."[8] But God dwells in the darkness, their ministers counseled them, and urged their flock to keep the faith. If defeat was the judgment of a stern but loving God, then He in His mysterious wisdom would see to it that such trials would only strengthen the faithful in the end.

And so white Southerners kept a white-knuckled grip on their self-image as a kind of non-Jewish Chosen People. Chapters of the United Daughters of the Confederacy commissioned stained-glass memorials to the Confederacy's generals in churches across the South, and a new generation of ministerial students learned theology from the lips of former Confederate chaplains. Does this sound like ancient history? It's not all that ancient. Bill Leonard, a professor of church history at Wake Forest School of Divinity, once had an older colleague who in his youth had been a student of John R. Sampey, a former president of the Southern Baptist Theological Seminary. Born in 1863, Sampey was of a post–Civil War generation that reverenced Robert E. Lee. One day in his class a student asked if it was possible that Lee could ever have lied. It was possible, Sampey replied, but there was no evidence that Lee had ever done so—and he launched into a long litany of sins that the pious Lee had never committed. What about Ulysses S. Grant? the student asked. "Son of a bitch, young man," the learned man of God snapped. "Son of a *bitch*." In historical terms, the Lost Cause was lost only yesterday. Black Southerners in the Jim Crow South seemed to have only two options when it came to matters of faith, sociologist W. E. B. Du Bois observed in 1903. One was to despair of the unfulfilled promise of true freedom, "to curse God and die"; the other was to trust in a faith that promised freedom and deliverance someday in the hereafter. "Some day the awakening will come" was his prescient prediction, and in fact the black church in the South would someday provide the resilience and strength of the civil rights movement. Meanwhile, black Southerners of the Jim Crow era—excluded from white houses of worship and alienated by a Lost Cause mythology that reduced their role in history to a walk-on—responded by creating a parallel evangelical universe that in its way exerted more influence on white culture than the other way around. The evangelical presence in the black community was, if anything, even more pervasive: "In the South, at least, practically every American Negro is a church member," Du Bois wrote.[9] More important, "the silent but potent influence" of millions of black evangelicals reinforced the political influence of the Baptist and Methodist churches, especially when it came to topics like liquor sales and gambling—and on those subjects, Pentecostals were of the same mind. (The Pentecostal movement wasn't born in the South, strictly speaking, but it has been extremely influential there, and the Pentecostal churches were racially integrated from the very beginning.) The black church in the South was also a training ground for generations of black community leaders barred from using their gifts in society at large. "On Sunday, you weren't a maid or a butler," says Jonathan Walton, a scholar of the black church in America who teaches at

Harvard Divinity School, "you were a deacon or Trustee Jones. You were *somebody*." [10] The black church, in short, was the means by which a social system based on racial segregation unwittingly nourished the seeds of its own destruction.

Whether it was the black church or the white church, evangelical religion and politics have always been twins in the South. But they exerted influence in different ways. The white evangelical church's control worked via its sheer pervasiveness: a person couldn't get elected dogcatcher without being an evangelical church member in good standing somewhere. Periodically, white churches would get energized about specific causes—opposition to teaching evolution in schools, for instance, or to some local proposal to allow beer sales on Sundays. But up through the 1960s, white churches in the South saw their mission as saving souls, not involving themselves in earthly concerns. (There were some notable exceptions to this rule: black and white Methodist women formed an interracial lobbying effort in the 1920s to campaign for a federal anti-lynching law, for example, but though the historical import of that was huge, the numbers involved were tiny.)

This—white evangelical Southern religion—was the religion of my childhood, large chunks of which were spent in the classrooms and sanctuary of a nondenominational fundamentalist congregation in a suburb of Atlanta. East Point Christian Church traced its theological provenance to the Christian Restoration movement of the 1830s and the fundamentalist movement of the late nineteenth century—the first from Pennsylvania and Kentucky, the second a product of the Midwest. All of that would have been news to me at the time; I thought "evangelical" and "fundamentalist" meant the same thing, and were both synonymous with "Southern." William Faulkner, describing his childhood in turn-of-the-century Mississippi, wrote that religion "was a part of my background. I grew up with that, I assimilated that, took that in without even knowing it. It's just there. It has nothing to do with how much of it I might believe or disbelieve—it's just there." In that respect, he might have been describing my childhood sixty years later; in its essentials, not that much had changed.

The fierce doctrinal battles I recall from my childhood were a product of the overall uniformity of the religious landscape— a phenomenon Sigmund Freud once called "the narcissism of small differences." Devout brothers and sisters in Christ could disagree vehemently on questions like whether baptism should immediately follow one's confession of sin or if it was okay to wait until the end of the month, whether it was scripturally correct to address ministers as "Reverend," and whether to use real wine or Welch's Grape Juice at Communion. (The consensus in my church was for grape juice, mainly because none of us could imagine Jesus in a liquor store.)

It was a culture that drew no practical division between church and state, no particular boundary between private belief and public expression. Years later, I was surprised to learn that the Supreme Court's decision on school prayer had been in 1962; as a former Georgia public school student in the 1960s, I can authoritatively say that the law of the land was being ignored in that state at least a decade later, and probably much longer. In elementary school, I sang in a chorus at a regional convention of public school music educators that welcomed visitors to Atlanta with "Praise God from Whom All Blessings Flow"; in high school I attended a school-sponsored pep rally in which a local youth minister invited people down front to give their lives to Jesus. Today, these things would cause an uproar, even in the South; back then, anybody who objected would have been shunned. Were Jews offended? Probably, but Southern Jews had long ago resigned themselves to life among the evangelical goyim. Every city council meeting, every school graduation, every bridge dedication began with an invocation "in Jesus' name," and a standard conversational icebreaker when you were just getting to know someone was, "What church do y'all go to?"

But larger events were about to intrude on this cloistered little world. Had I been born in the Atlanta of 1855, as opposed to the Atlanta of 1955, I might have grown up with the same sense of having arrived at the end of one historical epoch and the beginning of another, with a front-row view of a battle over contested terrain. The nineteenth-century battle was political; the twentieth-century version was both political and religious, as white evangelical religion in the South took on a tone of grievance. In 1962, the year I was in second grade, a concrete barrier went up across a street in a southwest Atlanta neighborhood about ten miles north of us, marking a division between black and white ends of the street. It was a foolish gesture; it would have taken the Berlin Wall to withstand the post–World War II demand for housing among Atlanta's black middle class, who had been penned up inside the city limits for decades. Starting in 1948, when restrictive racial covenants on real estate were declared unconstitutional, black home buyers finally gained access to white neighborhoods that had long been denied them. The tide of transition and white flight headed toward those areas of the city and its close-in suburbs where property values were the most affordable—west and south, straight toward us. Week after week, I would hear the same conversation among adults at church: so-and-so was moving down to Fayette County, or Newnan, or somewhere even farther out, because his neighborhood was—"*you* know." Racism was the prevailing virus; one way or another, we all suffered from it, or for it.

There's an old story, possibly apocryphal, in which Lyndon Johnson turned to an aide after signing the 1964 Civil Rights Act and said, "We have lost the South for a generation." For the past fifty years, the conventional explanation for the South's political shift from Democratic to Republican was simple: the minute Democrats became the party of black Americans, white Southerners left en masse. It's a tidy formulation that has always driven conservative white Southerners nuts, since the more vigorously you deny you are a racist, the more likely it is you are one. Nevertheless, racism was not the whole story, as the resurgence of modern conservatism and the culture wars in general have made increasingly clear, and in recent years a new generation of scholars has been adding some much needed nuance to that picture.

To Princeton historian Kevin Kruse, the explanation lies in a definition of "rights" which attaches to the individual, not to groups—a point of view not unique to the South, but which has found a more receptive audience there than anywhere else in the country. When the U.S. Supreme Court ruled that restrictive racial covenants in real estate transactions were unconstitutional, Kruse said, conservative Southerners could appreciate the court's logic even if they didn't like its conclusion. "The rationale [was that] a home is private property—you can't lock a person into a commitment to the neighborhood. You can't tell people who they can sell their house to."[11] For racist white conservatives in the South, who hated "big government" even more than they hated black people, this made sense. But when the 1964 Civil Rights Act went further—when it said, in essence, that the government *could* tell owners of department stores or restaurants which customers they must serve, those same Southern whites were outraged by what seemed to them a blatant inconsistency in logic.

The mind of the white South of the 1960s saw the issue of residential integration not in terms of the rights of black Southerners as a group, but in terms of the rights of white homeowners as individuals. The middle- and working-class whites like the ones I grew up among on Atlanta's Southside "were fighting for rights of their own—such as the 'right' to select their neighbors, their employees and their children's classmates, the 'right' to do as they pleased with their private property and personal business, and, perhaps most important, the 'right' to remain free from what they saw as dangerous encroachments by the federal government,"[12] Kruse writes. It's an argument that has too often been dismissed as a fig leaf for baser motives. But racism and Southern-style political conservatism could be, and often were, separate entities. As the past fifty years have shown, the South has gone a long way—maybe further than any other region—toward divesting itself of overt racism, while the hatred most white Southerners have for federal mandates and "big government" burns hotter than ever.

So what do Atlanta's residential integration wars so many years ago have to do with Southern religion today? It was a hinge moment in history, emblematic of the way in which white evangelicals in the South woke up to the passing of an era when their culture and their religion had constituted a seamless whole. Suddenly, their ownership of their culture was under threat, and the realization brought home for them the necessity of a kind of grassroots political involvement they had never needed to bother with before. They weren't the first white Southern evangelicals to face this moment of truth; something very similar had happened to other members of the tribe three thousand miles away, in southern California—and here, we need to double back in our story for just a moment.

There's an old joke in the South: the Great Depression happened without our noticing, because it came in the middle of hard times. In the 1930s, the South was home to vast tracts of poverty that had been poor since the Civil War, and when the Great Depression came, hundreds of thousands of Southerners, white and black, began a mass exodus. The most famous chapter of this Great Southern Diaspora was the one that took millions of black Southern sharecroppers from the old plantation belt north to Chicago, Detroit, Baltimore, or Washington. Less well known is the one that took hundreds of thousands of white Southerners in the "western South" (Arkansas, Texas, and Oklahoma) west to find jobs in the defense industry plants and car factories of southern California, where they were to have a huge impact on the new suburbs sprouting in the still rural areas just south of Los Angeles.[13]

Transplanted from the insular, rural culture they had always known, ridiculed by their new California neighbors for their uncouth rural ways, the migrants formed communities organized the way they had been back home—around church membership—and began work on what evangelicals call the Great Commission: bringing unsaved souls to Jesus. But these weren't your standard-issue Deep South evangelicals; these were a new and more militant species—Southerners who had reacted to the national ridicule heaped on evangelical religion in the wake of the famous Scopes "monkey trial" in Dayton, Tennessee, by reasserting their belief in the "fundamentals" of evangelical religion. They were, in short, fundamentalists—and their reaction to their strange new surroundings was to become more so.

They had arrived with the Southern Yellow Dog Democrat political affiliation (as in "I'd vote for a yellow dog as long as he was a Democrat"). That began to fray after World War II, when liberal New Deal Democrats in California allied with labor unions to challenge hiring practices that discriminated against blacks, who were in direct competition with the migrants for jobs. The Democratic establishment's tilt toward expanding New Deal–style social programs also triggered the newcomers' ingrained Southern distrust of anything that smacked of "big government." At the same time, a new crop of evangelical preachers (including a handsome young man from North Carolina named Billy Graham) were raising alarms about communist takeovers in China and North Korea. To the evangelical mind in those early years of the Cold War, the sudden emergence of Soviet-style communism looked very much like the coming of the Antichrist prophesied in the Book of Revelation—a clear warning of the imminent Second Coming of Christ. The establishment of the modern state of Israel in 1948, also seemingly foretold in Revelation, cemented that interpretation. Evangelical preaching took on an increasingly urgent tone; what was at stake, believers were told, was nothing less than the fate of humanity.

In this atmosphere of paranoia and social unrest, the migrants began a steady defection to the Republican Party. This

was the 1950s, a period of prosperity in which a successful business entrepreneurs teamed up with evangelical preachers to pour
money into a growing network of schools devoted to conservative religious precepts and a belief in laissez-faire capitalism—
places like Pepperdine University in Los Angeles and Bob Jones
University in South Carolina. (Oral Roberts University in Tulsa,
part of same phenomenon, would follow in 1963.) These were
years in which the groundwork was being laid for the resurgence
of right-wing conservatism in the 1960s—most notably, the
1964 presidential election, when Republicans broke the Democrats' century-long lock on the Deep South.

The voters who made that happen were white middle-class
Southerners like my parents—and because those people were
overwhelmingly evangelical Protestants, that historic political
shift marked the fusion of conservative politics with a particular subtype of evangelical religion. Put another way, by the time
the South was ready to break its generations-long allegiance to
the Democratic Party, those West Coast Southern migrants had
already begun to alter the genetic makeup of the Republican
Party, whose success in the South in the 1960s proceeded to
alter the genetic makeup of Southern evangelicalism—making
it more fundamentalist in tone, more political, and overall less
hospitable to so-called "moderates" or "liberals." It was a subtle
but inexorable development, which eventually would cause formal ideological schisms among Southern Baptists and Presbyterians and tear the evangelical church loose from its moorings as
a Southern cultural institution.

This may come as a surprise to people under the impression
I once was—that the South has *always* been the land of fundamentalism. That may be because fundamentalist religion is such

a natural fit with certain aspects of Southern culture that, like kudzu, it's hard to imagine a time when it wasn't there. It's contrarian, in that it places a higher value on personal conviction than on government authority, a trait that fits right in with that stubborn Scotch-Irish antiauthoritarian streak I mentioned earlier. The fundamentalist insistence on a literal interpretation of the Bible and the "originalist" school of Constitutional interpretation reflect a similar psychological mind-set. Fundamentalists also place a high value on obedience to authority—which may sound like a contradiction, but it's not: Southerners are all in favor of authority as long as we are the ones exercising it. In the 1960s, the fundamentalist admonition that "the powers that be are ordained of God" (something I heard a lot about in Sunday School) fit right in with a society that ranked people according to skin color, social class, and gender.

Most important, though, is the fundamentalist emphasis on being set apart, called to fulfill a particular moral mission. Paul's admonition to the Christians in Corinth to "be ye separate" from non-Christians was another thing I heard in church as a child more times than I can count; we were constantly reminded that Christians were to be "*in* the world, but not *of* it." The fundamentalist emphasis on "family values" and moral purity fit naturally with the remnant of that fusion of evangelical religion and Confederate nationalism I described earlier, which was built on the assumption that the South was a land of superior civilization and moral values.[14]

Still, this was not the fundamentalism I had grown up with. That had been otherworldly and apolitical; this was media savvy and intent on making its political presence felt. By 1976, pollster George Gallup had declared that it was the "year of the evangelical"; in 1979, Jerry Falwell founded the Moral Majority. That year, Christian broadcaster Pat Robertson announced, "We have together, with the Protestants and the Catholics, enough votes to run the country. And when the people say, 'We've had enough,' we are going to take over." [15]

The strength of the religious right was its passion, which was also its fatal flaw: people who are in direct communication with God are not always good at taking orders from each other. By the 1990s, it was becoming clear that the movement's hard-line rhetoric on issues like abortion and homosexuality was producing a backlash; in the eyes of a lot of people, including a lot of evangelicals, "fundamentalist" was becoming synonymous with "intolerant." And other issues were beginning to distract conservatives from their "family values" preoccupation: 9/11, the war in Iraq, the roller-coaster economy, income inequality. In the 2008 presidential race, the cohesiveness of the religious right vote had clearly fragmented.

But the imprint of the fusion between Southern evangelical religion and conservative politics has been lasting, and nowhere more evident than in the South. Shortly after the 2008 presidential race, I saw an article on the *Daily Yonder*, a blog devoted to news about rural America, about rural and exurban counties that had "flipped" from one party to another in the election. Most of those flips had been from Republican to Democratic and had been associated with the enormous black turnout in a historic race. The exception was a striking band of red counties across the rural South, from southwest Arkansas through Tennessee and into eastern Kentucky and southwest Virginia. Not only had those counties flipped from Democratic to Republican, some of them had voted Republican for the first time in four or five election cycles. This was the upper South, a mostly white swath of the United States that has historically been the home of small farmers, coal miners, and Appalachian residents. It's deeply conservative, with a populist streak, and devoutly religious, with evangelical roots that go all the way back to those eighteenth-century Baptist and Methodist missionaries. What was it that had made this particular stretch of the South so emphatically reject Barack Obama for John McCain? The answer can be summed up in a concept that straddles the worlds of religion and politics: moral values.

In 2007, the Pew Forum on Religion and Public Life conducted a poll called the U.S. Religious Landscape Survey, covering a range of topics about religious affiliation and stands on various social and political issues. With the help of the people at Pew, I extracted the results on the McCain Belt (for lack of a better term) from the Pew poll. I found that on many questions, the McCain Belt wasn't that much different from the rest of America. But it was emphatically different on a narrow range of issues of particular importance to fundamentalist Christianity—the morally corrupting influence of mass media, creationism vs. evolution, homosexuality, and abortion. On those subjects, folks in the McCain Belt expressed conservative opinions that differed from the national average by anywhere from 9 to a whopping 29 percentage points.[16] More important, the McCain Belt was strikingly different from other parts of the South—the Black Belt, most notably, and the urban-suburban South.

Those numbers are just a snapshot, but they illustrate a huge, if subtle, shift in Southern culture that Samuel Hill, the dean of Southern scholars of religion, was trying to describe in a provocative 1998 essay. The rise of fundamentalist religion in the South in the late twentieth century, he wrote, "has wrought more changes in Southern society and culture along some lines at any rate than did the Civil Rights Movement in its prime."[17]

Considering the qualifiers he threw in ("along some lines at any rate"), Hill may have been engaging in a little bit of Southern hyperbole, but there's no doubt that in the South, religion has gotten a lot more like politics and politics has gotten a lot more like religion. Conservative political figures urge ideological purity with slogans like "principle over party," tout their "servant's heart" as a qualification for office, forecast imminent doom if prescribed remedies are not taken, and warn their followers about the dangers of consorting with unbelievers (also known as "liberals"). A candidate's born again experience is now viewed as an essential part of his or her political résumé, and every campaign involves a revelation of the candidate's most intensely personal come-to-Jesus moment. Collectively, Southerners still love Jesus with as much passion as ever, but these days we are not at all sure Jesus is crazy about our fellow Southerners.

"Fundamentalism's great achievement thus far has been to make Southern religion less Southern," Hill wrote. Evangelical religion had once been a big tent that all Southerners could live under, but once it was divided into "liberal" and "conservative" camps, it divided Southerners, too. "The old tribalism of Southern life, a product of its history and its heritage ... is being replaced by a new tribalism that represents a coalition of the right-thinking, the correct-minded, the doctrinally and ethically pure."

Hill might have been describing an experience I had when research took me to Mississippi, and I decided to drop in on the Sunday morning service at Clarksdale Baptist Church. I don't miss the apocalyptic religion of my childhood, but there are things about the church itself that I miss, and I was feeling nostalgic. I had reason to think that at Clarksdale Baptist there would be familiar hymns in a familiar order of service, the same kind of church architecture, the same kind of people in the pews. And I was right, up to a point. The service was familiar, and people went out of their way to be friendly. But something was slightly . . . off. It might have been just a small-town curiosity about the appearance of a stranger, but I kept wondering if I detected something else in those friendly greetings that was new—a faint edge of suspicion, not just a "Hey, how are you?" but a "Hey, who *are* you?"

Maybe I imagined it; maybe it was there and I misread the motive. Still, the sermon that morning was enough to make a person wonder. It was based on the parable of the tares and the wheat, a New Testament story about a farmer who is sabotaged by a neighbor who secretly scatters weed seeds all over the farmer's freshly planted wheat field. Wheat seeds and tare seeds only *look* alike, the minister warned us; likewise, "There's a difference between cultural Christians and true Christians," between real believers and those who call themselves Christians but who "are too smart and too sophisticated" to believe that the Bible is literally true. In the parable, he noted, the tares were sorted from the wheat on the threshing floor, then bundled up and burned—clearly, a metaphor for the eternal judgment awaiting all but true believers. "Folks," he said earnestly, "we are to be *separate*."

There it was, the old fundamentalist admonition. In my youth, it was a warning against the secular world and the enticements awaiting us outside the church walls: premarital sex, illegal drugs, rock music, liquor, dancing, gambling. It was also not something you would have heard in your standard Southern Baptist church. Back then, Baptists were far more interested about getting people in the door. If a few doctrinal impurities sneaked in, the thinking went, either some good Baptist preaching would set those people straight or God would sort things out in His own time. This was different—a warning against subversive thoughts that might be entertained by fellow Christians sitting in the same pew. I had come hoping for nostalgia; what I got was a message of exclusion, and from fellow members of my tribe. Here I was in a Southern Baptist church in the Mississippi Delta, the most Southern place on earth, and I did not feel the least bit at home.

Just as evangelical religion has always been entwined with politics in the South, it has also had a close working relationship with what Southerners refer to as "bidness." The origins of this idea are neither new nor Southern: back in the 1920s, a New York City advertising executive named Bruce Barton popularized Jesus as a marketing genius and "the founder of modern business" in his best-selling book *The Man Nobody Knows*. But the evangelical church is particularly hospitable soil for this notion, for an obvious reason: when your mandate is to "go ye therefore into all the world and preach the Gospel," you need the most effective and efficient means of getting the word out. In short, you need the tools of business. This is the reason evangelicals have always been ahead of the religious curve in adapting to new technology and inventing new marketing techniques. Evangelicals pioneered the use of radio as a medium in the

1920s; in the 1940s, they invented the concept of parachurch organizations like Campus Crusade for Christ or the Full Gospel Business Men's Fellowship; in the 1970s, they created vast media empires.

Then there's another persistent strain of thought in the evangelical world—that is, the subset of evangelicals who belong to charismatic or Pentecostal churches. It's a merger of the Christian belief in the "gifts of the Spirit" and the biblical idea of a covenant between God and man, which reaches the conclusion that faith is a kind of contract with God, who bestows His gifts in direct proportion to the believer's faith. The "gifts" in question can be spiritual, like the gift of speaking in tongues, or they can be material—an idea popularized in the early twentieth century by a Baptist evangelist named E. W. Kenyon with his "Word of Faith" movement. A version of this message came into our house every Sunday morning when I was a child via Oral Roberts's "The Abundant Life" television show, which my mother liked to watch before Sunday School. Roberts was one of the evangelical church's television pioneers, and his pitch was simple: *Send me your money and God will bless you with more money.* Loosely characterized as "prosperity gospel" theology, this is a vein mined by a long line of evangelists from Jimmy Swaggart to Jim Bakker to T. D. Jakes.

The next step in this logic is obvious: if business practices can be put to use in building a religious empire, why can't religious practices be put to use in building a business empire? Christian businessmen's fellowships had been a feature of the evangelical landscape since the 1940s, but my first exposure to this theology came sometime in the late 1970s, when I heard Truett Cathy, the founder of Atlanta-based Chick-fil-A, give a talk at a suburban Atlanta junior college. Cathy told us that walking with the Lord was a sure route to business success, and he used as his text the New Testament verse in which Jesus advises his disciples to "seek ye first the kingdom of God, and all these things will be added unto you." I don't remember exactly what Cathy meant by "all these things," but one stuck in my mind: the new luxury car he had recently bought. This was a theology tailor-made for the Reagan era of laissez-faire capitalism, especially in the increasingly Republican Deep South.

An Arkansas businessman named Sam Walton took things to the next level. Walton had founded his chain of five-and-dime stores in the early 1960s, and by the 1970s he was beginning the expansion that would make Walmart a global retailing superpower. Walmart's origins in the small-town South of the Arkansas Ozarks meant that its first employees were farm wives, products of an agrarian economy in which everyone in the family contributed to the household upkeep. As Bethany Moreton recounts in her book *To Serve God and Wal-Mart: The Making of Christian Free Enterprise,* what later generations would regard as sex-based wage discrimination was to these ladies just a chance to augment the family income and still be home in time to cook dinner. Those women also brought to work with them a kind of Southern church lady mentality, in which being helpful to the customer was just another way of putting the evangelical ethic of "Christian service" to work in their daily lives.

Inadvertently, Walton had stumbled onto the ideal labor pool for the late-twentieth-century service economy: cheerful, service-oriented employees who worked cheap. The South was a particularly deep pool of this kind of worker; every year, small Bible colleges in Oklahoma, Texas, South Carolina, and

Tennessee turned out a crop of bright young men and women who understood the ethic of Christian service, were strangers to labor unions, and didn't mind starting at the bottom of the corporate ladder. The institutional culture that made Walmart a global powerhouse, Moreton writes, was honed "in the aisles and break rooms of Southern discount stores, in small-group Bible study and vast Sunday-morning worship services [as well as] through the marketing classes and mission trips of Christian colleges, through student business clubs and service projects."[18]

The merger of business and religion finds its apotheosis in the megachurch, and it is no coincidence that the South is home to more megachurches than any place on the planet: 43 percent of the 1,400 churches in the United States that fit the (arbitrary and unofficial) two-thousand-member minimum are located in the eleven states of the Old Confederacy. (I counted well over thirty in the Atlanta area alone.)[19] "Megachurch" and "prosperity gospel" are not synonymous; in fact, the pastor of the nation's biggest megachurch, Rick Warren of southern California's Saddleback Church, has said flatly that the prosperity gospel is "baloney." If it were true, he asks, "Why isn't everybody in the church a millionaire?"[20]

But the prosperity gospel is prominent strain these days in evangelical circles, where most megachurches reside, and it's a philosophy that seems to be particularly attractive to blacks and Latinos. One scholar of the prosperity gospel has written that "proportionate to the entire American population, which is anywhere from 75 to 80% White/non-Latino, a larger percentage of African Americans and Latinos are involved in [prosperity gospel] churches than Whites"[21]—although this is not to say that white people don't find it plenty attractive, too: overall, prosperity gospel congregations seem to be models of ethnic diversity.

I'd never been to a megachurch before I went to Creflo Dollar's World Changers Church International in the suburbs of Atlanta—I hate crowds and loud music—but destiny seemed to have dictated that my path and Creflo Dollar's would someday intersect. For one thing, his church was right down the street from where I'd gone to high school: somehow, a tract of land I remembered as a dense pine thicket had sprouted an imposing $18 million, 8,500-seat World Dome. For another, Creflo Dollar and I were both alumni of Kathleen Mitchell Elementary, the cafeteria of which had served as the first meeting place for his fledgling religious empire. In fact, the church website told me, Dollar had been the first black student ever to attend Kathleen Mitchell. I did some quick math, deduced that Dollar is at least five years younger than I am, and realized I had caught him in what politicians call a "misstatement": I attended Kathleen Mitchell with the Strozier kids, who were black, several years before the future reverend skipped through the front door in short pants.

But let he who is without sin … So one morning in early June I arrived at the World Dome a full fifteen minutes before the service—ample time to get a good seat, I thought. I was wrong. There wasn't a parking spot to be found within a football field's distance of the front door, and already cars lined both sides of the street. Eventually, I parked in the far-flung outer lot about a quarter of a mile down the road, where shuttle buses were available to take slackers like me to the front door. By the time I got there, the service had started; I could tell this because even in the parking lot, I could feel the faint bass vibrations of the music inside the World Dome through the soles of my feet. My fellow congregants were an orderly, polite crew, and I'd say about 85 percent of them were black. In that sense, I'd picked a highly atypical megachurch: nationally, membership in such churches is more than 80 percent white, and blacks are actually underrepresented compared with their numbers in the general population. But World Changers is in College Park, a suburb of Atlanta that is overwhelmingly black and Latino these days. People were friendly, but in an impersonal sort of way; I didn't have the feeling that I was in a crowd of people who saw each other regularly every week.

The decibel level increased exponentially once I was inside the door. I followed the crowd through a large front hallway, past a combination bookstore/gift shop and into the Dome itself, where curving rows of seats sloped stadium-style down to a carpeted dais where six or seven women were doing a modern dance interpretation of the music. It was a combination church service/television show taping, with all the electronic gizmos associated with cameras and sound equipment and stage lights. Nobody had a bad seat: there were a dozen television screens mounted on columns throughout the audience, and two huge screens on either side up front. During pauses in the service, infomercials and testimonials were played on them. "At this church, we can't stand religion, but we love God," said one ad; in another, a church member told a story about how he had been unhappy at his job, feeling unappreciated and underpaid, until he realized that he simply needed to trust God's principles and "speak from a position of increase—you have to *speak* things into being." Shortly thereafter, he said, he got a 23 percent increase in salary, a promotion, and a year-end bonus that was almost double what he'd received the previous year. "The Word works if you work it," he said, with evident satisfaction.

At some point during the preliminaries, the Reverend Dollar made his appearance without any fanfare; one minute he wasn't there, and the next minute he was, with his wife, Taffi, seated off to one side of the dais. He looked nothing like the 1980s-era evangelists like Jim and Tammy Faye Bakker, who had made prosperity gospel synonymous with sequins, false eyelashes, and all things tacky; Dollar's suit was of a subdued ocher shade, with a pale yellow shirt and a pale blue tie—an ensemble that bespoke both sophisticated taste and money. Dollar has told reporters that he does not get a salary from his church, which took in $69 million in 2007, the last year for which that information was made public. His personal income comes instead from real estate and business investments as well as what he has described as "million-dollar deals" for books. But he's not hurting: he owns a Rolls-Royce and flies on church business in a ten-passenger Learjet. The church income is presumably spent on its many outreach ministries, which include a home schooling program, adult literacy classes, record and publishing companies, entrepreneurship classes, housing and legal help for low-income people, and many others. The day I was there, a church bulletin listed among its upcoming activities a "marriage boot camp," student mentoring sessions, and a food bank drive, as well as an advertisement for the Taffi Dollar Women's Cruise, a five-day Caribbean getaway scheduled for the following year. There was also, I noted, a small announcement that World Changers did not accept any postdated checks.

The reverend's sermon this day was the last in a series of five based on a theme: the wounds inflicted on Jesus' body just before and during his crucifixion. Today he was focusing on the spear wound inflicted in Jesus' side by Roman soldiers who were making sure he was dead. Its title: "Drinking from the Fountain of His Side." The fixation on blood as a symbol in evangelical or Pentecostal Christianity—and Catholicism, for that matter—probably seems macabre compared to more decorous religious traditions, but this was familiar ground to me. "Put your seat belts on, because I have the wonderful pleasure, by the power of the Holy Spirit, to get up in your *business* this morning," he told us, and I heard chuckles around me. So cleansing from sin by the blood of Jesus was the theme, but most of the sermon was spent homing in on certain sins in particular. It didn't strike me until later how much of what he said revolved around themes of material and emotional security as they applied to marriage and parenthood.

"You have *Christian* men who don't support their children," he said, and I heard *mmm, mmm* in agreement around me. By now, the reverend was warmed up and had left the pulpit to pace back and forth directly in front of the audience. "You have *Christian* men who are arrogant and prideful and not accommodating, who have the *nerve* to tell their wives they fat." More *mmm, mmms.* A Christian man can't just sit back and be the biblical head of the household, he went on; a woman whose man doesn't treat her right will find a man who does. "An *un*saved man will open the door for her." *Amen!* "An *un*saved man will wine her and dine her!" *Say it, preacher!* "You have to get your mind right with God and treat your woman like she *need* to be treated! If you drink from the fountain, you ain't gonna *need* no Viagra!" The crowd loved that, but Dollar stopped abruptly, as if the word "Viagra" had reminded him of where he was. He managed to look charmingly abashed. "Y'all forgive me. I'm still a work in progress." More laughter. "The point is, these women need to be *cherished*"—the applause was building—"and they need to be treated like precious *jewelry.*" More applause.

After much more in that vein, the reverend began to make his way back to his starting point: sin and salvation. "The reason why people sin is not the devil made them do it. It's because they *want* to do it." He imitated a pothead, in a whiny tone: "'I don't *wanna* stop smokin' weed. I *like* smokin' weed.' Well, your body belongs to God. It was bought with a *price* ... You will have to give an accounting for the deeds you have done in this body someday. Your body is on *loan* to you, for a little while." Then, abruptly: "Turn with me to I Thessalonians 5:23 and read along."

All around me, people were bringing out their Bibles. As a former ace at the Sword Drill, an old Sunday School exercise where we kids competed to see who could look up a verse the fastest, I could tell that these were folks who were deeply familiar with the text; most of them flipped open directly to the back of the New Testament, where Paul's epistles to the early Christians are found, without any need to go to the index. They read aloud in unison: "And the very God of peace sanctify you wholly; and I pray God your whole spirit and soul and body be preserved blameless unto the coming of our Lord Jesus Christ."

Dollar had been talking for a solid hour by now, and it was time for the windup. It is possible to be "blameless, whole in soul and body," he told them, if they apply the blood of Jesus to the sin in their lives. "Start *applying* the blood to that mess! I plead the blood of *Jesus* on that mess! You stay with the Word, you will look up one day and you will not even have the *taste* for sin anymore!" The applause had begun again and now was rising to a crescendo; his tone was urgent. "You don't *have* to be defeated by the Devil one split second, but you *do* have to drink from the fountain! Now, look at your neighbor and say, 'I'm delivered from sin!'" As all around me people were doing just that, I suddenly discovered an urgent problem with my sandal strap. "Now look at me when I say, 'How?'" And all around me, I heard, *"By the blood of the Lamb!"*

He paused, letting a feeling of release percolate through the crowd. In my childhood, I once heard a minister boil down everything he had learned at seminary about giving a sermon into three easy steps: *Tell 'em what you're gonna tell them, tell them, and then tell 'em what you've just told 'em.* We were now at that third step. When Dollar spoke again, his tone was conversational and friendly. "Now, when you go home today, people gon' ask you, 'What'd you talk about in church today?' And you gon' say, 'Sin.'" While he was talking, people began to stir, and I saw ushers with paper buckets emerge from the back and fan out among the crowd. *Here it comes*, I thought, and when it did, it was a straightforward pitch: he had given them something spiritual today that was of value; in return, they should give something of value back.

And it was working: people were getting up from everywhere in the arena and coming down front in a steady stream with white envelopes in their hands, depositing them in front of the pulpit, while others were putting theirs in the buckets the ushers were passing along the rows. When it came to me, I threw in a five-dollar bill, which was all the cash I had in my wallet. While this was happening, Dollar addressed his critics. "Now, some people say, 'I like your preaching, Reverend. I just don't like all this talk about prosperity and healing.' I say, fine. You *want* to be broke and sick?" And the money flowed down the aisles like a river.

"The last fifty years has seen the greatest redistribution of a religion ever in the history of the world," Rick Warren, Saddleback Church's pastor and author of *The Purpose-Driven Life*, told a 2009 forum on the future of evangelicalism held in Washington, D.C. At the beginning of the twentieth century, 71 percent of all Christians were in Europe, and only 10 percent of Africa's population was Christian, he said; by 2000, Europe was only 28 percent Christian, while Africa's 360 million Christians represented over half the population of that continent. If you want to know the future of evangelicalism, he told his audience, it is in Africa, Asia, and Latin America.

If you are an evangelical, this is good news: the world is hearing the Gospel. If you are a Southerner of my generation, especially one who hasn't spent a whole lot of time in church for the last thirty years, it presents a strange inversion of the way things used to be: mosques in Tennessee, Hindu temples in Georgia—and folks in Ghana singing from the Baptist hymnal. When I was a kid, we sent missionaries *to* China; now they're sending them to us.[22]

The megachurch is here to stay, Warren thinks, but it will be a kind of franchise operation, with fifteen or twenty or thirty small sites administered by a large central organization—and as they try to appeal to a more diverse group of potential members, they will inevitably lose some of their Southern cultural tradi-tions: it's hard to imagine five thousand people standing in line for homecoming dinner in the Fellowship Hall. The presence of a more ethnically and geographically diverse population will have the same effect.

"It's more difficult for conservative Christian churches to set the cultural current in the way they would have twenty or thirty years ago," says Brad Wilcox, a sociology professor at the University of Virginia whose specialty is research into the influ-ence of religion on family life in America. Take family values, for instance. Wilcox's research, and research done by University of Michigan sociologists Ron Lesthaeghe and Lisa Neidert, shows that contrary to what people may think, divorce is actu-ally *more* common among nominal conservative Protestants and Southerners than it is in the nation as a whole.[23] In fact, Wilcox thinks that one reason conservative Protestants are so concerned about "family values" is that they are acutely aware of the threat in their own homes, and the reason that there is so much stri-dent rhetoric about homosexuality and same-sex marriage from this group is that there are far more divorced evangelicals than there are evangelicals who identify themselves as homosexuals. (Even Charles Stanley, pastor of Atlanta's First Baptist Church, was divorced in 2000, after forty-four years of marriage.)

The changing global economy—the shift of manufacturing jobs from Western to Eastern countries, the growing disconnect between the type of jobs available in this country and the skills of the available labor force—has changed things, too, Wilcox says. "As a practical matter, more and more working-class rural Southerners are detached from the life of the church." Why? In part, because they are more likely to be unemployed. "Men have lost ground in the last thirty years and men are more likely to be churchgoers when they are successful [providers]."[24]

So where does that leave us? At the dawn of a new era. There are signs that the pendulum has swung as far to the right as it can, and that the fundamentalist influence on evangelical religion may be waning. What's likely to replace it will be a far more global, socially conscious evangelicalism. "The generation of the [Jerry] Falwells and [Pat] Robertsons and Billy Grahams is passing us by," says historian Darren Dochuk. He thinks that the Tea Party, for all the noise it has made in recent years, especially in the South, may represent the passing of an era. "I think it's very representative of the older Cold War generation of upper-middle-class suburban evangelicals across the South who are coming to the end of their careers, coming to the end of their lives, coming to the end of their political power."[25]

What will replace them? Their sons and daughters, of course—but the current generation of evangelicals now in college are tired of the culture wars, disillusioned with Republicans and Democrats, and, with the exception of abortion, not particularly energized by the issues that galvanized their parents. In 2011, for instance, Belmont University, a Christian school in Nashville, announced the formation of the school's first gay student organization;[26] Wheaton College, whose most famous alumnus is Billy Graham, now has an alumni group of gay and lesbian graduates. Evangelicals as a group remain firmly opposed to gay rights, at least in principle; what seems to be changing is the willingness to make that opposition a top priority. Among the "signature issues" of Rick Warren's Saddleback

Church, for instance, are an outreach program for people with AIDS and a global initiative aimed at attacking poverty, disease, illiteracy, and political corruption.[27]

The old fusion of evangelical religion and Southern culture is mostly gone; where it survives, it's living on borrowed time. But two essentially Southern traits have not changed. One is the degree to which religion permeates the culture, even if it's not the monolithic evangelical religion of my childhood. The other is a very Southern kind of emotional fervor.

A while back, my cousin Butch told me about an incident at his church in Chattanooga, which at the time was allowing a neighboring Korean Baptist congregation to use its Fellowship Hall for its early Sunday morning service. One Sunday morning Butch pulled into the church parking lot just in time to see some Asian men spill out of the Fellowship Hall and onto the sidewalk, pulling hair and throwing punches.

"What on earth were they mad about?" I asked.

"I dunno," Butch said. "A fight over First Ephesians, maybe?"

6.

The Sorting Out

Driving south from eastern Arkansas into the heart of the Mississippi Delta, I entered a landscape of two-story-high tractors, flat vistas, and no people. It was February, and the fields were still bare and soggy from recent rains. Huge flocks of black starlings wheeled and swooped across the sky, looking for last season's leftover seeds. It was mid-morning on a weekday, but in one fifty-mile stretch of U.S. Highway 61, I counted exactly twelve cars, two tractor-trailers, and, except for the birds, no other signs of life. From time to time I drove through a small town, identifiable by a gas station, a few businesses, and a town limits sign; sometimes it was just the remnants of a small town, with dried kudzu vines covering a rusty Citgo sign. After a while, I began to get the creepy sense that alien robots disguised as John Deere tractors and grain silos had staged a secret invasion and devoured all human life while nobody was looking.

If there are alien robots out there, they could probably get away with it. Rural America is invisible to us urban-suburbanites, except when there's a presidential election, a natural disaster, or—in the South—some kind of gothic event like a church burning or an all-white high school prom. This invisibility is why, outside a small network of academics and policymakers, very few Americans have ever heard of something called the "rural brain drain"—the steady mass migration of people out of rural areas into urban and suburban areas, caused by the encroachments of industrial farming and the loss of manufacturing jobs. From the interstate, you wouldn't notice. But from the back roads like the one I was on this day, it was hard to miss the boarded-up gas stations, the falling-down barns, the desolate small-town main streets, the overall sense that some slow-motion catastrophe was under way—which it is.

The rural-to-urban population movement is a global phenomenon, but in the South it has transformed a part of the landscape that has been an integral part of Southern identity for generations. Southern identity and an agrarian way of life are two concepts so intricately linked that it's still hard to contemplate one without the other. Have you ever heard of a "big-city Southerner"? Me neither. Southerners may live in the heart of Manhattan, in a penthouse in Paris, or in a condo in Buckhead—but if they identify themselves as Southerners, it means that somewhere, and probably not very far back, they have a close personal connection with the land: relatives who still live in the rural South, a grandfather who farmed, a small town that is the ancestral family home, a cousin up in some holler who still talks with a twang. Lifelong residents of, say, Kansas may also lay claim to agrarian roots, but they don't celebrate it the way Southerners tend to, laboring as so many of us do under the delusion that we have a special, mystical attachment to The Land. (And this *is* a delusion: time after time, Southerners have demonstrated that for the right price we can divest ourselves of our attachment to Grandma's peach orchard faster than you can say "upscale retail opportunities.") It is our nostalgia for peach orchards we have known, rather than any clinging to some particular tract of real estate, that helps define us as Southern. And up to now, this tenacious memory has put its taproot deep into the rural South.

And of all the things that have changed in the South over the past fifty years, none has changed more profoundly than the rural South. For one thing, its population is shrinking: urban-suburban residents in the South outnumber rural residents almost two to one. But the biggest change, by far, is physical and demographic. What used to be a mosaic of small communities has largely become a series of broad, sterile zones of the "haves"—a land of subdivisions, freeways, and malls—and the depopulated countryside of the "have-nots." This phenomenon is very much in evidence in the Midwest, too, but in the South the effects are magnified—first, because the rural South has such a long history of poverty to begin with, and second, because the enclaves of poverty it creates also tend to be racially isolated. In the Mississippi Delta and in the crescent-shaped zone of old cotton plantation country that stretches across the Deep South from southern Mississippi to South Carolina, the poverty is overwhelmingly black; in the upland South and in Appalachia, it's mostly white; in scattered rural communities all over, you can find Hispanic poverty. The antebellum South had vast wealth inequality, but at least poor and rich, slave and owner lived in close proximity—and that remained true certainly up through my childhood in the 1960s, if for no other reason than the South has never been big on zoning. Today, however, zoning is done by the invisible hand of global capitalism—and in the rural South, the poor have been banished to live far away and out of sight. Driving through this weirdly depopulated landscape, it's tempting to conclude that, finally, they've found a way to assimilate the South into the rest of the country: they just relocated all the Southerners.

Or . . . maybe we're just witnessing another evolution. Maybe that taproot of Southern identity I mentioned lies deep in something that just happened to grow in the rural South. Maybe Southern identity does not derive simply from agrarian culture, but from a uniquely Southern version of agrarian values. This was the crux of an argument made eighty years ago by a group of writers who called themselves simply "12 Southerners" but who are better known as the Nashville Agrarians. In reality, they were a group of writers, historians, novelists, and poets who knew each other as students and/or faculty at Vanderbilt University in Nashville, in the first decades of the twentieth century. The 1930 manifesto they created, *I'll Take My Stand*, was a radical challenge to the American worship of technology, progress, and personal fulfillment—and not from a leftist perspective, where such challenges usually come from, but a profoundly conservative one.

The writers of *I'll Take My Stand* can't be credited with being the first to challenge the American culture of materialism. Henry David Thoreau considered the problem at Walden Pond; a couple of thousand years before that, Jesus asked pointedly, "For what shall it profit a man, if he shall gain the whole world, and lose his own soul?" They were, however, the first to draw a set of moral principles from the values implicit in agrarian life, to link those specifically to the health of the soil from which we

144

derive our food, and to hold up the South as an example of what such a society might look like.

This, obviously, is dangerous territory. Even assuming that Southern identity derives from the values of the agrarian South of the early twentieth century, it's another thing entirely to discern them at work in the urban South of today. *I'll Take My Stand* is also a tainted masterpiece: woven into its elegant prose are some passages that read like a Ku Klux Klan recruiting pamphlet. For that reason, among others, some of the authors began distancing themselves from the book not long after publication, and one—Robert Penn Warren—later repudiated his contribution altogether. Anyone who takes this book seriously today risks a certain amount of guilt by association, not to mention outright ridicule, since holding up the South as an example of anything worth imitating is dead certain to bring out the redneck jokes. Why, people will ask, are we paying attention to a bunch of old white guys from eighty years ago who never had sense enough to get out of Dogpatch?

To answer that question, it seemed reasonable to start with exploring what Dogpatch actually looks like these days. And that's how I wound up in Mississippi.

At six o'clock on a Saturday evening, the courthouse square in Oxford, Mississippi, had the vibe of a place where a party was about to start. The art galleries and dress shops had closed for the day, but the lights were blazing at Square Books, and the restaurants were doing their first seating of the evening. Two young women and their dates passed me in a nimbus of chatter and perfume, clearly on their way to some dressy event, while a couple of families with kids in strollers navigated the uneven sidewalks. From somewhere nearby came the aroma of meat on the grill. High on his pedestal, like some Confederate traffic cop, a marble Rebel soldier contemplated a steady stream of cars coming into town down Lamar Avenue.

Oxford is a very cool place. Besides being the home of Ole Miss and the place where William Faulkner wrote his novels, it is one of the most livable small towns in the country—rich in cultural amenities, blessed with a low crime rate, possessed of top-tier medical facilities for retirees and some of the best college football on the planet. Its neighborhoods look like a cover for *Southern Living*: broad streets with towering old trees, shady lawns, and houses with wide, welcoming porches. I'd come to town purely on a mission to find a bookstore, never expecting to be so charmed. Much as I wanted to stay, I couldn't: my suitcase was waiting for me sixty miles away in Clarksdale.

It was late when I started the drive back. After the lights of Oxford and its outlying shopping malls faded behind me, I entered an inky blackness. The moon was new and the night was cloudy; except for a very occasional passing car, there was nothing but me, my headlights, and a few dozen feet of the road ahead. After I turned off U.S. Highway 278 to take a small shortcut back to my hotel, there was no ambient light, no reflections in the clouds from some distant shopping center, no way to tell where the horizon met the sky. I felt like a small boat on an immense, dark sea—an impression reinforced by the appearance, after a while, of the lights of Clarksdale way off to my right, like the sight of a distant coastline. The road I was on ended abruptly at Highway 49. When I drove straight across the highway, crossed the railroad tracks, and pulled into the parking lot of the Shack Up Inn (more about that later), I felt as if I had crossed some kind of abyss.

In a way, I had. Clarksdale and Oxford are on opposite sides of a demographic chasm. Oxford epitomizes the land of the haves. Clarksdale, which sits only fifteen miles from the Mississippi River, as deep in the Delta as it is possible to get, is a poster child for the land of the have-nots: 39 percent of its population live below the poverty level, which makes it only the *sixth* poorest county in the state. Yet in terms of cultural riches, it rivals Oxford: the intersection of Mississippi U.S. Highways 278 and 61 in Clarksdale is where (so goes the legend) a young black man named Robert Johnson sold his soul to the devil one midnight a long time ago in exchange for the knowledge of how to play a kick-ass blues guitar. Muddy Waters grew up here, as did Ike Turner; playwright Tennessee Williams lived here as a boy. But even before blues music, this was farming country, the kingdom of Big Cotton. It was the land around Clarksdale that Big Daddy described in *Cat on a Hot Tin Roof* as "the richest land this side of the Valley Nile."

Farming today is still a major industry around Clarksdale, but it has mostly passed into the hands of big corporations with headquarters in other places. It's Clarksdale's cultural heritage that keeps it in economic existence. Tourists these days come to tour its fascinating blues museum, housed in the old railroad depot, or catch some music at the Ground Zero nightclub, or attend one of its many music or literary festivals. But aside from those enterprises and a few tourist shops, Clarksdale is mostly a monument to what used to be. Its downtown is pockmarked with abandoned buildings and shuttered businesses. Along U.S. 61, the main commercial artery, entire strip malls sit vacant, and the once bustling Greyhound bus terminal is empty. The only drugstore downtown stocks a disproportionate inventory of aluminum canes, bedside urinals, and adult diapers. Downtown traffic is sparse. I wouldn't go so far as to say that a dog could nap in the middle of Yazoo Street at noon on a weekday, but he would definitely have time to set a spell.

Clarksdale is the seat of Coahoma County, which has lost 11 percent of its population since 2000. In the same period, its white population fell 27 percent. It's a story repeated throughout the Mississippi Delta—a vast area encompassing northeast Louisiana, western Mississippi, and southeastern Arkansas—where statistics show declines in population in county after county dating back for decades. In more recent years, the declines have been double-digit (and in places where there are roughly equal numbers of whites and blacks, most of the people leaving are white). Imagine a large map of the southeastern United States with the outlines of every county in every state, and then imagine that the counties losing population are marked in green. What you would see is a broad swath of green that tracks both sides of the Mississippi River from New Orleans almost to Little Rock and, with some small interruptions, roughly follows the broad crescent of the Black Belt up to South Carolina. There would also be smaller pockets of green in eastern North Carolina, southwest Virginia, and patches of west Tennessee.

But, you say, haven't people always left the small town for the big city? Yes, they have. People have been leaving the Mississippi Delta in droves for much of the twentieth century. The Great Migration of blacks to Northern cities like Detroit and Chicago that began in the early twentieth century and lasted, off and on, up to the 1960s, drew largely from the Delta. The difference is that those earlier migrants were poor—and while they represented huge untapped human potential, their immediate value was in their physical labor, which could be cheaply replaced by machines. People leaving the rural South today tend to be middle-class retirees, college-bound teenagers, young adults with job skills—in short, brains, money, and skills, irreplaceable assets and the very things small rural communities can least afford to lose. In 1940, college-educated people were more or less evenly distributed between cities and small towns; today, there's roughly a 15 percent difference between the most educated areas of the country and the least educated.[1] Education and money go hand in hand: there's roughly a $10,000 difference in annual average income between counties that have the highest percentage of college graduates and the counties that have the lowest.[2] And even though black Americans are remigrating back to the South in significant numbers, they are young people drawn to cities like Atlanta or Nashville, or middle-class retirees looking to live out their golden years in the region their parents or grandparents once called home.[3]

The depopulation of the rural South is easy to miss if you are a city- or suburban-bred person zooming down I-85 through the Carolinas, or I-55 through the heart of Mississippi. Even on the back roads, a person might miss the signs. But if you know what to look for, they are everywhere. They are in the weeds and scrub pines you can see beyond some dilapidated fence—a farm driven out of business, or where an aging farmer has died. It's now owned by his heirs, who are looking to unload it because nobody in the current generation has the skills or the capital to get a farm running. What looks like rolling pasture is really a berm that conceals a four-thousand-hog farming operation, leased by the folks who sell Smithfield hams; that man-made "lake" off in the distance is actually a hog lagoon, where the tons of shit those hogs produce is turned back into fertilizer, which, at least in theory, never ever leaches into the local groundwater. That picturesque cornfield sprang from genetically modified seed and was planted by a two-story-tall machine on a grid laid out by satellites in space—and that's why it looks subtly different from the cornfields of my childhood; the cornfields I remember had rows wide enough for a human being to walk down, but these plants will never be touched by human hands. Those dense piney woods may *look* like a forest, but are in fact part of a vast farm under cultivation for Georgia Pacific, destined to be turned someday into toilet paper, maybe, or pressed board you will buy at Home Depot. The woods look artificial, too: there are no oaks or dogwoods or pecan trees or even so much as a holly bush to break the monotony. This also may explain why you don't hear that many birdcalls, either: monoculture on such a vast scale seriously screws with the ecosystem.

As devastating as Big Ag has been to community life in the rural South, it's had help: the other major force at work here is the loss of manufacturing jobs, which were relatively plentiful up through the early 1990s. But in the late 1990s those jobs began to leave in search of cheaper labor in places like China and India—and then came the Great Recession, which began in rural areas a full year before the November 2008 stock market meltdown and hit the rural South harder than almost anywhere else. Today, the small-town and rural residents cheerfully extolled by Sarah Palin as the people who "grow our food and run our factories" are either unemployed, working in a service industry, or making hundred-mile daily commutes to work.

Those who haven't been driven out of agriculture altogether are usually beholden in some way to a major agricultural business—growing corn or chickens or cotton under contract with some corporation that tells them what seeds they can use and how many chickens they must cram into one barn. Everybody else has left to follow the jobs.

Increasingly, that leaves a population skewed toward the very old, the very young, the chronically unemployed, and—not least—the unhealthy. Remember that map of the Southeastern United States where counties losing population were marked in green? Now imagine an overlay in which counties where more than 30 percent of adults over twenty are fat are colored blue. The overall result is aqua—green plus blue—because there's a high correspondence between counties that are losing population and counties with high obesity rates,[4] not to mention the incidence of diabetes and other obesity-related diseases.[5] It's hard not to gain weight when you live in a depopulated rural area: aside from the lack of things like bike trails or sidewalks or community gyms, it can be amazingly hard to find sources of fresh, locally grown fruits and vegetables. (And no, those factory-processed unnaturally green pole beans at Walmart don't really count; there's no telling where those came from.) It's one of the great ironies of life that in the ocean of fertile farmland we call the Mississippi Delta, there are only about eight farmers markets, and not all of them operate year-round. In Coahoma County, fast food and/or convenience stores outnumber groceries three to one.[6] In terms of mortality rates, access to health care, availability of recreational facilities, smoking rates, and premature births, it's one of the unhealthiest counties in an unhealthy part of the state.[7]

But health is just a part of the picture. As a county's population declines, its property tax base erodes; as that happens, the first institution affected is the school system. State and federal funding for education is based on the number of students, so counties with the smallest enrollment have the least money with which to supplement teacher salaries. That, in turn, makes it harder to keep and attract experienced, first-rate teachers. Once a school system starts to decline in this way, an area's economy enters a death spiral from which it is nearly impossible to recover, since there's no hope of attracting businesses that pay a living wage without an educated workforce.

Adding to the problem is white flight. Even in areas where the racial demographics are fairly balanced, there seems to be an invisible tipping point at which many white parents are unwilling to send their kids to majority-black schools, and figure out a way to get them into other school systems. A good example is Lee County, Arkansas, a small county on the edge of the Mississippi River about sixty miles southwest of Memphis. The 2010 census shows that 41 percent of Lee County's 10,770 residents are white. Its schools, however, are over 90 percent black. It's been that way for years, assistant superintendent Wayne Thompson told me; at this point, not even white school system employees send their kids to county schools. Some enroll their children in private schools, which are mostly white, or resort to some subterfuge to enroll their child in a nearby county where the school demographics are more to their liking. If anybody asks, Thompson said, it's easy to explain: "You just say, 'My kid doesn't live at home anymore, he lives with my sister.'"

In 1967, Lee County had fourteen schools. Today, thanks to an ongoing population exodus, it has three. Four hundred students rattle around in its only high school, where the building could accommodate 1,200. Students don't remember when their school had things like a drama program or a marching band. The county depends on volunteers from the Teach for America program, which puts recent college graduates in rural and/or poor school systems across the country, to supplement its teaching staff, as well as on a program that pays retired teachers who come back into the classroom. One of those "retired" teachers is biology teacher Wayne Phelps, who told me that his budget for supplies for all his classes, for an entire year, was $200. His biology students will never get a chance to dissect a frog: there's no money to buy specimens. The county has attempted to fill the gap by providing computer software for "virtual dissections," but the computers in Phelps's classroom are so old that they can't run the software. One of Phelps's students was so eager to do a dissection that Phelps told him he would stay after school to teach him, provided he came up with something to dissect. The student went into the woods with his rifle and showed up the next day with a dead possum.

Schools everywhere are a reflection of the overall health and vitality of a community, but in the South they are also monuments to history. One of those sits a few miles outside Clarksdale—a bland brick building rendered in an architectural style millions of baby boomers would recognize from their childhood. Andrew Carr, a retired Clarksdale cotton planter and a prominent civil rights activist back in the day, told me its story: built in 1962, it was designed to replace the run-down, one-room wooden schoolhouse (with adjacent outhouse) that up until then had served most of the black children in Coahoma County. County leaders at the time hoped that by giving black kids a new school, they could forestall court-ordered integration of the all-white elementary school in downtown Clarksdale. Their plan worked—for a while. But then, thanks to declining population, there just weren't enough children out in the country to justify keeping the new school building open. It closed while it was still relatively new, and today sits abandoned, engulfed by weeds. The irony is that schools in Coahoma County are almost as segregated as they were in 1962—only in reverse. The formerly all-white elementary school in town is all-black, and Clarksdale's white children attend the private school begun during the days of school busing. (Though these days a few black families now have the means to send their children there, too.)

And so we arrive, as we always do in the South, at the subject of race. This kind of racial sorting out is one of the unforeseen consequences of the rural brain drain in the Deep South. In fact, one reason there's a growing number of majority-minority counties is the fact that in many poor rural counties, there are more whites than blacks leaving. (Another reason is the growing influx of Hispanics into areas where there is already a sizable black population.) It may be true that Mississippi leads the nation in the number of local elected black officials, but quite a few of them are running shrinking governments or school systems—in effect, elected to oversee a kind of governmental going-out-of-business sale. Fifty years ago, Andrew Carr and his fellow civil rights activists thought they were working toward a world in which skin color would not be the main determinant of a person's chances in life. And, to a significant extent, they succeeded: there are black doctors and lawyers in Coahoma County now; a majority-black council runs the county, and a black mayor runs the city. In Clarksdale's lovely old Oakhurst neighborhood, where black people once worked as maids or gardeners, there are now black homeowners. A lot of them, in fact, because Oakhurst is now 85 percent black. Most of the white people have left, and thanks in large part to the declining local economy, the market value of those lovely old homes is a fraction of what it once was.

If there is any small silver lining in all of this, it's that the economic pressures of the rural brain drain have forced many areas to scour their histories for something, anything, with which to lure some tourist dollars. Hence the idea of civil rights tourism, born of the need to generate income for places like Dallas County, Alabama, home of several key events of the Montgomery-to-Selma civil rights march of 1965; or Dougherty County, Georgia, where Martin Luther King was once put in jail. People who might otherwise have been content to live their whole lives without seeing Neshoba County, Mississippi, now have an inducement to visit: there, they can pick up a brochure directing them on a driving tour of notable civil rights sites, including the place where civil rights workers James Chaney, Andrew Goodman, and Michael Schwerner were murdered in the infamous "long, hot summer" of 1964. The need for money is powerful enough to overcome the lingering reaction of many whites—and blacks, for that matter—that some chapters of local history are best laid to rest. "Tourism has been forced on these places," Jim Carrier, a Montgomery, Alabama, author of *A Traveler's Guide to the Civil Rights Movement* told the *New York Times* in 2004—but in the end, the result has been a fuller, more complex, and more honest picture of the South.[8]

In Clarksdale, which cannot boast of any significant local

civil rights–era history, imaginative entrepreneurs have found a way to market something else: rural poverty. Hence the Shack Up Inn—a collection of authentic sharecropper shacks that businessmen Bill Talbot and Guy Malvezzi moved to the site of the old Hopson Plantation a few miles outside town, retrofitted with some modern necessities like indoor plumbing, heat, and air conditioning, and then rented to tourists traveling down Highway 61 on the Mississippi Blues Trail. It's a hit among the musical and literary set: when I was there, most of the other guests were students in a New York City documentary filmmaking class that comes to Clarksdale once a year. Not everybody has been charmed: Malvezzi told me about one National Public Radio reporter who compared it to an Auschwitz-themed bed-and-breakfast. Overall, though, the concept has been so successful that it has spawned an imitator—Tallahatchee Flats, a few miles away in Greenwood.

The number of black visitors has been few, Malvezzi told me, and he and Talbot were concerned at the beginning about perceptions that they were exploiting a painful part of black history. But they have taken pains to uncover what they can about the stories of the families who lived in their shacks, and each shack bears the name of its last full-time resident. "Last summer, I had an African American family reunion on the grounds here," Malvezzi told me, and shortly after the reservation was made he got a visit from one of the granddaughters of the organizer. The granddaughter was incensed at the very idea. "She was a seventeen- or eighteen-year-old who had a real chip on her shoulder. I went into defensive mode and I said, 'Before you fire off any more questions, let me walk you through the Robert Clay shack. We're trying to honor a man who raised seven sons in this place.'" The reunion was a success, and Malvezzi hopes that the word-of-mouth advertising they have always relied on will now start percolating into a wider market. Considering the growing popularity of black family reunions and the millions of black families in the United States who can trace some part of their origin to the Delta, Malvezzi and Talbot may be onto something.

So cultural tourism is a business model that works—for the owners and employees of the tourist attraction in question. Besides the Shack Up, there's Ground Zero, Clarksdale's major nightclub, and Messenger's, a pool hall over on Martin Luther King Avenue that is one of the oldest black-owned businesses in the Delta. Madidi, an upscale restaurant that is a business venture of the actor Morgan Freeman, also draws steady customers, and there are plans to renovate the old Alcazar Hotel and convert it into apartments. Those plans may make a few people a lot of money, George Messenger tells me, but they're unlikely to reinvigorate the larger economy. His own restaurant and pool hall would probably be out of business if it were not for tourist traffic. "We gonna end up with a few places really thriving," he said. "But I see Clarksdale dying every day. I don't see it getting better."

The missing ingredient in all the redevelopment plans is residents, the people who create the myriad small social encounters that nourish the life of a community: running into your child's third grade teacher at the drugstore, hearing about the mayor's race from the man who sells you coffee. Those people aren't there, because the underlying industry that supports their presence—agriculture—has fundamentally changed. The number of white farmers is dwindling, and the number of black small farmers is so small as to qualify them for a spot on the Endangered Species list. When I asked people to estimate how many of the farmers in Coahoma County were black, people would start counting off individual names: lessee, there's Sam Miller, out by Friar's Point, and there's Franklin Wade, and . . .

One of the names on that list is Roosevelt Lee, who grows soybeans and wheat on 120 acres he inherited from his father, who never had more than a fourth grade education. Not only did his father manage to save money to buy the land while raising thirteen children, but he bought it out from under the nose of the white man he worked for at the time, Lee told me. When his father announced that he was quitting to run his own farm, the boss was irate: "If I'd a known that place was for sale, *I'd a* bought it!" was his reaction. The creases on Lee's face briefly deepen into a grin at the memory. For that reason, among others, the land is dear to Lee. Though he and his wife live closer to town, his farm still has the small wood-frame house where he and all his siblings grew up. He plans to fix it up someday, he tells me, even though the back porch leans at a perilous angle and the whole structure looks like it might not survive the next big thunderstorm. He is "a home boy," and his feel for farming is evident even in a casual description of the way a field of crops looks just before a rain: "You see 'em with their leaves flutterin' just before them clouds break. I think of that as a happy thing—We fittin' to get some rain, now." And yet, with each passing year, he sees less and less reason to keep on going. In recent years, he would have made more money by letting his land revert to woodland and taking a payout from a government conservation program.

All three of these men—George Messenger, Roosevelt Lee,

and Andrew Carr—are Clarksdale natives. They have lived and worked within twenty miles of each other for their whole lives, and experienced some of the most tumultuous years of the twentieth century from both sides of an important racial and economic divide. It would have been fascinating to sit down with the three of them over a beer and hear them talk about what all these changes have meant for them and their community. But that was unlikely unless I went out of my way to arrange it. The problem wasn't the social barriers that once kept blacks and whites from moving in the same social circles, because those are pretty dead, even in Mississippi. Now, the barriers are practical: distances are long, and there are no meeting places. The businesses and social institutions where people from different walks of life might meet—the civic groups, the scouting troops, the sports teams—have disappeared; in churches, where the congregations are skewing older every year and people are set in their ways, things remain pretty much black or white. The people who might have shaken things up have left, and they won't be coming back.

Carr is eighty-four, and he can remember a time when Clarksdale was a thriving center of commerce for the entire Delta, with its own luxury hotel—the Alcazar—and a Planters Club that had so many members they had to split it into Junior and Senior divisions. Today, he said, "we're hanging on by our fingernails.... We're depending heavily on tourism and the blues [music festivals], but I don't think that's going to get it."

Well, this is sad, you might be saying, but so it goes. The mule gave way to the gas-powered tractor, which yielded to a model with more horsepower, which was replaced by a two-story-tall machine equipped with a $30,000 GPS system and an onboard entertainment system. If feeding the world requires enormous efficiency of scale, if the entire Mississippi Delta must become one vast tract farmed by such devices, that is the price we must pay. To which the environmentalist replies: it is too high a price. Industrial farming has given us decades of cheap food, but it was possible only through the use of oil- and water-intensive methods. The era of cheap petroleum-based energy is over; even water is not a limitless resource. Trying to solve these problems by ramping up crop yields or expanding overseas markets is like thinking you can avoid running out of gas by driving faster.

This is a global debate, not a specifically Southern one, though it's worth mentioning that Southerners have done more than their share to define the terms. One of the major spokesmen for agricultural reform and the local food movement is Wendell Berry, a Kentucky-born farmer, poet, and essayist— and Berry's work, in turn, bears the clear imprint of *I'll Take My Stand*, a debt Berry acknowledged in his famous essay on agrarian values, "The Whole Horse."[9] In Berry's estimation, the statement of principles set out in the beginning of *I'll Take My Stand* is a cogent summary of the fundamental disagreement between the agrarian and the industrial ethos that remains valid to this day, and the authors' passionate opposition to the aims and methods of industrial agriculture was on record decades before the environmental costs of those practices became obvious. "A farm is not a place to grow wealthy; it is a place to grow corn," wrote contributor Andrew Lytle, who was fifty years ahead of his time in outlining many of the long-term economic effects of industrial agriculture: increased crop specialization, which results in large-scale production imbalances, requiring increased government intervention such as crop subsidies, which spawn artificially cheap food prices, which artificially inflate consumer demand for manufactured goods. Lytle did not foresee the advent of genetically altered crops or things like the huge dead zone in the Gulf of Mexico caused by the runoff of farm chemicals from the Mississippi River, but his critique is still remarkably prescient.[10]

Today, a small but significant number of people are coming to the same conclusions as the Nashville Agrarians, even if most of them have no idea who the Nashville Agrarians were. "With no fanfare, and indeed with hardly much public notice, agrarianism is again on the rise," writes Eric T. Freyfogle in the introduction to a 2001 compilation of essays on the subject entitled, appropriately, *The New Agrarianism*.[11] It's hard to measure the true breadth of this phenomenon, since farmers markets, organic growers who do not artificially preserve their crops for shipment, are, by definition, "selling local"—but according to figures from both the government and interest groups tracking this trend, it's significant, and growing. American consumers bought $1.2 billion of their food direct from farms in 2007, more than double the amount they spent a decade earlier—and while the overall number of farms in this country is declining, the number selling directly to consumers increased by 24 percent over the same period.

To Freyfogle, a professor of land use, natural resources, and property law at the University of Illinois at Urbana-Champaign, this phenomenon is born of "a rising sense of connection between people and working lands, particularly the lands that grow their foods." He sees the influence of this awareness in the suburbanite who converts his front lawn into a rain garden so as not to contribute to fertilizer runoff into the local watershed, in urban planners who design "walkable" neighborhoods, in a growing awareness among public officials about the need for formal land use policies. It's a sensibility that does not easily fit into a political pigeonhole, but instead is "a temperament and a moral orientation."[12]

And this is the point where the subjects of Southern identity, the disintegration of the rural South, and agrarian values all converge—because if there is any connection between Southern identity and agrarian values, it lies in the mores and values of a way of life that is, or was, specifically (a) rural and (b) Southern. So what are Southern agrarian values, anyway? If the rural South where those values were born ceases for all practical purposes to exist, will people still call themselves Southerners in fifty years? Why does it matter that when Wayne Thompson goes to the post office these days in the tiny Arkansas town where he has lived most of his life, he doesn't recognize a soul?

The easy twenty-first-century answer is: it doesn't. We live in a culture where we put our most intimate secrets on the Internet and have no idea who our next-door neighbors are, where we labor in cubicles all day and go home at night to update our Facebook page. What we lack—what most of us instinctively know we are missing, what makes so many of us log on to Facebook in the first place—is community. But virtual communities like Facebook cannot take the place of the real thing—an interdependent web of people, culture, economy, and nature, in Wendell Berry's definition, that is attached to a specific spot on this earth, a place where (as he puts it) it is possible to know "the histories of our families or of our habitats or of our meals."[13]

This concept of community lies at the heart of agrarian values—not because country folks are inherently nicer people, but because in a functioning rural economy, time and labor are the basic units of currency and the basic social safety net consists of neighbors. Southerners didn't invent this concept of community, but the South did create an important and highly influential variation on it. That's because in the rural South, the commonplace agrarian sense of community was reinforced by the steeliest of bonds. One was the bond that grows up among people who (if they were black) had to somehow survive an oppressive social and legal system; its white correlate was the bond created by the shared but unspoken knowledge that these systems constituted crimes against humanity. Among whites and blacks of the Jim Crow era, it was the bond created by the compelling need not to resist or question authority, lest you be branded as a (black) threat to public order or a (white) traitor to the status quo. For ensuing generations of Southerners, it was the shared and uneasy sense produced by this deafening silence—the nagging suspicion that history was missing a few chapters. Still another was the shared assumptions and values of an evangelical religion that saturated every part of daily life. Still another was the shared knowledge that we were all of us, no matter our skin color or economic circumstances, considered objects of ridicule to a lot of our fellow citizens[14]—and finally, on top of that, there was the shared conviction that, far from being inferior to everybody else, we were by God *better*.

This was the definition of community implicit in what the Nashville Agrarians called "the Southern way of life." If they did not explicitly define community the same way I have, it was because they were prisoners of their time and upbringing;

blinded by their own deeply imprinted racism, not even the most liberal among them could admit the fundamental evil of slavery ("Slavery was a feature monstrous enough in theory but, more often than not, humane in practice," wrote poet John Crowe Ransom[15])—much less acknowledge how effective a pattern of racial oppression can be in forging bonds among victims, oppressors, and onlookers alike. Still ensnared in the gauzy webs of Lost Cause romanticism, they were unable to separate their concept of community from the particulars of a time and place with which they were most familiar. In short, they conflated the concept of community with the real estate it was attached to.

This was a mistake everybody of their day was making; it's one people still make. You can see this confusion on display in *Gone With the Wind*, when Gerald O'Hara tells his daughter Scarlett, "Land's the only thing worth working for, worth fighting for, with dying for." Everybody who knows the movie remembers that scene, and Scarlett herself labors under the delusion that what's at stake here is the preservation of Tara, the O'Hara plantation. Possibly her creator was convinced of the same thing. But what makes *Gone With the Wind* so interesting a book are the truths it inadvertently reveals, the work of a gifted writer whose determination to be true to small facts while maintaining a larger cultural delusion put her at unconscious odds with herself. A much more telling moment comes when Scarlett returns at the end of the war to a ruined Tara and falls, hungry and exhausted (into a radish patch, I believe it was), then staggers to her feet and promises that, by God, the Yankees won't lick her; she will live through this war, and when it's over, "I'm never going to be hungry again. No, nor any of my folks."

My folks. Here is one of the most shallow, narcissistic, and

manipulative characters of twentieth-century popular fiction—
and yet over the course of the novel, the list of "folks" Scarlett
assumes responsibility for grows to include an elderly aunt in
Atlanta; Melanie, the wife of Mr. Fancy-Pants Ashley Wilkes
(when Scarlett is briefly married to Melanie's brother, they
become sisters-in-law), Ashley himself, Ashley and Melanie's
son, her own three children, her two sisters, one brother-in-law,
her elderly father, and, of course, Mammy—not to mention the
former slaves Pork, his wife, Dilcey, their daughter, Prissy, and
their infant son (who is never named). That's sixteen people, an
"extended family" by any definition, all fed, clothed, and housed
with hardly a murmur of complaint by a character who in every
other respect is a monster of selfishness. Why? Because it's her
job. Because it's what any self-respecting Southerner in her situation would have done, even if some of her reasons were born of
self-interest and blinded by racism (despite Scarlett's frequent
exasperation with her "helpless" darkies, it never occurs to her
how truly helpless she is without them). After you strip away
the Lost Cause sentimentalism, the revisionist history, and the
casual racism that make this book such a jarring experience
for modern readers, the basic structure of Margaret Mitchell's
flawed masterpiece is, at its heart, a story about the Southern
definition of community.

It took me a long time to appreciate this distinction—
perhaps because I spent so many years making the same mistake
everybody else did, and conflating the land I grew up on with
the community and the agrarian values attached to it. The window of my childhood bedroom window looked out over a cornfield, on the other side of which sat a small white frame house
where my mother's adoptive parents lived and farmed. My

grandfather, who was retired from a job as a carpenter at Southern Railways, and my grandmother grew most of their own food and a great deal of ours, too. Between their land and ours, which my grandfather had given to my mother on her marriage, we're talking about maybe thirty acres—a small, diversified farm kept partly in row crops, partly in pasture for cows, and the rest in timber. My grandfather kept a few hogs, a flock of chickens, and a white mule named Becky, which he used to pull the plow. (He had a tractor, but I never saw him use it.) He made shoes for the mule in his own blacksmith shop; he ground his own corn; we drank milk from his cows, ate breakfast with the eggs his hens laid, made jelly from the muscadines from his vines and the crab apples from his orchard. We weren't even connected to the College Park water system until I was seven or eight; up to then, we drank water pumped from the well behind my grandparents' house. While our house had a clothes dryer, my grandmother never owned one. But she knew how to milk a cow and how to wring a chicken's neck with one sharp twist; she was the one who told me that pouring used tea leaves on the ground around a blue hydrangea bush will make the blossoms turn pink, and that planting pole beans with the corn will give the bean vines cornstalks to climb on.

This was strenuous and often dirty work, a fact not lost on me even at the age of five or so, and in some ways it wasn't even a healthy lifestyle: when the cow got brucellosis, we all got brucellosis. But it had its compensations. For one thing, there was never any shortage of interesting things going on, whether it was watching little biddies take their first peck at water or admiring the way my mother rolled out biscuit dough. There was intimate daily contact with animals and growing things, and a kind of practical sense of their interconnectedness—so, for instance, tomatoes fertilized with manure and grown in soil rich in tannins from all those red oak trees miraculously produced tomatoes with an intensity of flavor I've never been able to replicate. Most important, there was talk. People who spend hours shelling beans or ironing or waiting for a big pot of plum jelly to boil down—repetitive manual labor of any kind—pass the time in a specific kind of conversation. They talk not to exchange information, not as shop talk or a form of one-upmanship; they talk for pleasure, to divert themselves by telling stories and recounting the day's events or commiserating over somebody's kidney stone, in a way that works itself into the brain of the child who is hanging out in the vicinity and, to all appearances, paying no attention at all.

This life took place in a specific physical and historical context—in the house by the railroad tracks I mentioned before, the ones Sherman's men tore up in August 1864. My grandmother's mother, the child who saw this, was a Hogan, and the Hogans had lived in those parts for long enough to have a road named after them. So had my grandfather's people, the Derricks. When we went to homecoming at Union Christian Church, which the Derricks had helped found not long after Reconstruction, I could visit the graves of my grandfather's twin brothers, Jacob and Esau, and a collection of more Derricks with tombstones that dated back to 1807, and each one came with a story. Driving north on U.S. Highway 29 would take us straight past the airport where my father worked and into Atlanta, where my mother's biological mother had toiled at a packing plant near the Nabisco bakery on Lee Street and where she died in the paupers' ward at Grady Hospital, not far from where my own mother would later get her first job, as a bookkeeper at Southern Railway. There were dozens of connections like that all around me, part of an unseen web that bound me not only to the world I could see but to its invisible past as well. And woven through all this tapestry, a distinct and recurring motif, was a particularly Southern brand of evangelical fundamentalist religion that to us was a matter of grave and eternal significance as well as something we took utterly for granted, like air. Our horizons were limited, but what my world lacked in breadth, it made up for in supplying an overall sense of order and belonging. Presbyterian or Methodist, Baptist, AME, or snake-handling Holy Roller, we all knew all six verses of "Just as I Am" without the need of a hymnal—and when Billy Graham came to town, we all packed into Atlanta Stadium to hear him, united in our belief that it was up to us to win the world for Jesus.

It was, in short, a complex web of community—and in addition to the specifically Southern traits I've already mentioned, it was also defined to a lesser but still important extent by one more: a concept of family that extended laterally instead of generationally, meaning that it encompassed not just one's parents and siblings, but aunts, uncles, cousins, grandparents, in-laws, cousins-by-marriage, and regular visitors. This is a feature of agrarian life in all societies, but since the South remained insular and agrarian longer than any other region of the country, it has Southern associations.

The confusion between "community" and "place" helps explain what I call Southern Sonar—i.e., the need Southerners seem to have to locate a person's physical origins, not just his current address, in order to completely identify him. When I was at Yale Law School in the mid-1980s, I remember hearing a third-year student from somewhere in the Northeast complaining bitterly about his job interview with former U.S. attorney general Griffin Bell, then a senior partner at Atlanta's most hoity-toity law firm, King & Spalding. "He asked me 'What does your daddy do?'" said my classmate. He perceived the question as a snobbish attempt to label him as "lower-class" because his father did not have an important-sounding white-collar job, but I knew that Judge Bell had simply been trying to "place" him in the way small-town Southerners of his generation instinctively did: by place of birth, father's occupation, mother's maiden name, and whether he'd played football for the University of Georgia, Alabama, Auburn, or Ole Miss. My classmate wasn't snubbed; he was merely pinged.

Southern Sonar is especially evident when Southerners encounter each other. The order of questioning in these meetings rarely varies much. "Where are you from?" Insert name of state or city. "Really? Whereabouts?" Further elaboration, followed with amazing frequency by "Do you know _____?"—on the assumption, apparently, that Charlotte or Knoxville is still a tiny burg the size of East Cowpaddy, Alabama, or that there is some GPS device that tracks the whereabouts of all the Southerners who live in, say, Newark, New Jersey. At the United Daughters of the Confederacy convention I attended in Richmond in the fall of 2008, as I was beginning research for this book, I talked to a delegation of ladies from Louisville, a small town nobody has ever heard of in central Mississippi, who had carpooled to Richmond. When they stopped for lunch at a Cracker Barrel in Chattanooga, the waitress asked them where they were from. They said Mississippi, and she said she was, too; further inquiry into the "whereabouts" issue established that the waitress was from Shuqualak, an even smaller town in central Mississippi nobody has ever heard of, except for people who live in Louisville. This led to even more intensive questioning, which revealed that the waitress was a distant relative of two of the ladies in the traveling party. "We just fell out!" one said to me—"fell out" being Southern idiom for the English idiom "died laughing."

It's a charming story, and the lady who told it to me also told me that she had grown up in Louisville, as had her husband, her parents, her grandparents, and her great-grandparents. But she had gray hair—very few of the women at the UDC convention looked to be under sixty—and the demographic and economic changes that are sweeping the South have reached Louisville, too. Just before the convention, her husband had been laid off from his job at a chemical company, which was cutting costs by closing its local plant. Louisville is in Winston County, Mississippi, which is part of the band of counties across the center of the state that have been losing population since 2000. The ties that have kept her family in one town for four generations are fraying; the easy assumption that *of course* grown children will settle down near their parents simply no longer holds, even in small-town Mississippi.

All of this may help explain why, when Wayne Thompson goes to the post office in the tiny Arkansas town where he has lived most of his life and fails to see a single familiar face, he feels a kind of existential anguish; it explains why a Clarksdale, Mississippi, packed with blues venues and museums celebrating an indigenous art form still doesn't seem like a real town anymore; it explains why driving through so many parts of the rural South these days is like driving through some sinister Matrix-like simulation of the real thing. So if giant machines till an unpeopled Mississippi Delta and Wayne Thompson's small town becomes a vacant lot, will there still be Southerners in fifty years?

Thirty years ago, sociologist John Shelton Reed, considering the question of the Agrarians' continued relevance, wrote that "whether [their] ideas can be translated into an urban and industrial context is an important question, and one, I believe, not yet answered."[16] Today, three decades later, I see some hope for agrarianism itself, and signs that Southern identity is morphing once again. But change never comes free, and the price tag for all this is excruciatingly high. Today's agrarian movement owes a debt to those 12 Southerners, but it's a debt unlikely ever to be fully acknowledged; they were prophets without honor in their own country. Their objection to the American notion of "progress" was that it turned human beings into nothing but workers and consumers, locked into a vicious cycle of production and consumption, a conclusion many of today's youth have come to share. To them, the Southern way of life was an agrarian one, achieving some kind of truce with nature; today, the urban-suburban South is a place of hideous suburban sprawl and snarled traffic, led by an aggressively pro-business political class that is only now beginning to grasp that political ideology is a pretty useless tool for dealing with issues like rising energy prices and climate change. Their utter failure to recognize that the highest and best use involved anything other than making a quick profit is the reason that my childhood paradise today lies under asphalt; of the woods I used to explore there remain exactly two of the big old red oak trees—both looking unhealthy—and a thin scrim of sickly-looking scrub pines overlooking a nineteen-lane freeway. The freeway is part of something called the Piedmont Atlantic Megaregion (PAM), a string of cities and suburbs stretching in a crescent from Raleigh, North Carolina, to Birmingham, Alabama. It's an ugliness I can't ignore: I look down on it whenever the plane I'm on makes a final approach into Hartsfield, and it makes me want to weep. All that destroyed, just so the world could have one more Econo Lodge, one more tacky strip mall.

And yet my own reaction, shared by so many others of my generation who grew up in the South, is instructive. If attachment to land was the only thing that mattered, then our identity would lie under asphalt, too. Yet here we are in the second decade of the twenty-first century, as attached to our Southern identity as ever, and struggling to understand in what form it will survive. To love a garden is to know that it is an essentially transient thing—broadly characteristic of a particular soil or climate, maybe, but essentially irreproducible; once it's gone, it's gone forever. Southerners are acutely aware of this feature of gardens and communities both, which goes a long way toward explaining our so-called resistance to change. It's not resistance. It's grief.

Yet the Southern sense of community is also a highly adaptable thing. It has survived slavery, war, and the upending of rigid social customs brought by the civil rights movement; today, it shows signs of surviving the severing of its last connection with its agrarian roots. One test of a community is whether members are able to recognize each other as members, and that certainly remains true; another is the survival of group customs and values, and for that we need only look as far as Paula Deen, who is creating an Oprah-size empire of cookbooks, interior decor, and recipes based on the precepts of "Southern hospitality." It's a cliché, certainly, but underneath the cliché is the historical reality that the South has virtually no tradition of public space—no Central Parks, no Public Gardens, no custom of the neighborhood pub. Hence the concentration of social life within the walls of private homes; hence the development of elaborate expectations for hosting and being hosted; hence a whole lot of recipes, just waiting for a Paula Deen to realize their money-making potential. Deen's success is built on many things, but one is her realization that all people, not just Southerners, instinctively crave community, and that sharing a meal is the most ancient foundation of community. It is this history that explains why when Southern people want to be friendly, they invite you *home*. So, for example, in the 1980s, a Jewish friend of mine from Memphis opened his bachelor's apartment every year for co-workers at the *Atlanta Constitution* whose work schedules kept them from going home for Thanksgiving. The Orphans Thanksgiving turned into a tradition, but it was just one of dozens of such events; communal Sunday dinners, seders, Fourth of July brunches—you name it, they happened almost every weekend, to a degree I did not appreciate until I lived outside the Deep South. Nor is it any accident that the South, one of the most politically conservative regions of the country, is also where there are more gay parents than in any other part of the country.[17] In the South, gay people don't parade; they organize potluck suppers and go to PTA meetings. In Atlanta's Candler Park, the decades-long presence of a lesbian community has transformed a neighborhood of run-down houses with a commercial strip of seedy bars and seedier laundromats into a gentrified neighborhood of organic food co-ops and an elementary school where test scores consistently top state averages.

But these are trivial examples, dwarfed by what is by far the most important evidence for the continued vitality of a distinctly Southern sense of community: the black remigration, which began in the 1970s and shows no sign of letting up. Thirty years ago, as the historic nature of this remigration was beginning to become evident to sociologists, John Shelton Reed took a look at more than a decade's worth of data from polls that had asked respondents to rate their feelings about various groups, including Southerners, on a scale of 0 to 100, 0 being cold and 100 being warm. In 1964, there were huge gaps between blacks and whites on this question—but as the 1960s became the 1970s, the gap steadily narrowed, thanks largely to warming attitudes among black respondents. By 1976, more than 80 percent of both Southern whites and blacks said they had "warm" feelings about Southerners; among non-Southerners, blacks were far more likely than whites to feel warmly about Southerners.[18] More recent poll results show that black people who live in the South are actually slightly *more* likely to identify themselves as Southerners than white residents—which is all the more remarkable considering that only thirty years ago "Southerner" automatically meant "white" (and still does, in the minds of many non-Southerners).

"The South was still deep within those who left, and the sight of some insignificant thing would take them back and remind them of what they once were," journalist Isabel Wilkerson writes, describing those earlier migrants—who, faced with oppression, poverty, and humiliations, went north and west (and, in the process, transplanted little pieces of the South to places like Bakersfield and Detroit). Now, decades later, a significant part of the black remigration is composed of their descendants. Between 2000 and 2008, 75 percent of the gains in the United States' black population occurred in the South; today, the South accounts for 57 percent of the nation's black population.

If ever there was evidence for a resilient and distinctly Southern sense of community, this mass movement of people would be it. It's safe to say that very few of its members are returning to reclaim any particular piece of land; the "Southern-ness" their ancestors possessed was not defined that way. It was instead a core of shared meanings, accents, folkways, and ways of doing things that they had always carried inside—and today, many of their descendants find more of that sense of commu-nity in the South than anywhere else. In fifty years, it may be that "Southern" is as automatically associated with black skin as it once was with white. Or maybe by then we will have finally disassociated Southern identity from skin color altogether.

That's the hope I feel when I talk to Paula Matabane. She is black, six years older than I am, and when I was growing up in the white Atlanta suburb of College Park, she was finishing high school just a few miles away, in southwest Atlanta near Morehouse University. An associate professor of television and film at Howard University in Washington, D.C., she has an academic career that has taken her to California and Pennsyl-vania, but her sense of a Southern identity remains as much a part of her as her skin. She feels at home among Southerners, and not just because in her experience Southerners are friendlier and more apt to be neighborly. It's also the shared experience—something she finds to be true even with white Southerners like me, who are old enough to remember what things were once like. We have seen and experienced things most Americans only read about in books; despite our differences, the same history has shaped us both.

"We struggled more with our humanity," she said. "We faced the realism of the social system we inherited. We know what we came through. And we have done better. We have not succeeded—we haven't overcome completely—but as Southerners, we have done so much better." Today, Paula lives not far from me, in the Maryland suburbs of the District, but she plans to move back to Atlanta in the next year or so. Why? "It's home. My extended family is [there]. It's the spiritual tie of who I am, remembering who I am, remembering the places that informed my development. It's spiritual. This is where my ancestors are buried."

The South is where my ancestors are buried, too; my mother's mother lies in an unmarked pauper's grave in Atlanta's famous Oakland Cemetery, alongside the city's founders, its mayors, and its social elite. I was born in a hospital almost within sight of that cemetery, and have known the city intimately for three decades: as a child in the 1950s and 1960s, as a student in the 1970s, as a reporter in the 1980s. Yet in the last two decades, Atlanta has been on the flip side of the "sorting out" of the rural South—the recipient of a vast influx of people, cars, skyscrapers, and money. Between 1990 and 2008, thanks largely to the black remigration, Atlanta more than doubled its black population; today, it has surpassed Chicago to become the city with the highest black population in the country. For better or worse, areas like the Atlanta metropolitan region will be the face of what constitutes the South in the twenty-first century—a South populated by people who have as much in common with all those "white Southerner" stereotypes as I have with Scarlett O'Hara, many of whom will trace their own family roots to places like Pakistan or El Salvador. Would the South I knew be transformed by all these changes? Or would it absorb them and morph once again into something different, yet still recognizably Southern?

I had left Atlanta in 1989. Though I'd passed through the city many times since then, it had been twenty years since I had seriously explored it. Now it was time to go back, to get a closer look at what the twenty-first-century South might be turning into.

7

Atlanta

To millions of Southerners, Atlanta is a blight on the landscape, an island of blue in a sea of red, the epitome of all that is not Southern. In truth, it's a very Southern city, although in ways that tend to elude even its natives. It is Southern in its inferiority complex, in its defensive need to be validated as a "world-class" city, Southern in its reflexive need to sugarcoat racial realities, Southern in its resilience and adaptability in the face of calamity. It is Southern in the same unintentional way Scarlett O'Hara was Southern: shrewd, afflicted with a remarkable incuriosity about its own past and an almost childlike attachment to its illusions. Over and over, it has been unafraid to morph into some new version of itself; over and over, it has chosen some kind of packaged myth—"the city too busy to hate," the Lost Cause fairy tale of *Gone With the Wind*, the tinsel glory of hosting the 1996 Summer Olympics—over authenticity.

It may also be an allegory for the twenty-first century South as a whole. At the moment, it faces a choice between two competing Southern traditions. One is a continuation of the "business first" model that created both its prosperity and its paralyzing suburban sprawl; the second is a new approach to land planning and conservation that draws on concepts of community familiar to an older, agrarian South. What happens in the next ten to twenty years in Atlanta will show how well this city—a mecca for young, educated, and upwardly mobile black people, with an unbroken forty-year history of black leadership—will be able to cope with increasing ethnic diversity, dwindling natural resources (like water), and some of the worst traffic congestion in the country, not to mention ingrained residential segregation that's a legacy of its Jim Crow past and the biggest gap between rich and poor of any city in the United States.[1] "We're at the point where we're either making some really good decisions and going to a really cool place, or we're not," says Ryan Gravel, an Atlanta urban planner who is the architect of a massive project that will, he hopes, eventually link forty-five intown neighborhoods by light rail. "One way or another, it's defining what we're going to be. It's scary and fascinating at the same time."

I find it scary and fascinating, too. For one thing, Atlanta is a creature of the South's die-hard belief in small government—the more small governments, the better. Its metropolitan region is a hodgepodge of ten different counties sprawling over an area that includes some sixty municipalities, some of which are small cities in their own right, as well as a state legislature dominated by people who aren't from Atlanta and who don't like it that much. Getting all those horses into one barn and coming up with something halfway sensible in the way of land use, transportation, and water conservation policies will be a huge challenge in itself, and that's not even counting the need to chop away at the symbiotic embrace that has historically existed between county commissions and real estate developers, and has thwarted so many efforts to stop overdevelopment and create affordable housing. But Atlanta survived Sherman; in the past, catastrophes—and Atlanta's urban sprawl, traffic problems, and looming water scarcity amount to an unfolding catastrophe— have brought out the best in its citizens. I also suspect that the solutions which emerge will be fundamentally fake. They will be beautifully landscaped but bland simulacrums of an imagined small-town South, complete with piped-in Muzak and upscale retail opportunities. And that, too, will be Southern—a reflection of Atlanta's corporate soul and its historical preference for packaging over content.

"Every time I look at Atlanta, I see what a quarter of a million Confederate soldiers died to prevent," Southern sociologist John Shelton Reed once remarked. It was not the late Confederacy he was lamenting, but a quality that crops up again and again in the Southern psyche—a result, maybe, of a history of being considered morally and intellectually inferior by so many outsiders for so long. Deep down, despite their many protestations of regional pride and easy relations between blacks and whites, a lot of Southerners feel a lingering unease in their own skins—a version, perhaps, of the "double consciousness" W. E. B. Du Bois described as afflicting people of color, an ever-present sense of how we look in the eyes of The Others. Atlanta reflects this fundamental unease. All those Confederate soldiers died for something that was compellingly real, at least to them. Atlanta prefers myth. It's the urban equivalent of an attractive woman who insists on slathering on too much makeup, a slave to its own public relations.

So this is it—the city where I was born and where I lived the first thirty-four years of my life. Welcome South, Brother (to borrow a 1960s-era slogan from WSB Radio, back when it broadcast from a faux antebellum mansion grandly named White Columns on Peachtree). Pull up a chair and make yourself comfortable. What follows is a brief tour of history.

We begin at a bronze statue on Marietta Street, one block west of Five Points, because the first thing you have to know about Atlanta is this: it is Henry Grady's city.

The man who first coined the phrase "the New South" is caught in energetic mid-stride, with one hand in his right breast pocket as if he were about to pull out a reporter's notebook. (Or, perhaps, something even more effective. Somewhere in the files of the *Atlanta Journal-Constitution* there's a picture of the city's first black mayor, Maynard Jackson, giving a speech at the base of the Grady statue. Jackson was a big man with an even bigger personality who was fond of long, florid orations. A copy editor proposed this caption: "Bored by Maynard's rhetoric, Henry goes for his piece.") When that picture was made, Five Points was a bustling city center, and the *AJC* newsroom was just up the street. But in 2010, after more than a century downtown, the paper relocated to an office park on the north side of town. Its departure left Henry to preside over a much quieter Five Points, one given over to Georgia State students by day, the homeless by night, and aggressive panhandlers virtually around the clock. Today, Henry looks less like the influential *Atlanta Constitution* editor he once was than like a guy with one hand on his wallet, afraid he's about to get mugged.

Born in 1850, Grady was a member of the business elite that seized control of the political machinery in the post-Reconstruction South. After studying law briefly at the University of Virginia, he turned his attention to newspapering. In 1880, he bought a quarter share in a fledgling newspaper called the *Atlanta Constitution* and became its managing editor.

Atlanta was a natural place for Grady: he was a born salesman, and Atlanta was a place where people sold things. Some cities are born because of their proximity to water or ancient trade routes; some, like Washington, were created out of a swamp by the force of an idea. Atlanta owes its existence to chance, and its prosperity to transportation. One day in 1837 an engineer for the Western and Atlantic Railroad drove a Zero Milepost stake in the ground and declared that this, the first stretch of flat land south of the Appalachians, would be the spot for the terminus of a spur originating in Chattanooga. Terminus, as Atlanta was originally known, happened to be at the same grade level for two other railroads then building across lands recently vacated by the forced expulsion of the Creek and Cherokee tribes, and so a railroad town was born. Today, a traveler in a jet on its final approach into Atlanta sees miles and miles of utterly mundane Southern Piedmont—roads and highways and shopping centers—and suddenly, like the Emerald City rising from the plains of Oz, a cluster of glittering skyscrapers. *Wow*, he thinks. *Where did that come from?* The answer is: nowhere. This is a fact that may help explain the kind of collective existential uneasiness that has driven Atlantans ever since to seek "national" or "big city" or "next great city" or "next great *international* city" status, or whatever it is that will once and for all validate the city's right to be where and what it is.

Grady made his newspaper into the voice for the Democratic Party in the South, which in his day occupied the same point on the political spectrum that some parts of the Republican Party hold today, in that it was enthusiastically and unequivocally pro-business. His temperamental and political opposite was a small, intense man with red hair and a fiery temper: Tom Watson. The son of an east Georgia family that had literally lost the farm in the aftermath of the Civil War, Watson is remembered—when he is remembered—as a Ku Klux Klan apologist, anti-Semite, and inciter of lynch mobs in the 1915 Leo Frank case.[2] But in the beginning, before racism darkened his mind, Watson was an eloquent spokesman for the legal rights of sharecroppers and a critic of the convict lease system, the practice of allowing prominent businessmen and state officials to get cheap labor by leasing convicts from state prisons. (The convicts were usually black; this was one of the practices writer Douglas Blackmon has described in his book, *Slavery by Another Name*.) In 1890, Watson was elected to the U.S. House of Representatives for Georgia's 10th District, and six years later his name was mentioned as a running mate to William Jennings Bryan, who was running on the third-party Populist ticket. The Populist platform was ahead of its time in proposing things like government ownership of railroads and laws barring speculation in farm commodities, and its early appeal was based on the radical proposition that all farmers—Southern and Midwestern, black and white—shared the same economic interests, which they did.

I am describing these two men in some detail because their lives illustrate two persistent themes in Southern history, and in Atlanta's history in particular: a distinctly Southern agrarian tradition, populist and deeply humane in instinct but fatally blinded by a romantic view of the past and crippled by racism, versus the hard, implacable engine of capitalism. It was never an equal contest. It was the ardently pro-business Democratic Party, in fact, that derailed Watson's political career in the 1890s, using a combination of voter fraud in the 1892 and 1894 House of Representatives elections and racist rhetoric warning that Watson was an advocate of Negro social equality.

While an embittered Watson retired to his family farm to brood and write increasingly anti-Semitic, anti-Catholic, racist diatribes, Grady's influence was rising. In 1886, at a meeting of wealthy New York City investors, he gave what became known as his New South speech. "We . . . have smoothed the path to southward, wiped out the place where Mason and Dixon's line used to be, and hung our latch-string out to you and yours,"[3] Grady told the group, which responded with "prolonged cheers." In newspaper columns written from his involuntary political retirement, Watson pointed out that Grady's promise of prosperity was meant for employers, not the workingman; he noted that Grady's vision of a "a hundred farms for every plantation" described a fantasy world in which there were no such things as starving cows or farm loans that came with exorbitant interest rates. Somehow, Watson's barbed critiques never got prominent play in Grady's newspaper. Across an impoverished South, desperate for a respite from two decades of hard times, skeptics were simply drowned out. Wilbur Cash later described the proliferation of the New South gospel as "a crusade preached with burning zeal from platform and pulpit and editorial cell."[4]

The deal Grady proposed to those New York investors was simple: you give us money, we'll give you cheap labor. It's a Faustian bargain that has dominated the South to the present day,[5] and its early success was due to the South's historical antipathy to unions. The standard historical interpretation, once again, is simple white Southern racism: labor solidarity meant biracial alliances, which working-class whites wanted none of. The truth isn't nearly so simple. It goes without saying there were plenty of working-class white racists, but there were also many working-class whites and blacks who were acutely aware of the fact that, in Tom Watson's blunt words, "You are kept apart that you may be separately fleeced of your earnings."[6] It was a biracial coal miners union in Birmingham—very rare for its time anywhere in this country—that organized the 1908 coal miners strike in Bimingham, Alabama. The strike was defeated only when white coal mine owners whipped up public support for their side by resorting to inflammatory racial rhetoric.[7] The success of such tactics, over and over, betrays the fatal weakness on the part of all too many Southern whites for appeals to emotion rather than reason—in particular, the fixed belief that racial cooperation would open the way for lustful black men to get their hands on white women. (In individuals, the trick of seeing one's own unconscious guilt in another person is called "psychological projection"; in Southern history, the only term for it is "mass psychosis.")

But there are other, more subtle, reasons for the South's historic anti-unionism—the most interesting and mysterious of which, at least to me, is the Southern attitude toward individual and property rights. These are red-blooded American values, obviously, but Southerners defer to none in their passion on this subject. This is an attitude with a long history in the South, and my theory is that it's one more legacy of our history as a slave society. When some human beings are classified *as* property, it stands to reason that the ability to *own* property is the ultimate mark of personhood. Slaves aspired to own themselves; non–slave owners aspired to own slaves; slave owners were men of consequence; freed blacks knew that owning their own livelihood was the key to independence. Property ownership made a man of you, literally. Then throw in the religious emphasis on obedience, also dating from slavery days but useful as well for keeping workers in line, and add the South's Scotch-Irish heritage. Those immigrants from the border area between England and Scotland were landless, quarrelsome folks who eked out an existence herding cattle or sheep. Societies where one's entire worldly estate might walk off during the night are societies that take the defense of property as a matter of life and death.

These are just suppositions on my part, but cultural attitudes embed themselves in the collective unconscious and survive the economies that spawned them; we are products of our history whether we know it or not.[8] Whatever the link between history and current attitudes may be, there is without a doubt a kind of ingrained cussedness in the DNA of white working-class Southerners in particular—a streak of individualism and antiauthoritarianism that bristles at the notion of "worker solidarity" and "collective bargaining." Just as they would later do in the 1960s turf wars over real estate, those Progressive-era Southerners tended to see "rights" of any kind as accruing to the individual, not the collective; it follows that an individual's right to run his business the way he sees fit amply justifies whatever it takes to bust up a picket line.

And so industry came to the nonunionized South, and Atlanta grew fat and prosperous shipping the goods that industry made—and then, in the mid-twentieth century, it edged Birmingham out to become an air transport hub, which turned it into a convention city. Along the way, there developed a uniquely strong and extraordinarily effective working coalition of politicians and corporate power brokers that has been the fascination of social scientists for fifty years, ever since University of North Carolina sociologist Floyd Hunter coined the term "power structure" to describe it. The marriage of business and politics in Atlanta is until death do them part, and it has dominated the city's history—deciding the geographical direction and parameters of its growth, charting a course through the social turmoil of the civil rights era, setting its financial priorities. To think of this coalition as some kind of backroom cabal, though, makes it sound more sinister than it is; there are no great power dynasties in Atlanta and no rivals ever take a midnight swim in the Chattahoochee while wearing cement overshoes. It's just that when the big corporate players decide they want something, they get it. Governance in Atlanta is like a family where a doted-on favorite child gets anything he wants—the convention centers, the stadiums, the new skyscrapers, the underground game arcade. Meanwhile, the toilet leaks, the paint peels, and the rest of the kids wear hand-me-downs.

By the time I was a child growing up in the Atlanta suburbs of the 1960s, we were on our third or fourth version of Henry Grady's "New South"—it's a slogan that by definition requires regular updating—but the theme had not changed. Bigger was better; bigger was the only means to the goal. "Forward Atlanta" was our slogan, though a more accurate one would have been "*Fast* Forward Atlanta." We were in a race, and if nobody knew where the finish line was, who cared? New skyscrapers leapfrogged each other in a scramble to dominate the skyline;

construction began on the Perimeter; the minor league Atlanta Crackers and several poor black inner-city neighborhoods were given an unceremonious heave-ho so the city could acquire the National League's Milwaukee Braves and put them in a brand-new stadium. When the metro region's population topped the one million mark in 1959, there were high-fives all around. Ha! Take *that*, you hicks in Birmingham!

Yet the city I knew also maintained the pretense that it was an oasis of Old South custom—which it was, though not in the genteel ways it liked to celebrate. In the spring, hoopskirted young ladies were presented to society at the Piedmont Driving Club, which as the most exclusive club in town naturally did not admit blacks or Jews. In Druid Hills and Buckhead, people lived in white-columned mansions set far back from the road on lush green lawns; white housewives ended shopping expeditions at Rich's by lunching in the Magnolia Room, served by (outwardly) deferential black waitresses. I lived on the fringes of this world; the money in Atlanta has always migrated to the Northside, and we lived on the Southside. But every other Saturday, my father would go downtown for a haircut at one of the barber shops founded by Alonzo Herndon, the city's first black millionaire. There, black barbers in starched white smocks tended to an all-white clientele in a long room with marble floors and crystal chandeliers; at one end of the shop there was a shoeshine stand, where white men lounged reading the sports page while black men polished their shoes to a glossy sheen. The barbers fussed over me and my sister; I could spot them running around the second we entered, scooping up girly magazines and putting out comic books. We waited for Daddy in a row of green vinyl chairs with springy seat cushions by the front window, so high that my feet dangled. At the end of every shave, every customer was dusted with talcum powder, brushed off, smartened up, and sent out the door with a smile.

In that moment, as a deferential black man handed my father his coat, I could see the clear outlines of a social order that was even then in the process of crumbling. It was a world in which white people deluded themselves that they understood the black people they lived with and affectionately accepted their foibles; black people, possibly with better reason, often thought the same thing about us. Racism thrived in a show of civility. It was in this era that former mayor William B. Hartsfield came up with that brilliant public relations slogan: "the city too busy to hate."

It played well outside Atlanta, and there were no doubt lots of white people in Atlanta who believed it. But the real story was more prosaic. What kept us from turning into another Birmingham, with its fire hoses and snarling police dogs, was simply that racial turmoil was bad for business. This is an often repeated part of the story, but it's usually presented as a cosmic revelation that struck Atlanta's enlightened white citizenry: "Wait! We can't afflict those Negroes—they shop here, too!" What Atlanta had and Birmingham did not have was a sizable black middle class with economic clout, and a critical mass of black leadership. Those leaders understood that Atlanta's white leaders weren't too busy to hate, but that they were dying to be perceived that way. And they knew leverage when they saw it.

The existence of this black leadership class—people like John Wesley Dobbs, Maynard Jackson's grandfather and "the mayor of Auburn Avenue"—was a direct result of the economic success of a few. It is one of the complexities of Atlanta's history that at the very same time it hosted one of the nation's worst race riots, in 1906,[9] it was also the home of black businessmen who were already millionaires. (The reason Auburn Avenue became known as a black "millionaires' row" was that it was the part of town where black businesses were forced to relocate after white mobs burned down and looted black-owned businesses elsewhere.) In the 1920s, black real estate mogul Herman Perry's Standard Life Insurance Company was one of the very few financial institutions willing to make home loans to black people, and Perry's development of Atlanta's West End made it into a middle-class enclave.

The black community also had its very own local think tank and reservoir of political activism, otherwise known as Atlanta University—which by the 1940s consisted of the campuses of Morehouse, Spelman, Clark, and Morris Brown colleges. When the U.S. Supreme Court ruled in 1944 that white primaries were unconstitutional, Atlanta's black leadership had read the tea leaves and had already put in years conducting voter registration drives. Before the ruling, Mayor Hartsfield had bluntly told a delegation of black leaders that he had no plans to put black officers on the city's police force. Shortly after the Supreme Court ruling, faced with a renewed request and thousands of newly enfranchised black citizens in his city, Hartsfield had one question: "How many do you want?"[10] If all those Negroes were going to be voting, the mayor cheerfully explained later, he figured they might as well vote for him. In reality, it was a transformative moment in American politics, and a classic example of how white Southern conservatism worked in real life: resist change to the bitter end, then pivot adroitly and act like it was your idea all along.

Yet as central as race has been in Atlanta's history, events would not have played out the way they did had it not been for a very Southern case of class consciousness. I know of no way to accurately define class in the South, and I know of no empirical way to prove my belief that Southerners are more class-conscious than other Americans. All I can say is that I've never met a Southerner who did not know precisely what class his people belonged to—and we're talking about distinct groups like "aristocracy" or "gentry" down to "redneck" or "yeoman farmer," too, not some vast catchall phrase like "middle class." Just as important, class is something Southerners actually *talk* about.

Class in the South was and is a complex mixture of accent (a coastal drawl, for example, is considered higher-status than a Tennessee twang, and a black person who says "ax" for "ask" has signaled something about his origins), family education, church affiliation and attendance, personal morals, manners, and prison record (although having one of the latter is not necessarily a disqualifier for anything; murdering your wife's lover might actually be a social asset). Wealth had something to do with class distinctions, but as one look at Graceland in Memphis could tell you, money alone could not buy status. If, on the other hand, you grew up in a shack but managed to make a pile, there was a fair amount of social mobility; there has been many a Southern millionaire who could recall a childhood in which he or she owned exactly one pair of shoes. As murky as all these definitions were, one thing was clear: the lowest was "poor white trash." Used by blacks and whites alike, this was a withering term that told the world that even given the fifty-yard head start of being born with a white skin, the person in question had still never managed to amount to a hill of beans. (You don't hear either "poor white trash" or "hill of beans" much anymore, but good luck finding anyone raised in the South who doesn't know what they mean.)

In a class- and race-conscious culture like this, it was a natural corollary that some people were simply born to lead. In another time and place, that status might have been based on family name or landholdings; in Atlanta, the city of business, the natural aristocracy has always been the Business Elite. In the 1960s, that elite was all white—a group of people who lived mostly on the city's Northside, in neighborhoods like Druid Hills and Ansley Park and Morningside and Buckhead. They played golf with each other at the Bobby Jones Golf Course, went to the same schools, dated each other's sisters, partied together, belonged to the same clubs. They all spoke with a peculiar type of Southern accent known as Buckhead Lockjaw—a syrupy drawl with elongated vowels and lots of emphasized words, all produced with next to no lip movement: "It's a little *waw-um* today" or "Somebody really should speak to Dawson about his wife's *wardrobe*"—the last two words pronounced "waff's wawa drobe," without parting the lips. (Try it. It takes skill.) Some of the class differences between Northside and Southside began to dawn on me when as a teenager I went with a church youth group to a social gathering held at the Buckhead home of former Atlanta mayor Ivan Allen Jr., whose fortune derived from his family's office supply store. Mayor Allen used to say, "I inherited money, I made money, and I married money" with a huge grin that looked (as my grandmother would've said) like a jackass eating briars. It wasn't his house that got my attention so much, or the pool, or the tennis courts; it was the enormous *meadow*—there's no other word for it—stretching out for acres behind his house into the gauzy summer twilight, a private Eden carved out of some of the most expensive urban real estate in the South. As I gazed out at that vista, my own place in the larger social hierarchy of my world suddenly became a whole lot clearer.

In the black community, class was determined by all of the above—with the added subtleties of skin shade factored in. Light skin wouldn't automatically vault a poor person of color into a higher social stratum, but it did promote him to the top of whatever class he was in; conversely, having a dark complexion could work as a brake on the aspirations of a person who was educated and well-to-do. Maynard Jackson, elected in 1972, was not only the grandson of John Wesley Dobbs but also the nephew of Mattiwilda Dobbs, an internationally known opera singer. The Jacksons weren't rich the way the Allens were, but they were prosperous, educated, and cultured, which counted for a great deal—and light-skinned. Despite his bespoke suits and the freshly laundered handkerchief he always carried in his front pocket, Jackson did care about the working class, and the major accomplishment of his time as mayor was a huge increase in the percentage of city contracts awarded to minority firms. On the other hand, as a member of Atlanta's black elite, he was also perfectly prepared to issue instructions for the betterment of his social inferiors.

In 1981, when I was a new reporter for the *Atlanta Constitution*, I covered a speech Jackson made at the Hungry Club, a venerable forum for black community leaders. Then at the end of his second term, Jackson could not run for a third and had endorsed former U.N. ambassador Andrew Young as his successor. It was a three-way race that also featured a black former police chief, Reginald Eaves, and a white state legislator, Sidney Marcus. With no candidate getting 50 percent of the vote, a runoff was called between Young and Marcus, and on the day in question Jackson was determined to stop any defections of Eaves's supporters to Marcus. I had a fork load of steamed cabbage on its way to my mouth when I heard the mayor say something about "Nee-groes" who were "shuffling and grinning" around the Marcus campaign; even as the novice I was, I instantly realized that was the end of my lunch; the next deadline was forty-five minutes away, and I had a story to write. The speech royally pissed off most of the black people in the city, who didn't like being patronized or having the black community's dirty laundry aired in public—but to Jackson this was simply a logical use of political power and social clout. What kind of kingmaker failed to keep the peasants in line?

The evolution of black leadership in Atlanta over several decades gave a lot of white Southerners a chance to do something black Southerners had been doing for a long time, which was to get an up-close and personal look at political leaders of another race. Shockingly, they proved to be human. While the giants of the civil rights movement were morphing into larger-than-life icons in other places, the pedestals they occupied in Atlanta were considerably closer to the ground. People in Atlanta knew that Martin Luther King's children were living examples of the disappointing fact that extraordinary men can produce very ordinary offspring; they knew about Julian Bond's wandering eye, and Andy Young's tendency to put his mouth in motion before his brain was in gear; they saw how the long battle for respect black women had waged made them insistent on being known as "Mrs. John So-and-So" long after white feminists had declared that such titles were relics of an outmoded patriarchy, and how certain black men who were noted spokesmen for civil rights treated their own wives as second-class citizens. They saw lighter-skinned black politicians use that fact against darker-skinned rivals. They heard rumors about which ones drank too much or partied with drug dealers or put the moves on women they weren't married to, and it all seemed oddly . . . familiar. As Julian Bond, then a sexy and incredibly young spokesman for the Student Non-Violent Coordinating Committee, observed at the time, "Look at that girl shake that thing / We can't *all* be Martin Luther King."[11]

Today, forty years after Maynard Jackson's election, Atlanta has enjoyed the longest uninterrupted black leadership of any city in the United States, a record that makes it as close to being "post-racial" as anyplace in the country. Yet what's interesting about all these black Democrats is how, if you stand back and squint slightly, they look so darn Republican (in the old-fashioned, non–Tea Party sense of that word). Jackson was the most old-line Democrat of the lot, and in his first term he went head-to-head with the city's white business establishment. When Coca-Cola president Robert W. Woodruff—Atlanta's version of Cardinal Richelieu, a corporate titan whose behind-the-scenes influence was the single most important force in Atlanta's political and philanthropic scene for the better part of fifty years—offered to pay off Jackson's campaign debt, Jackson courageously said no, recognizing the offer for what it was: Woodruff's attempt to own him.

But in the end, Jackson could not prevail against Atlanta's powerful business interests, who never stopped cultivating a back channel to the conservative white Georgia legislators at the state capitol down the street from city hall. It was during Jackson's first two terms that the city poured 85 million taxpayer dollars into Underground Atlanta, a section of the city that had been roofed in by a proliferation of viaducts and that downtown developers hoped to turn into a tourist attraction. (It failed.) Jackson did open up city contracts to minority businessmen, but that was a benefit to the black middle class, not the poor, and when he left office he became a bond salesman. Andy Young's conservative personal politics earned him the label of the civil rights movement's "closet Republican"; as mayor, he spent most of his time abroad, wooing foreign investors. His successor, Bill Campbell, presided over the demolition of the city's public housing; Campbell's successor, Shirley Franklin, worked for both Jackson and Young before running for mayor herself, and made herself known as a friend of the downtown business establishment.[12] The city that prides itself as the birthplace of the civil rights movement has given birth a deep pool of black political talent—but so far, not a single authentic champion of the poor in the bunch.

And so we come to the present.

First impressions of a returning native:

Traffic—everywhere, a rush hour that began in the predawn hours and lasted until late at night, an endless crawl that sometimes extended so far out from the city limits that it seemed like just one leg of some transcontinental convoy. And new faces, speaking new languages. It used to be that it was unusual to hear anything besides English on a downtown Atlanta street, but that hasn't been true for a while now. On Buford Highway, Atlanta's immigration freeway, I could find a cluster of Chinese and Vietnamese supermarkets and restaurants in one strip mall, and a cluster of Mexican and Salvadoran ones a mile down the road. In Gwinnett County, which in 1990 had been largely rural and more than 90 percent white, I shopped at an International Farmers Market, where I bit into the glistening white flesh of a lychee from China and tasted its cold, sharp sweetness. Lost in a babble of Spanish and Chinese and several other languages I didn't recognize, I cruised past huge platters of meat cuts and fish, some as familiar as catfish and others strange to me—cow necks, sheep heads, shark fillets. Forty miles south, the State Farmers Market in Forest Park was now row upon row of empty stalls. The market is still busy early in the mornings and on weekends, but these days a lot of Georgia farmers sell their crops by the field directly to companies like Dole or ConAgra; high fuel costs make it impractical for smaller farmers to drive their produce all the way to Atlanta. On a Tuesday afternoon, the few stalls that were open were run by Hispanics—and they were resellers, not farmers.

The farmers market was one sign of the demographic changes sweeping the South, but there were plenty of others. Atlanta's most affluent neighborhoods have always been on the Northside, but the central core of downtown was always considered Five Points, on the south end of the city's famous Peachtree Street. Atlanta's Southside, once a mostly white suburban haven for the middle class, had devolved into vacant lots, run-down houses, and strip malls, interspersed with little islands of gentrification or heavily fortified gated communities. The whole Northside-Southside dichotomy had become starker and somehow more ominous. The downtown core had moved a mile north of Five Points, to Midtown—and if skyscrapers could somehow detach from their foundations, I got the feeling that they would be clunkily edging farther north, away from all those poor folks, to join all those spanking new towers clustered on the north side of the Perimeter.

And then there were the black people. *Lots* of black people—significantly more than I remembered seeing when I lived in Atlanta in the 1980s, and far, far more than I remembered seeing when I was growing up on the Southside of the city in the 1960s. Memory can play tricks on the mind, but figures from the 2010 census show I wasn't imagining anything. In 1990, the ten-county metropolitan Atlanta area had been 67 percent white, with the vast majority of its black population living within the city limits of Atlanta. The 2010 census figures showed that today whites are a decided minority—38 percent, in fact—and are outnumbered by natural population growth among blacks, an incoming wave of black newcomers, and a significant increase in Hispanic and Asian immigrants. Nearly one-fifth of the black population gains in the country's hundred biggest metropolitan areas went to the Atlanta metropolitan area alone. Decades ago, more than five million poor blacks walked out of the South, driven by the cruelties of Jim Crow to look for jobs and a better life up north. Today their descendants are returning by choice, with education, money, and job skills— and even on the most superficial level, their increasing numbers are hard to miss.[13]

Nowhere is this more true than in the new majority-black suburbs, which stretch out for miles past the point where, at least in my memory, "nowhere" used to begin. They range from acres of brand-new townhouses in south Fulton County to $2 million luxury homes in east DeKalb County—imposing mansions the size of a country club, fronted by velvety lawns big enough for a putting green or three. Downtown, many of the street names I had once known had been changed to commemorate black civil rights leaders, or the 1996 Olympics, or the city's self-proclaimed international status, or sometimes the international status of black civil rights leaders (hence, Andrew Young International Boulevard). Other street name changes had erased old distinctions between black and white neighborhoods. In the 1960s, black Hunter Street on the Westside became Mozley Park Drive once it crossed Chappell Street into an all-white neighborhood. Today, it's all Martin Luther King Jr. Boulevard. A few blocks south of Martin Luther King, a glittering complex of high-rises marked Morehouse Medical School, replacing what I had known in the 1970s as borrowed classroom space in a run-down building. Nearby, brand-new loft apartments have sprung up on what had once been blocks of serious urban blight—all of them built by H. J. Russell & Company, an Atlanta-based company and the largest black-owned construction firm in the nation.

It's a little misleading to characterize the black remigration to the South as the descendants of those who left during the Great Migration; demographers don't know how many of the new arrivals are actually grandchildren or great-grandchildren of those migrants, though undoubtedly many of them are. What they do know is that the remigration is two distinct streams: one of young, highly educated single people and younger married families who are already in the labor force and who have never lived in the South, and another of older people who are returning to the South after decades of living elsewhere. The latter are more likely to be divorced or widowed, a fact that suggests they are returning in their retirement years to a region where they have family connections.[14] The unanswered question is to what degree the first group is also driven by some older connection to the South—the memory, perhaps, of grandparents who lived there, or simply the desire to live in a place where they don't have to be a minority.

"Atlanta is a metaphor," writes William Jelani Cobb, a professor at Rutgers University who lived in Atlanta from 2001 to 2011 while teaching history at Spelman College. "Inside of five minutes here you can't help but notice that this place is a scale model of black America with all of our glories, vanities, contradictions and failures. The precise status of black America [today] can be found somewhere between the old Bankhead Highway—inspiration for a thousand hip-hop references and home to even more hard realities—and Cascade Road, bourgeois landing strip and metaphor for black success."[15] Since the death of Martin Luther King, he thinks, "we've seen black people move in two directions, simultaneously and rapidly. One is the growth of an educated middle class and the emergence of a fairly well established, financially secure group of people. And we also see a broader and more intransigent type of poverty. When you look at Atlanta you see both of those things."

Obviously, all cities have wealth disparities; Atlanta's is notable only because it's such a good illustration of what black wealth disparity looks like. The gamut runs from neighborhoods of entrenched poverty to the palaces of entertainment and sports moguls like Evander Holyfield, actor and hip-hop artist Ludacris, and filmmaker Tyler Perry. All cities have poor people, too—but not many go to the lengths Atlanta has gone to in an effort to keep them out of sight. Few people know as much about that as Anita Beatty.

Beatty, who runs the Metro Atlanta Task Force for the Homeless, is a white-haired lady with a pale pink complexion who looks like central casting's idea of what she in fact is: a Methodist minister's wife. "I'm really just a sweet little granny, but that's not what a lot of people say," she told me, and in fact her genteel demeanor conceals a steely will and a sharp tongue; people find her either inspirational or infuriating. Her organization's headquarters are right on Atlanta's Peachtree Street, fronted by what was once a 1920s-era Packard automobile dealership showroom. Behind the showroom, in a warren of interconnected buildings that takes up most of a city block, there is a shelter with beds for five hundred men, along with a network of offices, conference rooms, and waiting areas. On the morning in June when I visited, hundreds of unemployed and/or homeless people sat in a cavernous, sweltering space in the former garage. Some were sleeping; others were filling out applications for jobs, drug treatment programs, or emergency housing—all the tedious paperwork that comes with being poor. Outside, a group of fifteen or twenty homeless people, mostly men, gathered in the shade of a pin oak tree on the corner or paced up and down the sidewalk, whiling away the long hours until evening, when the shelter doors would be unlocked and they could go back inside.

To Atlanta's government leaders and corporate titans, the sight of all these homeless people loitering right on the city's main drag—or at least its symbolic main drag—is intolerable. They equate homelessness with panhandling and panhandling with serious crime, and they have a point. Complaints about Atlanta's downtown panhandlers come a close second to its traffic problems on the list of things visitors say they dislike about Atlanta; people understandably feel threatened when some smelly, disheveled stranger insistently asks for pocket change or approaches a woman with "Hey, Red, gimme some pussy." City officials say Beatty's organization contributes to the problem by simply warehousing homeless men—in effect, enabling the self-destructive behavior that underlies homelessness, like substance abuse and untreated mental illness. Beatty's response is that the city has no statistics to back up its claims that homeless people commit disproportionate amounts of petty crime; in fact, she says, homeless people are most often the victims of street crime, not the perpetrators. In her view, Atlanta's programs for the homeless amount to window dressing: they're underfunded, they're much too small to meet the actual need, and they're tucked away in hard-to-find parts of downtown. City officials may talk about homelessness being a complex social problem, she said, but their actions say something different. "Their strategy is always 'contain, control, move out of sight,'" she said.

In fact, over the years, the city has gone to extraordinary lengths to sweep its homelessness problem under the rug. In the months before the opening of the 1996 Summer Olympics in Atlanta, police went around offering a one-way bus ticket out of town to any homeless person who agreed to leave; about the same time, a sympathetic police official gave Beatty and her confederates access to police records, which was how they discovered piles of arrest citations printed up with descriptions already inked in: "African American homeless male." The Atlanta City Council has made valiant efforts to come up with a law that somehow contrives not to violate the First Amendment while making it illegal to walk around giving the impression of being poor and unemployed. So far, its efforts have earned the city a number four ranking on a 2009 list of the "ten meanest cities" compiled by the National Coalition for the Homeless[16]— and bonus points for legal creativity: one ordinance made it illegal for anyone to be in a parking lot unless he or she was parked there, another law barred carrying a pillow on city property, and another banned anyone from asking for money in the downtown "tourist zone." The first two fell to legal challenges, and Atlanta police quit writing citations for "tourist zone" violations because nobody really knew where the "tourist zone" was. At one point it included the plaza outside the Martin Luther King Center for Nonviolent Social Change, where there is a statue of Mahatma Gandhi—the father of peaceful resistance and a man who spent much of his life with a beggar's bowl in his hand. "I said, 'You're making it illegal for somebody to ask for a quarter in front of the *Gandhi* statue?'" William Jelani Cobb told me. "Nobody recognized the irony."

This, of course, is not the image of Atlanta most people see. The face that Atlanta shows to the world is one you might see in a *Cooking with Paula* photo spread or an episode of *The Real Housewives of Atlanta*—a city of sports franchises, upscale barbecues, swank shopping malls, and over-the-top baby showers. It's no accident, Cobb notes, that the prosperity gospel has caught on so spectacularly in Atlanta, or that one of the biggest churches associated with that theological mind-set, Bishop Eddie Long's New Birth Missionary Baptist Church, is in suburban DeKalb County. The idea that God rewards his followers with financial well-being is not a black phenomenon or even a Southern one, but it would be hard to find a place more ripe for the picking than Atlanta—a city deep in the Bible Belt, obsessed to the point of collective insanity with image and appearance.

Why, you ask, should this be? It has to do with that existential uneasiness I mentioned, as well as with the stubborn persistence of a Southern inferiority complex. But another reason is simply that Atlanta is a city of business, and business is not government; its job isn't solving social problems, but making profits and maintaining an image. If it looks good, it must *be* good. Exhibit A of this mind-set would be the 1996 Olympics, a project undertaken by a group of Atlanta businessmen led by a (white) local estate lawyer named Billy Payne.

The idea, Payne said, came to him in a dream in 1987, just as he was finishing a big volunteer project for his church and looking for something else to do. Payne was not an insider among Atlanta's ruling business elite, but he had one or two friends in that group; through those connections, and his own relentless public relations campaigning, he succeeded in mobilizing a critical mass of support from the major corporate and political players. There was just one problem: unlike, say, Los Angeles, which had hosted the 1984 Summer Olympics, or Barcelona, which hosted the 1992 games, Atlanta lacked the infrastructure needed for such a mammoth event. And bigger cities far better equipped with transportation systems and existing sports venues, like Los Angeles and Montreal, had lost hundreds of millions of dollars hosting the Games.

Not to worry: Payne assured state and city leaders that the 1996 Games would be paid for entirely by private donations—and, more important, he promised that hosting the Games would finally and beyond all doubt mark Atlanta as a "world-class city." The last part was the clincher. Soon, a groundswell of popular support had materialized—plenty of willing volunteers, at least, even if the wealthy weren't exactly queuing up to buy those $4 million individual sponsorships. In 1992, crowds gathered in front of huge television monitors in downtown Atlanta to watch as Juan Antonio Samaranch, president of the International Olympic Committee, announce in Tokyo that the host of the 1996 Games would be . . . Atlanta! Women shrieked in joy; strangers embraced each other; grown men wept.

From the promoters' standpoint, the Olympics was a huge success, bringing in an estimated $5.1 billion to the Georgia economy. People made out like bandits. That is, some people did—those with insider connections who managed to snag a job or a lucrative contract. For everybody else, including the hundreds of sidewalk vendors who showed up only to be relegated to distant side streets, the Games were "a vehicle for patronage," according to a postmortem by the *Journal-Constitution*.[17] Atlanta's debut as a "world-class city" was marred by logistical problems and transportation foul-ups, all recorded with savage glee by the out-of-town media.

The Games did leave behind a half dozen new sporting venues and spiffed-up neighborhoods, but taxpayers wound up footing another $1 billion in infrastructure costs (sewers, streetscaping, job training, demolition expenses, airport expansion, and so on). However, even that figure omits administrative costs, which ran into more millions. Critics like Larry Keating, a professor of urban planning at Georgia Tech, also pointed out that $5.1 billion, even if every dollar of it was real, represented only a minuscule fraction of the state's $900 billion–plus economy. Demolishing the city's dilapidated public housing created some attractive new mixed-use apartment complexes and improved the look of some eyesore blocks. But the demolitions also displaced an estimated thirty thousand low-income people, according to estimates made by advocates for the homeless. The displaced families were given housing vouchers, but vouchers aren't much good unless there are apartments to use them on. In Atlanta (as in most major cities) there's a dearth of one- and two-bedroom apartments, and suburban zoning laws effectively ban the construction of any more.[18] In August 2010, when thirteen thousand vouchers for federal housing assistance became available in the Atlanta suburb of East Point, thirty thousand applicants showed up.

Today, the most visible reminder of the '96 Games is Centennial Olympic Park, a twenty-one-acre open space near Five Points. Centennial Park is popular with tourists; they like the fountains, where their kids can play and which provide a welcome respite from the inferno that Atlantans call "summer." But calling it a park is a bit of a stretch; it's actually a sculpture garden and public amphitheater with a small kids' playground at one end. Occupying a central position is a bronze statue of Billy Payne himself, holding an Olympic torch. In order to build the park, Olympic planners razed an old industrial section that was beginning to show signs of becoming a funky, urban-pioneer kind of neighborhood and replaced it with upscale high-rise condominiums. But the city's streets are as deserted as ever at night, and in order to lure residents to downtown, the city has had to offer subsidies to private developers to encourage continued building in the area. The biggest "gift" to the city, then, actually comes with a rather hefty, and ongoing, price tag.

Meanwhile, the city's bridges are crumbling, its sewer system is dangerously outdated, and test scores among its public school students are so abysmally low that a July 2011 report from the Georgia Bureau of Investigation found that 178 educators had helped their students cheat in order to boost the passing rate.

The Olympics saga is just one example of what Keating indicts as the "pursuit of narrow, immediate interests without the leavening influence of the broader public interest"[19] by the business-political axis of power. It's a situation that endures despite Atlanta's transition from white to black political power—and even the latter is sometimes less than it appears. During the planning for the Olympics, Keating noted, the organizing committee did an end run around then-mayor Maynard Jackson by going to the Georgia General Assembly to get the legal authority to create Centennial Olympic Park. The mayor learned about the proposed creation of a major city landmark smack in the middle of his downtown the same way everybody else did—by reading the morning newspaper.

"Can you imagine that?" Keating marveled. "If you did that in Chicago, your knees would be broken in the morning."[20] But nobody breaks any knees in Atlanta; that would be *rude*, and Atlanta strives above all things to be pleasant. This reflexive need to be nice is a deeply Southern trait, but it can lend itself to charges of being phony—which may help to explain the sense that many visitors to Atlanta get that it's not a real city, merely a very lifelike, somewhat Disneyfied movie set, interspersed with some very untidy back lots. This is the city where in the late 1960s architect John Portman created the first "open atrium" hotel (the Hyatt Regency), a much imitated design that turns

inward and away from the street. It's the architectural embodiment of the cop who says, "Move along, folks. Nothing to see
here." The assumption that people want to be in this kind of
hermetically sealed environment, where they can get all their
food and entertainment needs met in one place and feel "safe"
from the unruliness of random human encounters, has been
the underlying idea of every huge development in downtown
Atlanta in the last four decades. It's never worked. In fact, it
runs counter to basic human psychology—when have humans
ever *not* wanted to stare at other humans walking by?—but
Atlanta developers gamely kept at it for decades, convinced
that someday it would catch on. In more recent years they have
finally abandoned that theory; their latest effort is a 138-acre
office/condo/stores/entertainment district called Atlantic Station, built in what was then a run-down industrial part of the
city. The last part was a nice idea; the problem is that this part
of town is separated from Midtown by the gigantic north–south
chasm that is I-75/85. In an effort to lure shoppers and tourists
to its fine array of hotels, movie theaters, restaurants, and stores,
Atlantic Station has adopted a kind of suburban shopping mall
ambience, complete with music piped from speakers hidden in
the shrubbery. New York City's Soho it ain't.

Lurking under all these attempts to create a vibrant downtown is the old, persistent real issue: race. Any authentic urban
environment in Atlanta is going to draw black teenagers—
specifically, young, male black urban dwellers, the mere sight
of whom causes many suburbanites to turn in their tracks and
head for the parking lot. How to get these groups to mix com-
fortably is *the* basic problem facing urban planners in Atlanta,
and it's exacerbated by the long-standing difficulty many white

people have in distinguishing between a black college student and a black teenage urban gangbanger. Mix it all up, and you get a situation where whites understandably object to being branded as racists just because they are afraid of crime, blacks understandably bridle at being branded as criminals just because they are black, and they all want to kick the criminals out—if they could just figure out who the criminals are. It's a fundamental reality of the twenty-first-century South: whites and blacks work together, enjoy genuine friendships, date and even marry each other—but all that is mostly one-on-one. In the presence of groups, ugly racial memories awaken from their slumber. In 1987, writing about downtown crime, *Atlanta Journal-Constitution* political columnist Frederick Allen noted that "even if the troublemakers are eliminated, most white people are still going to be uncomfortable among unemployed and working-class blacks."[21] The only difference is that these days lots of middle-class black suburbanites are uncomfortable, too.

So while the owners of Atlantic Station try to find the tweaks that will transform their downtown oasis into a financial success, the lack of honest conversation about race and class stifles their attempts. Atlanta would benefit enormously from just one black leader who could speak plainly, even at the risk of being labeled crude or déclassé—somebody along the lines of New York City mayor Ed Koch in the 1970s, who was willing to deviate from what people expected and who if nothing else started conversations about the burning issues of the day. But that's not going to happen—not in Atlanta. Instead, newspapers editorialize about surrogate issues like "crime" and developers speak vaguely of "fostering an urban ambience." Atlanta's long history of clueless attempts to manufacture spontaneity reminds me of the old joke about the English officer who was asked what it was like being at the Battle of the Somme. He replied: "My dear, the *noise!* And the *people!*"

It was late afternoon in Mary Mac's Tea Room on Ponce de Leon Avenue, and the sunlight through the shuttered windows made bright bars on the far wall. It was quiet, too early for the dinner rush, but that was the way I liked it: cool, dusky, a respite from a long, hot day of navigating Atlanta's freeways. My plate was loaded with sweet potato soufflé, macaroni and cheese, collards, a couple of corn muffins, and beside it was a tall glass of sweet tea. My waiter, a thirtyish black man with a pierced ear, wearing an impressively clean and starched white shirt and a red bow tie, glided over with another pitcher of tea in hand. "Is everything all right here wi' chu, baby?" he asked. In another context, that "baby" might have sounded sexist, but not here. This was a very Southern "baby"—almost maternal in connotation, managing to convey a kindly regard for a stranger's welfare and a level of informality that people are trying to describe when they use the cliché "Southern hospitality." Hearing that, I suddenly felt homesick.

Sometimes appearances are exactly what they seem: there *is* a friendly vibe here. New York City may be just as friendly in its own way, but in New York you never get the fleeting sense that the polite stranger giving you directions might invite you home for dinner. In Atlanta, you do. Years ago, I ran out of gas on a residential Atlanta street; without much thinking about it (this was before cell phones), I went to the nearest house, where an elderly lady invited me in and offered me a glass of tea while she got her neighbor to pour some gas into my tank and then prime my carburetor so I could get to a gas station. Not long after this incident, I moved to New Haven, Connecticut, where one winter afternoon I found myself with a dead battery in a grocery store parking lot. I had jumper cables, but when I asked the lady in a nearby car if I could use her battery for a jump start, she looked at me as if I were a scam artist. "Don't you have Triple A?" she said. A single anecdote doesn't prove anything, and there are plenty of rude people in Atlanta; still, there is a certain unspoken expectation of civility here—and in the South generally—which you cannot count on finding in other places. Charmaine Ward, the director of community relations for Georgia Pacific, has felt it. Born and raised in Chicago, she came to Atlanta for the first time with her high school senior class on a tour of Spelman College. She returned the next year to attend Spelman, and has been in Atlanta ever since. "This was the one place I wanted to be," she told me. "Everybody was friendly. This was October, and it was still warm and there were still leaves on the trees, and it was beautiful. I've stayed here twenty-plus years. Every time I had a job where they wanted me to move, I switched jobs."

Other aspects of Atlanta's real character are more subtle. Some become apparent only in a study of a map of its housing patterns, which still bear the rough imprint of those created during the era of Jim Crow: majority-black neighborhoods are south of the east–west line drawn through the city by I-20, while neighborhoods above it are racially mixed or, farther north, majority-white. The influx of black arrivals to the metro Atlanta area has expanded the reach of black neighborhoods east and west below I-20, but not north. When you see it on a

map, the delineation is striking—as if there is still some anachronistic city ordinance on the books somewhere that says, "This
far shall you go, and no farther." Yet the degree of racially mixed
housing elsewhere in the city reveals that Atlanta is significantly
less segregated, overall, than Northern cities like Chicago, Detroit, or Cleveland—a stereotype-busting fact that is true of
Southern cities in general.[22] What's more, middle-class black
neighborhoods in Atlanta tend to have better access to amenities like schools, libraries, and grocery stores than comparable
neighborhoods up north (though they still rank below comparable majority-white neighborhoods).[23]

In any event, racial segregation in the twenty-first century is
no longer a result of overt bigotry; it's a secondary and insidious
reflection of income and wealth—and Atlanta ranks first among
all major U.S. cities in income inequality.[24] Even those segments
of the black middle class who are doing nicely on income don't
necessarily have the wealth socked away to weather a job layoff
or other financial crisis. Their wealth is in the roof over their
heads, and when something goes wrong, they lose it. DeKalb
County, home to some of the most prosperous black suburbs
in the country, is also home to one of the nation's highest fore-
closure rates. I saw the signs everywhere I went: boarded-up
garage doors, knee-high weeds on a block of carefully tended
lawns, front doors with official-looking notices taped to the
center. With statistics showing the wealth gap between whites
and minorities at a twenty-five-year high, it was likely that these
houses were the last chance many families would ever have to
live a middle-class lifestyle. No doubt most of them were back
on the low-income rental market—which is increasingly con-
centrated in the far-flung suburbs, as closer-in neighborhoods

become the territory of affluent families and young, upwardly mobile professionals.

I could see that phenomenon playing out in the parts of suburban Atlanta where I grew up: the Tri-Cities, composed of College Park, Hapeville, and East Point. Neighborhoods I knew as prosperous, white, and middle-class now bore the unmistakable signs of poverty: sagging porches, unkempt lawns, strip malls disproportionately given over to payday loan shops, pawnshops, and the offices of attorneys who specialize in car accidents and disability claims. I drove for miles without seeing anyone with skin as pale as mine. Yet the Tri-Cities has the advantage of sitting right on a rapid rail line, which in an era of rising gas prices instantly transforms it from suburban ghetto to a gentrification area waiting to happen. Already, I saw pockets of renovated housing in College Park and East Point—a sign that the cycle of prosperity, decline, and renovation was almost complete. In a few years, those neighborhoods will be as solidly black and middle-class as they were white and middle-class when I was growing up. In some ways, this will be progress, though I doubt the displaced will be thinking of it that way.

Another way in which Atlanta still bears the imprint of Jim Crow is more subtle: the lack of public space. Sociologists refer to this as the "third place" concept; after home and work, the third place is where people can go to just hang out, be with other people, socialize, and enjoy the neighborhood ambience. Usually, that's a park. But Atlanta has only about 4.5 percent of its land in public parks, less than half the national average for cities of its density;[25] if you were to combine its two biggest downtown parks, they would still be less than half the size of

New York City's Central Park. This may come as a surprise to people who think of Atlanta as a city of trees, which it is, or who have remarked on how leafy it looks from the air. It *is* leafy—but those trees they are admiring are in somebody's backyard. Atlanta has no tradition of "village greens" or downtown open-air marketplaces—and this deep in the Bible Belt, there's no tradition of a neighborhood tavern, either. (Until 2011, it was illegal for stores to sell alcohol on Sundays in Georgia, period; in Atlanta, you can still order a drink at a restaurant on a Sunday, but only after noon, a regulation presumably intended to give God-fearing church folks time to get home and off the streets before the drunks stagger forth.)

It was not always this way—at least, not for white Southerners. Up to the mid-1950s, their concept of "public space" meant ... well, space. The whole *world* belonged to white people, right down to and including sidewalks and streets and grass and air, though whites saw fit to "wall off" pieces of the physical universe for black people to use. It's no coincidence that those two big downtown Atlanta parks I just mentioned, Grant Park and Piedmont Park, were both created in the 1880s, at the beginning of the Jim Crow era; they weren't described as parks for white people only, but it went without saying that whites had first claim on their use. And that's the way things were for generations: golf courses, swimming pools, and parks were designated as either "white" or "colored" (though it goes without saying that "separate" was anything but "equal").[26]

When desegregation came, Princeton University historian Kevin Kruse points out, what happened was not so much peaceful integration as the abandonment by whites of public spaces they had been taught to consider their own. Integrate they would, if they had to—but share? *Hell*, no. And so a zero-sum system was created, in which every gain for blacks was the result of commensurate loss by whites. The result, he writes, was "a new division in which the public world was increasingly abandoned to blacks and a new private one was created for whites."[27]

In its history, its customs, its housing patterns, and its lack of public space—in all these ways, Atlanta is a deeply Southern city, no matter how much it tries to project a more cosmopolitan image. It's Southern in ways that Southerners rarely like to think of as Southern; in fact, its Southern-ness is the source of its most pressing problem: sprawl.

The faulty assumptions that have created urban sprawl—that gas will always be cheap, that natural resources are inexhaustible, and that people will always need to commute to jobs in a central urban core—have shaped cities across the country for the better part of the twentieth century. In the South, though, that error is magnified by four more factors. One is the geographical imbalances created by a long history of racial apartheid: Atlanta's historically white Northside became the side of the region where most of the job growth occurred, which created an outward push for development. Today, Atlanta's prosperous northern exurbs stretch practically to Chattanooga.

Another factor is just the sheer number of people moving to the South. Thanks in large part to the black remigration, the Atlanta area has been among the ten fastest-growing metro areas in the United States since the 1990s; though the city itself has lost population, its suburbs are still gaining people: immigrants, aging baby boomers, job seekers from all over. The more people, the worse the effects of sprawl.

Third, there's that Southern cussedness I mentioned, which combines with the Southern reverence for property rights to create a kind of grassroots resistance to anything that smacks of strong zoning laws or land use planning. Finally, there's the legacy of that Faustian bargain Henry Grady made: the South's desire to be attractive to business has also made it unfriendly to environmental regulation. Up to recently, it's been easier and less risky for a developer to bulldoze another stand of pines (or historic structure) and throw up another office building or self-contained subdivision of single-family homes than it is to think about abstract issues like sustainability or infrastructure or projected water scarcity. But a three-year drought that started in 2006 resulted in water wars among Alabama, Florida, Georgia, and Tennessee and focused everyone's attention on the fact that a region with an exploding population is saddled with a finite water supply.

Today the bill for all of this is coming due. Sprawl forces working families in the Atlanta area to spend an astounding 61 percent of their net income on transportation, making it a close second to San Francisco as the most expensive in the United States[28]—and those statistics are based on 2006 figures, *before* gas prices in this country began to approach European levels. In short, the people who most need the jobs Atlanta has had to offer are precisely the people who can least afford to live there. Lots of cities have sprawl problems as bad as Atlanta's, but only a handful—Dallas, Houston, and Phoenix, for example, in addition to Atlanta—are dealing with problems of sprawl at the same time they are coping with rapid population growth. It's a hellish combination, as anybody who has ever navigated Atlanta's infamous rush hour traffic on a blistering summer day can attest, and it's one that can cause a city to strangle on its own ozone fumes.

What's the solution? Not heavy-duty mass transit. Atlanta started an ambitious subway system back in the 1970s, but its development was hampered by that ingrained, knee-jerk distrust of "regional" government I've mentioned, and by ingrained white racism. Only two of Atlanta's seven metropolitan counties voted for the one-cent sales tax intended to fund the system, and a often repeated joke at the time was that MARTA (the Metropolitan Atlanta Rapid Transit Authority) actually stood for Moving Africans Rapidly Through Atlanta—and out to the lily-white suburbs. Today, it's a moot point: the cost of building a truly regional subway system would be the civic equivalent of mounting another Apollo mission. Politically, too, it would face heavy resistance. The only way to separate an Atlanta driver from his vehicle, a local joke goes, is to carjack it.

"People like their cars here, and that's a challenge," urban architect Ryan Gravel told me. "All that sort of cul-de-sac, strip mall lifestyle, the private neighborhood pool—that's the model here. And there are not a lot of models of something different." Gravel has thought of something different, though: his 1999 graduate thesis proposed linking a network of old railroads that forms a twenty-two-mile loop around the central part of downtown into a light rail transit system. His thesis became the Atlanta BeltLine, a $2 billion project now in its early stages that will eventually link forty-five in-town neighborhoods and add a thousand acres of parkland to the city's existing seven hundred acres.

The theory behind the BeltLine is that housing demand in the next thirty years or so will be dictated by the price of gas, and that energy costs are only going up; the only question is how fast. Right now, if you look at a map of the Atlanta metropolitan area, the places where a family would spend less than 45 percent of its income on housing and transportation—and the generally accepted limit of what is "affordable" puts a cap at 30 percent—has shrunk well within the interstate perimeter of Atlanta on its Northside.[29] There's still some affordable housing to be found on the Southside, but as energy prices continue to rise in the coming decades that will shrink, too. Gravel worries that as close-in housing becomes more desirable, some of those suburban areas will simply become an urban version of the land of the "left behinds" that I saw in rural Mississippi—places where only the poor, the very old, and various immigrant communities will live. The nightmare scenario he paints is the worst of all possible worlds: close enough to the city to have urban problems like crime, far enough away from the city that it will take a long time for the cops to get there. "It's kind of scary to think about how we as a region are going to make that really work," he said.

One person's *Clockwork Orange* scenario is another person's blank slate. To Ellen Dunham-Jones, head of the architecture department at Georgia Tech, all those 1950s- and 1960s-era suburbs Gravel is talking about are full of what she calls "underperforming asphalt"—abandoned big-box stores and strip malls. This, she thinks, is the future: old Kroger stores turned into public libraries, aging Walmarts turned into churches, abandoned office parks turned into garden apartments, old strip malls turned into pedestrian boulevards.

Dunham-Jones is the coauthor of a book on exactly how to do this (*Retrofitting Suburbia: Urban Design Solutions for Redesigning Suburbs*). The New Urbanism, whose principles her book uses as its basic assumptions, has its critics: conservatives deride it as a form of Big Brother social engineering intent on telling us all exactly where to live and how; leftists say it doesn't do nearly enough to combat our dependence on cars. But you could make a case that New Urbanism is not a radical idea at all, but a return to an older and more conservative past. If you think about it, the only significant design difference between a twenty-first-century New Urbanist town and the 1930s-era Alabama town of *To Kill a Mockingbird* is the presence of fiber-optic cable: both are founded on the idea of neighborhoods where houses have front porches and sit close to the street, where "downtown" is within walking distance, and where there is enough commercial variety that only a few errands ever require a car. In fact, the Cotton District, a section of Starkville, Mississippi, now widely recognized as incorporating most of the important principles of the movement, was established by local developer Dan Camp in 1969, twenty years before Andrés Duany achieved fame as the father of the New Urbanism movement.

The Atlanta Regional Commission has recently hired Duany to look into places where Dunham-Jones's suburban retrofitting concept might work—and that in itself speaks volumes about a fundamental shift in the prevailing attitude toward land use in the South, the extent of which is still unclear. The ARC is a

quasi-elected planning body that has traditionally been dominated by the ten or so suburban county commission chairs who
are among its members—and they, in turn, have historically
been dominated by the bulldozer crowd who created sprawl in
the first place. For the ARC and Andrés Duany to get together
may seem at first glance as if Donald Trump had decided on an
Amish theme for his next casino.

Whether any of this will actually work will depend largely
on the political climate, and the increasingly mean tone of the
political rhetoric in the South, like everywhere else, is one of
the most sobering changes I noted from twenty years ago. The
Atlanta I knew was a deeply conservative place, but its political
stage still had room for public figures whose values were fairly
liberal—people like *Atlanta Constitution* editor Ralph McGill,
5th District congressman Charles Weltner, and Mayor Ivan
Allen, not to mention activists like Julian Bond and John Lewis.
With the exception of John Lewis, I couldn't imagine any of
them making a career in politics in today's Atlanta. Their brand
of concern for the poor and dispossessed would be instantly
construed as an attempt to pick the pockets of the middle class;
they'd be booed off the stage.

Politics in the South reflects the increasing national divisions and rancor, and in the red state–blue state dichotomy, the
divisions are increasingly along racial lines. Talk radio is conservative in Atlanta, as it is everywhere, but in Atlanta there's
no competing narrative: the local National Public Radio af-
filiate plays classical music during the day, and local television
news is given over to crime, politics, and "news you can use"
features. Looking at election maps going back to 1992, you can
see a clear evolution: Atlanta got bigger and bluer, and the rest

of Georgia—and large swaths of the South—got redder. The increasing sense of division reaches down into the most local of politics: in 2005, an affluent, mostly white section of north Fulton County known as Sandy Springs had won a long fight to incorporate—in effect, seceding from the county, at least in terms of police and fire services.

"There are a handful of prominent black Democrats, and I can't think of any prominent white Democrats who still hold office," an old colleague from my *AJC* days told me. "Not that Southern Democrats weren't always pretty conservative, but Roy Barnes [a Democratic governor who lost a bid for reelection in 2002, in part because he had incensed the Sons of Confederate Veterans by supporting a redesign of the state flag that downsized the Confederate battle emblem to the size of an address label] couldn't ride Obama's coattails to the governor's office. . . . Once you get beyond Decatur, Virginia Highland, Candler Park, all those intown neighborhoods, it's all Republican."

But here's the interesting thing, he continued: in social ways, the South today has changed more than any of us could have dreamed even twenty-five years ago, for liberals and conservatives alike. Take his next-door neighbor in Marietta, for instance—a navy guy, straight-arrow military, a right-wing Republican in every stereotypical way you can think of—watches Fox News and nothing else, listens faithfully to Rush Limbaugh. The neighbor and his wife, who are both white, recently adopted African American twins. To my friend, that in itself was not remarkable; what struck him was that this radical opening up of his neighbor's life, this intimate exposure to another culture and people with different life experiences and values, had done nothing to alter the neighbor's stance on, say, health care reform, or government funding for social welfare programs. "It hasn't changed their political universe at all," he said. "In fact it's acceptable in the South today, because it happens so often, that if you have a daughter and she dates a black guy in high school, you come to terms with that. And if you're in your late forties and you adopt Asian or Costa Rican or Hispanic children, that's okay, too. You can still like Fox News. These things are not necessarily at odds."

Then again, this is the *South*; cognitive dissonance is what we *do*. It takes some mental agility to argue with a straight face that most masters and slaves were really friends, or that thousands of black slaves fought for the Confederacy—assertions that it seems no amount of scholarly research can kill; maybe the same mental agility explains the Southern knack for creative adaptation. To Dunham-Jones, who moved to Atlanta in 2000 from Cambridge, Massachusetts, Atlanta is remarkably open to newcomers and new ideas, in large part *because* of its corporate culture. After all, business follows the marketplace, and demographics foretell major changes in the marketplace: the aging of the baby boomer generation, the population bulge known as Generation Y (people born since the mid-1980s), all those new immigrants. Gravel, too, is guardedly optimistic.

"Atlanta isn't like Chicago or Boston," he said. "Those cities already are what they're going to be. Atlanta still has room for pretty significant identity changes." In 2012, Atlanta-area voters resoundingly defeated a $6 billion bond issue devoted to transportation, but Gravel sees a silver lining in that cloud: the strongest opposition came from the outlying suburbs, he notes, where most of the money would have gone to roads, not public transit. But were the voters saying no to sprawl, or just no to more spending? Nobody knows. Meanwhile, talk about a rapid rail that would run from Chattanooga to Macon via Atlanta seems caught up in the old white-rural versus black-urban politics. It was Chattanooga, by the way, where that railroad engineer set out from back in 1837, back when Atlanta was a stake named "Terminus" driven into the ground. Sometimes history really does come full circle; the only question is whether it offers a chance for a do-over, or to make the same old mistake.

On my last day in Atlanta, I stopped by the sexton's office at Oakland Cemetery to see if they had any records of where my grandmother was buried. As I expected, it was a lost cause: paupers at Oakland were interred without headstones in a section of the cemetery adjacent to the north wall. I found my way there and found a single granite monument sitting at the edge of a large open field. I was on a slight hill, and when I looked up I found myself with a spectacular view of the city skyline. The towering giants I knew from childhood—the Equitable Building, the old Life of Georgia tower, city hall, the Polaris Lounge atop the Hyatt Regency—now looked like step stools for the newer skyscrapers looming over them.

Twenty years earlier, I had left with a promise to myself that someday I'd be back. Now I knew that would never happen—and yet, it didn't seem like goodbye. For one thing, there was the history that lay (quite literally) under my feet. For another, there were the people I had known here. They were old classmates, fellow church members, work colleagues, old friends of my parents, a far-flung cousin or two. The community of friends I had here had survived all the uprootings and displacements and life changes two decades had brought. Partly that was because so many of them were newspaper people, who are a tribe unto themselves, especially in an era when newspaper reporters are an endangered species. But an equally important reason, I think, is that most of us were born and raised in the South.[30] We belonged to that complex web of community I described earlier; we were bound together by racial memories, by acts of racism seen and experienced and practiced, by our shared awareness of our collective secrets, by historical memory, by shared religious rituals and Sunday dinners and football team allegiances and a thousand other tensile threads of custom. My connection with these people had been born in this city and nurtured against the backdrop of its history, but its existence no longer depended on my zip code.

"Atlanta rubs some people—journalists in particular—the wrong way," my friend Frederick Allen, the former political columnist and CNN commentator, had said when I'd paid him a visit a few days earlier. "The journalists look at these corporate titans and say, 'Oh, you're just trying to make money.' Oh yeah? Well?" He fixed me with an inquisitive look, waiting for some rebuttal. We were talking in the living room of the mansion Rick and his wife, Linda, occupy in one of Atlanta's leafier and more affluent neighborhoods; one of the things I value in Rick, aside from the fact that he knows a lot about Southern politics, is that, unlike me, he has money; he also understands other people who have it. "Atlanta rubs journalists the wrong way," he continued when he saw I had no answer, "because journalists don't care so much about money. If they did, they'd find a different line of work."

Well, that *used* to be true. Though there are nowhere near

as many print reporters as there once were, the ones who are left tend to be graduates of elite schools who pal around with Wall Street stockbrokers. (Some of them used to *be* Wall Street stockbrokers.) But Rick was right about one thing: Atlanta's relentless commercialism does rub me the wrong way. After just a week back in my old hometown, I was beginning to get the feeling that I would find ads on the inside of my eyeballs when I dozed off at night. But there are things I love about Atlanta, too. Mainly, I love the people here, and the neighborhoods they have created, and the social norms that have their roots in an older, agrarian concept of community. Somehow, something essentially Southern has managed to survive here, like grass growing in cracks in the concrete. But is that evidence of its persistence, or just the dying remnants? Is it possible to take the failing parts of a city and rebuild them with these fundamental values as the basis, and convince business that it can be economically self-sustaining?

If such a thing were to work, it would have to work for middle- and low-income people as well as the more affluent, because any community that walls out certain groups of people, no matter how beautifully landscaped it is, is not a community; it's a ghetto. The people behind the BeltLine project are at least saying the right things: the project's literature says that affordable housing is "a vital component" of the overall plan, and it includes $240 million to build some 5,600 new low-rent apartments over the next twenty-five years. It's billed as "the most significant investment in affordable workforce housing in Atlanta's history," but it's an unintentionally revealing boast. This historic investment will offer some low-income people who meet a stringent set of requirements up to $50,000 in forgivable loans toward buying their own homes—but that's the top amount, and $50,000 for a house in a gentrifying neighborhood is pretty much chump change. Overall, the project's affordable housing budget is less than 10 percent of its total, and 5,600 housing units over twenty-five years is a pitiful effort in a city where thirty thousand people in need of affordable housing showed up on one day. And this is assuming everything happens exactly the way it's laid out on paper, which it won't; in Atlanta, affordable housing projects have a long history of morphing into upscale condos for the urban gentry.

Still, Atlanta is hardly the only city to neglect its poor, or to have crummy schools, or to allow its infrastructure to fall apart while it spent money unwisely on frills. I don't hold it to any higher standard on that score than I do any other city, and ignoring the poor is something most of us are complicit in anyway. What I hold against Atlanta is its pretense.

I don't mind that Atlanta's white power structure despised Martin Luther King when he was alive; many Americans did at the time. What I mind is the retroactive glow of racial enlightenment thrown over that whole chapter of our history, and the pats on the back Atlanta gives itself for embracing its native son—when the real story (which is hardly a secret here) is that the famous banquet the city gave King when he won the Nobel Peace Prize happened only after Robert Woodruff decided that the alternative would be bad for Coca-Cola's image. If Billy Payne brings the Olympics to Atlanta and well-connected people make a lot of money from it—well, that's how the world works everywhere. What I mind about the Olympics is the public relations hype, which so many movers and shakers in Atlanta actually seem to believe to this day, about how the

Olympics benefited all Atlantans and symbolically ushered the
city into the pantheon of the world's great metropolises, right
up there with Paris and Rome—while they ignore the existence
of all those people who were forced into an unforgiving housing
market when the urban renewal wrecking ball arrived. It makes
me crazy that *Gone With the Wind* and its Lost Cause version
of history are still considered Atlanta's "brand," rivaled only by
Coca-Cola, while hardly anyone here has heard of Sam Hose,
the black man lynched down in Newnan, or knows that a thousand people took the train down from Atlanta so they could
watch the spectacle of a human being hacked up into pieces
and roasted alive. It appalls me that I *grew up here* and studied
Southern history and literature at Emory University, which
considers itself a first-rate Southern institution of higher learning, yet not a one of the many books I was assigned to read so
much as mentioned that historical incident, notable not just for
its savagery but because it radicalized a preeminent black intellectual who went on to help found the NAACP.

What I hold against Atlanta is its willingness to trade on a
reputation as a city where the civil rights movement flourished
when it has never owned up to being what it was, or acknowledged the bitter struggles it took to change people's hearts
and minds. The real history of what made Atlanta what it is
today—a place where black people and white people really do
have hard-earned and valuable experience in learning how to
see each other as human beings, an authentic accomplishment
that only a handful of Southern cities can rightfully claim—is a
remarkable thing. But Atlanta doesn't seem able to own its real
history. White people here would rather dress up like Scarlett
O'Hara or mount campaigns to keep the Stars and Bars in the

state flag—and black leaders know not to complain too loudly, lest it mess up some state contract or queer a business deal. I find it tragic that Southerners, who are so in love with their own history, are so careless and so willfully blind about which history they choose to love.

I stood for quite a while on that hill somewhere in the vicinity of my grandmother's unmarked grave, thinking these thoughts and looking at a city whose skyline I once knew by heart, until it was time to go.

8.

Old Times There Are Not Forgotten

J uly 13, 1864, would have been one more sweltering day in Atlanta, but it was hard to think about the weather with an invading army camped on the city's doorstep. Various Union divisions and scouting parties had been spotted for days in the outlying farmland east and west of the city, including some soldiers from Stoneman's cavalry who had camped just outside Palmetto, a mile from the Thompson farm. It would have been no surprise, then, when the two Thompson boys— William, fourteen, and James, twelve—saw a group of Union soldiers outside the house that morning. *Where's your horse?* one of the soldiers asked when he saw the boys, and William pointed toward the pasture. After that there was nothing to do but watch as the men rounded up the livestock, cleaned out the kitchen pantry, and loaded up the contents of the barn. They took the horse, the cow, 240 dozen bundles of oats, 80 bushels of corn, 250 pounds of bacon, and 280 pounds of flour. But then something unusual happened: the next day, a soldier returned with a written receipt. It wasn't payment—this was war; nobody was getting paid—but it was at least the promise of repayment, a small courtesy to acknowledge the family's status as Union sympathizers. Samantha Thompson refused to take the paper from the soldier's hand. A few weeks earlier, her husband had been driven into hiding by the neighbors' death threats; if those neighbors learned the Yankees had done her a favor, there was no telling what form their retaliation might take.[1]

For a long time, I could not explain exactly why my family's little shard of Civil War history fascinated me the way it did. And then one day, apropos of something totally unrelated, my eight-year-old daughter asked from the backseat of the car, "Mom, what does an American look like?" She was studying Europe in social studies, and being a very literal child, she wanted some picture in her mind to go with "American," the way she had filed away other national factoids—things like *Norwegian people have blond hair* and *French people eat croissants.* "An American could look like anybody," I said. "Like a Chinese person or an African person or just like us." I could see her face in the rearview mirror; she looked irritable and confused. "But what do they *look* like?" she said, and I said, "Sweetie, being American is not about how you look—it's a *choice.*"

Later, as I thought about that conversation, I realized that what she was really asking was: how do you define "American"—and this pointed me in the direction of a deeper meaning lurking in that Civil War story: it was about the practical consequences of choosing a particular definition of "American." The Thompsons were Southerners. They were also Americans who considered themselves Unionists; the Thompsons came from Randolph County, Alabama, a well-known hotbed of Unionist activity. To them, the urgent need to keep the nation intact was something that outranked local political and economic interests—and in fact four Thompson cousins fought for the Union. Thomas Thompson tried once to cross over to Union lines but was captured; as it was, his resistance consisted of refusing to fight for the Confederacy and helping other resisters hide from conscription officers. "Any man that would fight against Washington ought to be hung," he once said, in public. For holding this opinion in a time of sectional division, he endured the harassment and bitter enmity of his neighbors for four long years—and then, on top of everything else, his farm got picked clean by Sherman's army like everyone else's. His thoughts about how to define "American" was never an idle inquiry or abstract issue. They were personal, with immediate practical implications, which is what makes this such a quintessentially Southern story.

And my own need to understand it, to trace the way in which that tiny thread of history has woven itself into my own identity, is a very Southern compulsion. People raised by parents who were a complicated mixture of brilliance, violence, oppression, and love often spend their lives trying to make sense of their childhoods, and so do people raised in that kind of culture. Think, for example, of an unemployed newspaper reporter pecking away at a typewriter in the unheated and unlit backroom of the post office in Boiling Springs, North Carolina, in the dismal early years of the Great Depression, trying to turn a magazine article into a book that would explain something called "the mind of the South"—trying, that is, when he wasn't periodically chasing away the kids who pecked at his window and made faces at the plump, oddball loner who at thirty-two still lived at home with mama and daddy. Why would anyone take on such a foolish task? Speaking for myself, I'd say foolish ambition, fueled by compulsion. I suspect Wilbur Cash would have agreed.

And so we come to *The Mind of the South*, the book whose

title I have so audaciously tinkered with to make my own. Ever since its publication in 1941, Cash's masterpiece has been required reading for anyone who hoped to understand this region—most of all for Southerners, who were his primary audience. *The Mind of the South* has held an honored place in my library for years, but when I was starting out on this book, I made a conscious decision not to reread it. I didn't want to be intimidated or unduly influenced by it; for better or worse, I wanted my conclusions to be entirely my own. But if you use a title that invites comparisons—well, then, let us compare.

It was after I'd written most of this book that I revisited Cash's book and his life, and only then that I realized the similarities in our backgrounds. By noting this, I'm not anointing myself as his literary heir; I'm just describing the kind of person who is likely to have the perspective and the temperamental inclination to be consumed by the peculiarly Southern habit of defining "Southern identity." Cash thought the ideal person for this task was "the man in the center," a description I'll update to "the person at the center." He, or she, is a white Southerner, for the simple reason that white Southerners are the ones who have been swilling the historical Kool-Aid for generations—lied to, basically, and thus more apt to be obsessed with the truth. This observer has no personal connections to any part of the Southern myth—no stories of grand plantations or lost fortunes, no military heroes, no dim ancestral memory of defensiveness or guilt about the institution of slavery. Yet we are, as we had to be, products of a deeply racist culture. The history I learned growing up in the Atlanta suburbs of the 1960s might have been a somewhat more diluted version of the Lost Cause myth than what Cash heard growing up in the Piedmont of South Carolina in the first two decades of the twentieth century, but the differences would not be huge. (For a recent case in point, I give you Paula Deen: when in 2013 the well-known Southern cook and author innocently admitted that she had once considered catering a party with an Old South theme, complete with black servants in livery, her obvious bafflement at the resulting public outcry offered a rare public display of a white Southerner completely blindsided by her own ignorance of history.)

The person at the center is from plain folks, raised in a middle-class home where books were valued, even if those books were likely to be religious tomes or encyclopedias or the kind of fiction once collected in gilded sets of Readers' Digest Condensed Books. The person at the center is also deeply familiar with, and yet an outsider to, the religion of his culture. For anyone who grew up in an environment dominated by one kind of religious belief and practice, the painful discovery that the assumptions taken for granted by the people you love the most do not fit the reality you see is the beginning of a kind of internal exile, a necessary precondition for observation.

Then there are a couple of more personal parallels which are of some relevance: both Wilbur Cash and I could both be described as bookworms, homebodies, late bloomers, products of Southern universities (which were small oases of intellectual ferment in a deeply conservative region), hypochondriacs, and social wallflowers who did not find the safe harbor of a happy marriage until our late thirties. Both of us began our careers close to home, burdened with some high-flying literary ambitions; both of us found our talents more suited to literature's déclassé cousin, journalism. But it was a fair enough trade: the adventures of newspaper work pierced the social cocoon in which we were raised, and the tools of journalism proved invaluable in making sense of a complicated and many-layered culture. Results may vary, as the old advertising disclaimer goes; all I know is that when I look at photographs of Wilbur Cash, I immediately recognize a member of my tribe.

"The South, one might say, is a tree with many age rings, with its limbs and trunk bent and twisted by all the winds of the years, but with its tap root deep in the Old South," Cash wrote—the Old South in this case being not the one of myth but the real one of the gritty frontier and the yeoman farmer. It was an apt analogy: trees, like cultures, have finite life spans, but barring some catastrophe both can survive for centuries, even millennia. Were Cash alive today, he might see some gnarled limbs of his aged tree dying or broken off altogether, but he would also see vigorous new growth sprouting in unlikely places.

The most obvious new growth comes from immigration. The South Cash knew—the South I knew in my own childhood— was the most insular part of the country, a place where nearly everyone was a product of the native soil and the vast majority of the gene pool was made up of two major streams: one from Africa, the other from the British Isles. Today, although their absolute numbers are small, the Hispanic population of the South is poised to exert an outsize influence in coming years, as the electoral influence of white native Southerners—especially those in rural areas—wanes relative to that of the rest of the region. It's an effect that will be magnified as the baby boomer generation ages in the South, as it is everywhere, and as younger Hispanics continue to produce babies at a higher rate than whites. The political consequences of this could be profound. In the 2012 presidential election, Latinos comprised 11 percent of all eligible voters, up from 8.2 percent in 2004—and 17 percent of all eligible Hispanic voters live in so-called battleground states, three of which are in the South: North Carolina, Virginia, and Florida. The change is noticeable: if he were to drive today through the Carolinas he knew so well, Cash would see clear evidence of an increasing Hispanic presence: a Mexican bakery even in a one-intersection town like Briscoe, North Carolina, or an imposing new Catholic church under construction in downtown Spartanburg, South Carolina.

With his usual prescience, Cash foresaw that the invention of the mechanical cotton picker, just coming into mass production at the time of his death, was going to send millions of rural African Americans out of the South to look for work, on top of the hundreds of thousands who had already left during the years of Jim Crow. But I don't think even he could have foreseen the extent of the black re-migration into the South, powerful testimony to the enduring pull the South still exerts on its natives and their descendants. A product of his time and its racist conventions who once refused to sit next to a black person on a train, Cash probably could not have foreseen the political and economic tsunami that was the civil rights movement, the hundreds of black Southerners it launched into public office, or the pace of social change that has transformed interracial marriage from a felony into a non-issue.

The political landscape Cash would see today would be a complete upending of the one he knew. The Democratic Party, in his day a fully owned subsidiary of Southern white culture, is now the home of the majority of Southern black voters; the vast majority of Southern whites long ago drifted to the starboard side of the Republican Party; Southern religion has become fragmented and politicized, while right-wing Republican rhetoric has adopted the rhetoric of fundamentalist religion.

Right-wing Republicans are not limited to the South, of course, and its most visible manifestation, the Tea Party, is a national phenomenon. But whether you believe the Tea Party has its roots in Southern conservatism or in flinty New England individualism, it goes without saying that the wing of the Republican Party ideologically opposed to "big government" would find a hospitable reception in the region which has spent the last 200 years elevating the concept of "states' rights" into a civic religion. Today's "strict construction" school of constitutional interpretation is basically the fundamentalist belief in a literal, inerrant Bible transferred to the realm of social policy, and the deliberate fusion of right-wing ideology and "Christian values" emerged in the late 1960s as a strategy aimed specifically at wooing Southern whites. It's not surprising, I guess, that the many books written about the so-called Southern strategy have interpreted it strictly as a political phenomenon, since that's what it is—but a person like me, immersed from the cradle in fundamentalist preaching, hears the music as well as the words. When at the 2012 Values Voters Summit in Washington, D.C., someone in the back of the room yelled, "We love you, Ted!" to Texas senator Ted Cruz as he stood onstage, Cruz replied, "I receive that blessing"—an exchange straight from many a Wednesday night prayer meeting of my childhood. Washington has always been a town where politicians find it in their interest to display a conventional kind of piety, but it hasn't always been the kind of place where Republican caucuses begin with prayer and a singing of "Amazing Grace," which is the kind of thing that passes for normal these days. When it does, most of the folks in the room are from the South.[2] When Wilbur Cash was alive, the answer to the question, "What church do y'all go to?" told you something about a person's neighborhood and social class; today, it tells you about their politics.

Wilbur Cash worked on *The Mind of the South* off and on for most of the 1930s, a time roughly as far from Reconstruction as we are today from the civil rights movement. While he might be astonished at the exact nature of the changes that have happened in the last fifty years, the existence of massive change itself would not surprise him at all. The ability to weather such change and yet retain certain distinctive features was the essence of the South he was describing—a conclusion that is as true today as it was in 1941.

Which of his themes endure? Religiosity probably tops the list: churchgoing habits are in flux, but the South still has far more evangelical Protestants than any other region, and more than 80 percent of residents in every Southern state say they believe in God "with absolute certainty."[3] Next would come the South's brand of militant individualism, along with its fierce attachment to certain economic premises: that property rights are sacred, that employers have an inalienable right to make their own bargain with employees free from outside interference (otherwise known as "unions"), and that Progress depends on preserving a ready supply of cheap labor. (When Southern legislatures began passing laws aimed at ferreting out undocumented workers, the most effective push-back came not from civil rights groups, but from Southern farmers, who suddenly found it impossible to find cheap agricultural labor.)

He would also see the quintessentially Southern "let's you and him fight" political tactic still thriving. For the last 150 years or so, Southern politicians of both parties have found it advantageous to distract low-wage workers from certain realities of their plight by creating some looming catastrophe. (Race mixing! Outside agitators! Secularism!) Tom Watson's unforgivable sin in the eyes of the political elites of his day was that he dared to explain exactly how this worked to integrated audiences. "You are kept separate," Watson told groups of black and white farmers in his early Populist career, "that you may be *separately fleeced of your earnings*." But fear is a far more primal emotion than logic; likewise, the pro-business advocates of Cash's era diverted attention from abysmal working conditions and low factory wages by convincing Southern whites that, as Cash formulated the argument, "labor unions + strikers = Communism + atheism + social equality with the Negro." The specific issue Cash was referring to was the Gastonia, North Carolina, textile mill strike of 1929, but it's not hard to see the same technique at work in the rancorous public debate over the Affordable Care Act, when Tea Party opponents diverted attention from a broken health care system with dire warnings that the new law would, among other things, create government "intrusions into the private lives of America on a scale never seen before"—conveniently ignoring the fact that the advent of the Internet had already taken American society down that road years earlier. No matter: "Logic, as we know, scarcely was the forte of anybody here," Cash wrote, pointing out that the very factory workers who would have most benefited from collective bargaining in the Gastonia of 1929 were frequently the ones who most violently opposed unionization. The traditional Southern suspicion of things like labor unions back then, like the anti-Obamacare "socialized medicine" screeds of today, are both examples of the Southern mind Cash described, one characterized by "an exaggerated individualism," an "incapacity for analysis," and "too narrow a sense of social responsibility."

Another enduring theme: violence. Parsing the Federal Bureau of Investigation Uniform Crime Reports of his day, Cash found examples of Southern cities whose murder rates were 18 times those of similarly sized cities in New England. Since then, we've narrowed the gap: the murder rate in Albany, Georgia, today is only about twice that of Albany, New York. Crime statistics are notoriously difficult to parse, but the South has always had a higher incidence of violent crime than any other region of the country—and, as in Cash's day, the victims of most African American perpetrators are other African Americans. Cash's theory about this—that violent crime rates are partly a reflection of public distrust in the justice system's ability to correctly identify criminals and impose meaningful penalties—was not only ahead of its time, but could also help explain why today every Southern state except Virginia and Arkansas has some kind of "stand your ground" gun law on its books.[4]

The Mind of the South was published on the eve of World War II, and its author was oppressed with a sense of looming catastrophe. It's a familiar feeling. Like Cash, we don't know the exact scope of the economic and environmental catastrophes we are all so dimly afraid of, but there's a pervasive sense today that tough times are coming, that maybe they have already begun. Gridlock in Congress, growing wealth inequality (most pronounced in the South), aberrant weather patterns and rising sea levels, the threats posed by tiny numbers of terrorists with the means to kill large number of people—it all gives us the sense of being on the cusp of profound change.

Will that be the end of the South as we know it? Yes—*as we know it*. But that twisted, weathered tree with the deep taproot will survive in some form for the foreseeable future. The vices Cash saw in the region we both call home—violence, intolerance, suspicion of new ideas, impulsivity, an aversion to analysis, and a deep capacity for self-delusion—are still abundantly in evidence. So are the virtues: pride, courtesy, a tradition of military honor and service, loyalty. And I would add one more virtue he did not mention, which unites black and white Southerners equally: a unique and profound sense of community. The test of any group identity is whether members of that group can recognize each other, which we do—and the beating heart of Southern identity is the Southern attachment to the idea of community. The fact that this attachment has given birth to some pathologies—the concept of white supremacy comes to mind—only emphasizes, not diminishes, its importance. "To me, the South is family," a middle-aged white lady at the United Daughters of the Confederacy convention told me when I had just started my research, just as Paula Matabane said to me much later that she planned to retire to the South because "it's where my ancestors are buried." The tree changes; the roots endure.

I am old enough to remember the way the South marked the centennial of the Civil War fifty years ago. Those events took place at the height of the civil rights movement, in an electric atmosphere of white Southern defensiveness and grievance and a deafening silence about the existence of slavery. This time around, we are doing a much better job of seeing history as it really was. Historian Drew Gilpin Faust has noted that the Confederacy did not create the South; Confederate nationalism was just an organized attempt to justify and explain what was already there.[5] That is a subtle and scholarly kind of insight, but these days you can hear something very much like it from ordinary Southerners. Fundamental assumptions have shifted when even a long-time SCV member is able to say, as one said to me, "All things Confederate are Southern, but not all things Southern are Confederate." Moments like that make me believe we are on our way to achieving what has eluded us up to now—a way of seeing the war stripped of its myths and delusions, and finally arriving at what historian Andrew Delbanco has called "a truly convincing story, containing both admonition and inspiration, about the central event of the American past."[6]

"No Southerner, so far as I know, has yet seen fit to write about the 'two-ness' of Southerners," Carl Degler wrote. This "two-ness" once described the essence of my problem: how to express my love and respect for the South without pandering, apologizing, subscribing to racist delusions or drinking anybody's Kool-Aid. These are pitfalls that have always faced any person who identifies himself as a Southerner. Yet, because of this inconvenient fact, Southerners have had more opportunities than most to grapple with the definition and practical implications of our "two-ness"; over and over, we have had to give serious thought to exactly what this choice of being American really means. Over the past couple hundred years we've come up with various answers. We have defined ourselves by what we are not (Southern Americans, as opposed to Yankee Americans); we attempted to make the question moot by seceding;

we embraced that dual identity for Southerners with white skin while denying full citizenship to Southerners with dark skin. In recent years, this issue has come to seem almost quaint, maybe even irrelevant, in light of the bitter political divisions of our era; it sometimes seems more useful to think in terms of other kinds of distinctions, like whether a person gets his news from Fox or NPR, votes Republican or Democrat, goes to church on Sunday morning or heads off to yoga class. But even then, the whole issue of Southern identity refuses to go away—because as it turns out, a whole lot of people who get their news from Fox and vote Republican and go to church every Sunday happen to live in the South.

When "the South" comes up in public discourse these days, the reference is usually defensive, or disparaging: the South is that part of the country where true values still prevail, or where rednecks dwell. Both formulations miss the point. The South, I would argue, is where the ideals of democracy met the reality of race. The story of that clash, as ugly as it mostly is, is the South's unique contribution to American history, and the reason that only Southerners today can claim membership in a genuinely biracial society. By this I do not mean to say that the South is some postracial utopia; I mean only that we have finally arrived at a point where we are dealing with aspects of race as they apply to us personally without treating it like it's kryptonite—where interracial marriage is a non-event, where a seventeen-year-old black teenager named Trayvon Martin can be shot dead for no particular reason and white Southerners are among the millions who are outraged, and where family reunions feature branches with different skin color. After a difficult start, getting to this point has been surprisingly easy. What's left is coming to terms with the parts of our history that are excruciating to talk about or remember—and even this is a gift, because we are far enough away from those events to see them with some dispassion, but close enough to still feel the horror. The twenty-first-century South exemplifies the progress that has been made on race, and the distance there still is to go. There was a letter to the editor of the newspaper in Newnan, Georgia, a few years ago when the subject of establishing a memorial to Sam Hose, the victim of that horrific 1899 lynching, first came up. The letter's last line consisted of three words: "Let it rest." But the unacknowledged past can never rest. As powerful as the human tendency toward denial is, the arc of the moral universe really does bend toward justice. Someday, in the not too distant future, the Sam Hose lynching will be appropriately remembered and given its proper place in history.

I began this book by saying that a Southern identity is something I can't imagine myself without, and yet I've spent much of my life trying to figure out exactly what that is. My confusion was rooted in the willfully induced historical amnesia that characterized the South I grew up in, and my sense of a disconnect between what I knew about history, what I knew about my family, and what I saw happening around me in the South of the 1960s. It's a disconnect I have resolved to my own satisfaction. Understanding the South is the work of a lifetime, but I have divested my mental attic of a lot of junk, and I have a much clearer sense of what I still don't know. I know enough now to say to my daughters, "This is part of who you are; this is where a part of you comes from"—and to teach them that Southern history contains the purest essence of the American story. It's enough, finally, for me to pay some long-overdue respect to that stubborn Confederate draft-resister ancestor who was so heartily despised by his neighbors. You may not have been a Confederate, sir, but in your stubborn embrace of loyalty to both region and country, and in your refusal to let anybody dictate the terms of that loyalty, you were a true Southerner.

ACKNOWLEDGMENTS

A lot of the people to whom I feel most grateful are dead; others I've never talked to, though their books sit on my shelf, bristling with sticky notes and littered with underlined passages. To name them all would be an attempt to cover myself with their glory, so I won't, but I am conscious of following in some very large foot-steps. Among the living, there are also a lot of academics and journalists who put up with many e-mails and phone calls from me. All of them were courteous and helpful; some went out of their way to help guide my thinking, critique some early drafts, and steer me away from dead-end inquiries. First on the list is Margaret Storey, at DePaul University, whose work on Civil War–era Union loyalists in Alabama helped me understand my own family history. David Blight at Yale helped me think about how my small tidbit of history fit into a much larger story: the stranglehold the Lost Cause myth has had on how Americans remember the Civil War to this day. Larry Keating at Georgia Tech knows more about Atlanta's urban history than anybody else living, and was very generous with his knowledge and time. My thanks also go to Hodding Carter III and Howell Raines, distinguished journalists and fellow members of my tribe, who helped me thrash out some early ideas.

My friend and agent, Beth Vesel, helped to coax the small spark of an idea into a book proposal. When I say I don't know what I would have done without her, it's no hyperbole: I really don't. My editor at Simon & Schuster, Priscilla Painton, understands the South better than most Southerners do—better than any non-Southerner has a right to, in fact—and never failed to come up with some really sharp insight just when I needed it. She is not only a superb editor but a dear friend.

Finally, I thank my husband, David, for his love and unfailing support. For him, mere words are not enough.

NOTES

1. It's Complicated

1. Carl Degler, *Place over Time: The Continuity of Southern Distinctiveness*, University of Georgia Press, 1997, p. 127.
2. Testimony of Constantine Dodson and Isaiah Mosley before the Southern Claims Commission, Campbell County, Georgia, 1871.
3. C. Vann Woodward, *The Burden of Southern History*, Louisiana State University Press, 1960, Preface to the first edition.
4. Alexis de Tocqueville, *Democracy in America*, chapter XVIII.
5. Lincoln's Second Inaugural Address.
6. Alexander Stephens, "Cornerstone Speech," March 21, 1861, http:// teachingamericanhistory.org/library/index.asp?documentprint=76; "Declaration of the Immediate Causes Which Induce and Justify the Secession of South Carolina from the Federal Union," http://avalon .law.yale.edu/19th_century/csa_scarsec.asp; other secession convention records.
7. Jeffrey Passel, D'Vera Cohn, and Mark Hugo Lopez, "Hispanics Account for More Than Half of Nation's Growth in Past Decade," Pew Hispanic Center, March 24, 2011, http://www.pewhispanic .org/2011/03/24/hispanics-account-for-more-than-half-of-nations -growth-in-past-decade/.
8. Chris Kromm, "Analysis: A New South Rising," Institute for Southern Studies, Nov. 23, 2008, http://www.southernstudies.org/2008/ 11/analysis-a-new-south-rising.html.
9. Larry J. Griffin, Ranse J. Evenson, and Ashley B. Thompson, "Southerners All?" *Southern Cultures*, Spring 2005, p. 6.
10. So far, Tennessee, Texas, South Carolina, Kansas, and Wisconsin have such laws; Mississippi enacted a similar requirement via a state constitutional amendment. Alexandra Tempus, "Voter ID Drive Part of Quiet, Well-Funded National Conservative Effort," Associated

Press, March 5, 2012, http://minnesota.publicradio.org/display/web/
2012/03/04/voter-id-alec/.

11. This leaves out Kentucky, Oklahoma, and Missouri, which bear some
distinct Southern imprints, as well as the Eastern Shore of Maryland, which is undeniably Southern; it also leaves out sections of the
country that bear the imprint of the mid-twentieth-century Southern disaspora—the South Side of Chicago, for instance, and Orange
County, California. Readers will also notice that there's nothing in
here about New Orleans and its immediate environs. That's because
New Orleans is not so much the South as it is the northernmost city
of the Caribbean, a place like no other even before it suffered that
environmental catastrophe known as Hurricane Katrina. I couldn't
do it justice, but other recent books do, most notably Dan Baum,
Nine Lives: Death and Life in New Orleans, Spiegel & Grau, 2009.

2. Salsa with Your Grits

1. Leonard Dinnerstein and David M. Reimers, *Ethnic Americans:
A History of Immigration*, Columbia University Press, 2009, p. 129
(table based on figures from the U.S. Census Bureau).
2. U.S. Census 2010 figure.
3. Jeffrey Passel, D'Vera Cohn, and Ana Gonzalez-Barrera, "Net
Migration from Mexico Falls to Zero—And Perhaps Less," Pew
Hispanic Center, April 23, 2012, http://www.pewhispanic.org/2012/
04/23/net-migration-from-mexico-falls-to-zero-and-perhaps-less/.
4. These are 2009 figures from the Pew Hispanic Center, http://www
.pewhispanic.org/states/.
5. These are 2006 figures from the Centers for Disease Control, http://
www.cdc.gov/nchs/pressroom/06facts/birthfertility.htm.
6. Dinnerstein and Reimers, *Ethnic Americans*, p. 42.
7. James McBride Dabbs, *Who Speaks for the South?* Funk & Wagnalls,
1964, p. 3.
8. Adam Nossiter, "For South, a Waning Hold on National Politics,"
New York Times, Nov. 11, 2008.
9. Paul Taylor, "The Mexican-American Boom: Births Overtake Immigration," Pew Hispanic Center, July 2011, p. 5.
10. Interview with Carla Freemeyer, spokesperson for Asheboro City
Schools, Oct. 28, 2010.
11. Congressional Budget Office, "The Impact of Unauthorized Immigrants on the Budgets of State and Local Government," Dec.

2007, Pub. No. 2500, http://www.cbo.gov/ftpdocs/87xx/doc8711/
12-6-Immigration.pdf.

12. The question of how much, if anything, illegal immigrants cost U.S.
taxpayers is the subject of fierce, eye-gouging debate, and the numbers anybody uses are "prone to considerable error," the CBO study
cautioned. In the end, those numbers may matter less than people
think: the same CBO study concluded that even though immigrants
cost local governments money, the money is a "small percentage" of
what those governments already spend on legal residents.

13. Mark Hugo Lopez and Michael T. Light, "A Rising Share: Hispanics and Federal Crime," Pew Hispanic Center, Feb. 18, 2009, http://
pewhispanic.org/files/reports/104.pdf.

14. Paul Cuadros, *A Home on the Field: How One Championship Soccer
Team Inspires Hope for the Revival of Small-Town America,* Harper-
Collins, 2007.

15. John Egerton, *The Americanization of Dixie: The Southernization of
America,* Harper's Magazine Press, 1974, p. xx.

16. John Egerton, "A Mind to Stay Here: Closing Conference Com-
ments on Southern Exceptionalism," Southern Spaces, Nov. 2006,
www.southernspaces.org.

17. There's a grain of truth in the part about strangers helping travelers:
more than once in my travels in the rural South doing research for
this book, I would pull over to read a map or make notes, only to be
interrupted by a passing motorist asking me if I needed any help.
Maybe this happens in the Midwest, too, but my own experience is
that Southerners both black and white—even in cities—often go out
of their way to be helpful to strangers.

3. The Big Lie

1. Marjorie Kehe, "Textbook Controversy over Claim That Blacks
Fought for the Confederacy," *Christian Science Monitor,* Oct. 21, 2010,
http://www.csmonitor.com/Books/chapter-and-verse/2010/1021/
Textbook-controversy-over-claim-that-blacks-fought-for-the-
Confederacy. As with many historical distortions, there may be a
teeny little grain of truth in this one. There are eyewitness accounts
of black soldiers on the Confederate side at the First Battle of Bull
Run, for example. But Harvard historian John Stauffer, one of the
few scholars who give the assertion any credence, puts their number
at less than one percent of the army; he believes that most served

under duress or were biding their time for a chance to cross over to Union lines. Corydon Ireland, "Black Confederates: Their Numbers in Civil War Were Small, but Have Symbolic Value," *Harvard Gazette*, Sept. 1, 2011, http://news.harvard.edu/gazette/story/2011/09/black-confederates/.

2. "Civil War at 150: Still Relevant, Still Divisive," April 8, 2011, Pew Research Center for People & the Press, http://pewresearch.org/pubs/1958/civil-war-still-relevant-and-divisive-praise-confederate-leaders-flag.

3. Edward Ayers, *What Caused the Civil War: Reflections on the South and Southern History*, W. W. Norton, 2005, p. 132.

4. Membership in both organizations is limited to those who can prove that they are blood descendants of someone who fought for the Confederacy or "contributed material aid to its cause."

5. Karen Li Cox, *Dixie's Daughters: The United Daughters of the Confederacy and the Preservation of Confederate Culture*, University Press of Florida, 2003.

6. David W. Blight, *Race and Reunion: The Civil War in America Memory*, Harvard University Press, 2001, p. 279.

7. James Cobb, *Away Down South: A History of Southern Identity*, Oxford University Press, 2005, p. 128.

8. Blight, *Race and Reunion*, p. 283.

9. Conversation with the author, Jan. 29, 2009.

10. Cox, *Dixie's Daughters*, p. 160.

11. John Dittmer, *Local People: The Struggle for Civil Rights in Mississippi*, University of Illinois Press, 1995.

12. Mabel B. Casner and Ralph H. Gabriel, *The Story of American Democracy*, Harcourt, Brace, 1943, pp. 346–52.

13. Charles Grayson Summersell, *Alabama History for Schools*, 3rd edition, American Southern, 1965, p. 232.

14. Joyce Appleby, Alan Brinkley, and James M. McPherson, *The American Journey*, Glencoe-McGraw Hill, 1998.

15. Interview with the author, Nov. 4, 2009.

16. Interview with the author, Sept. 17, 2009.

17. Ireland, "Black Confederates."

Notes

4. Shadow History

1. "Carolina Mob Kills Woman's Attacker," *Washington Post*, June 22, 1930, p. M1.
2. "Old Negro Is Found Dead in Tiger River," *Atlanta Constitution*, June 9, 1906, p. 5.
3. Bruce E. Baker, *This Mob Will Surely Take My Life: Lynchings in the Carolinas, 1871–1946*, Continuum, 2008, pp. 18–19.
4. Appendix to *Congressional Globe*, 42nd Congress, 1st session, April 1871, pp. 293–94; Report and Minority views, Feb. 19, 1872, p. 35.
5. Interview with the author, June 15, 2010.
6. She will be eligible for parole in 2024, when she is fifty-three.
7. Paul Harvey, *Freedom's Coming: Religious Culture and the Shaping of the South from the Civil War Through the Civil Rights Era*, University of North Carolina Press, 2005, pp. 67–77.
8. Speech of Rep. J. H. Sloss, 6th District of Alabama, Appendix to *Congressional Globe*, 42nd Congress, 1st Sess., April 4, 1872, p. 268.
9. *Loewen v. Turnipseed*, 488 F. Supp. 1138, N.D. of Mississippi, 1980.
10. Sterling Stuckey, Linda Kerrigan, and Judith Irvin Salvucci, reading consultant, *Call to Freedom* (Texas edition), Holt, Rinehart & Winston, 2000, p. 636.
11. Interview with the author, Aug. 6, 2010.
12. Philip Dray, *By the Hands of Persons Unknown: The Lynching of Black America*, Modern Library, 2002, p. 14.
13. *The African American Desk Reference*, John Wiley & Sons, 1999, p. 317.
14. James Allen, *Without Sanctuary: Lynching Photography in America*, Twin Palms Publishers, 2000.
15. Interview with the author, Aug. 5, 2010.
16. Lillian Smith, *Killers of the Dream*, W. W. Norton & Company, 1949, p. 1.
17. One exception was Hodding Carter III, whose father was a Mississippi newspaperman well known for his progressive views on racial equality. Another was a friend of mine, Jim Auchmutey, an Atlanta journalist whose father was from Bartow County, which adjoins the county where the infamous anti-Semitic Leo Frank lynching took place. Auchmutey recalls hearing his father talk about that event, as well as a more obscure lynching of a black man in Bartow County.

251

18. This would have been the June 1940 lynching of Elbert Williams, a black resident who was involved in voter registration efforts. Source: Department of Justice Classified Subject Files on Civil Rights, 1914–1949, http://cisupa.proquest.com/ksc_assets/catalog/101768.pdf.
19. E-mail to the author, July 26, 2010.
20. Dray, *By the Hands of Persons Unknown*, p. xi.
21. James C. Cobb, *The Most Southern Place on Earth: The Mississippi Delta and the Roots of Regional Identity*, Oxford University Press, 1992, p. 158.
22. *Loving v. Virginia*, 388 U.S. 1 (1967), fn 5. In 1967, every one of the eleven states of the Old Confederacy had such laws; in addition, so did Delaware, Kentucky, Missouri, and Oklahoma.
23. Wendy Wang, "The Rise of Intermarriage: Rates, Characteristics Vary by Race and Gender," Pew Center for Research into Social Change, Feb. 6, 2012, p. 1, http://www.pewsocialtrends.org/2012/02/16/the-rise-of-intermarriage/2/#fn-10818-2.
24. Ibid., p. 46.
25. This is based on an analysis of 2007 U.S. Census Bureau statistics done for me by the National Institute for Computer Assisted Reporting at the University of Missouri.
26. Paul Taylor, Cary Funk, and April Clark, "As Marriage and Parenthood Drift Apart, Public Is Concerned About Social Impact," Pew Center for Research into Social Change, July 1, 2007, p. 25.
27. Wang, "The Rise of Intermarriage," p. 35.
28. Kenneth M. Stampp, *The Peculiar Institution*, Vintage, 1956, p. 351.
29. My preliminary research into this issue has yielded no real clues; later, when I have time, maybe I'll get back to it.

5. Jesusland

1. Figures from the 2007 U.S. Religious Landscape Survey, conducted by the Pew Forum on Religion and Public Life, http://religions.pewforum.org/.
2. © Don Peters/BMI.
3. Alison Pond, Gregory Smith, and Scott Clement, "Religion Among the Millennials," Pew Forum on Religion and Public Life, Feb. 2010, http://www.pewforum.org/uploadedFiles/Topics/Demographics/Age/millennials-report.pdf.
4. *The Carolina Backcountry on the Eve of the Revolution: The Journal and*

Other Writings of Charles Woodmason, Anglican Itinerant, University of North Carolina Press, 1953, p. 96.

5. Ibid., p. 53.

6. Christine Leigh Heyrman, *Southern Cross: The Beginnings of the Bible Belt,* Alfred A. Knopf, 1997, p. 6.

7. C. Vann Woodward, *Origins of the New South, 1877–1913,* Louisiana State University Press, 1951, p. 449.

8. Charles Reagan Wilson, *Baptized in Blood: The Religion of the Lost Cause, 1865–1920,* University of Georgia Press, 1980, p. 62.

9. W. E. B. Du Bois, *The Souls of Black Folk,* chapter X.

10. Interview with the author, Oct. 30, 2009.

11. Interview with the author, Oct. 7, 2009.

12. Kevin M. Kruse, *White Flight: Atlanta and the Making of Modern Conservatism,* Princeton University Press, 2005, p. 9.

13. Darren Dochuk, *From Bible Belt to Sunbelt: Plain-Folk Religion, Grassroots Politics, and the Rise of Evangelical Conservatism,* W. W. Norton, 2011.

14. The living embodiment of this religious-political fusion is Newt Gingrich—who was just starting his political career about this time and who, like the fundamentalist strain of religious thought itself, is not a Southern native: he was born in Pennsylvania and grew up on a series of military bases. When Gingrich became House speaker in 1994, he urged his newly elected Republican lawmakers to spend as little time as possible in Washington and not to socialize with Washington insiders, so as to avoid their corrupting influence. A former Bible-bred kid like me could easily detect the coded message, contained in II Corinthians 6:14, "Be ye not unequally yoked with unbelievers."

15. Daniel K. Williams, *God's Own Party: The Making of the Christian Right,* Oxford University Press, 2010, p. 159.

16. Only 23 percent of those in the McCain Belt thought that homosexuality was a way of life that should be accepted by society, compared to 52 percent of all Americans; 37 percent thought abortion should be legal in most or all cases, compared with 53 percent of all Americans; 62 percent disagreed with the theory of evolution, compared to 44 percent of all Americans; 51 percent thought that "Hollywood values" were a threat to their own values, compared to 51 percent of all Americans.

17. Samuel Hill, "Fundamentalism in Recent Southern Culture: Has It Done What the Civil Rights Movement Couldn't Do?" *Journal of Southern Religion*, vol. 1, 1998.
18. Bethany Moreton, *To Serve God and Wal-Mart: The Making of Christian Free Enterprise*, Harvard University Press, 2009, p. 5.
19. Statistics are from the Hartford Institute for Religion Research, http://hirr.hartsem.edu/.
20. David Van Biema and Jeff Chu, "Does God Want You to Be Rich?" *Time*, Sept. 10, 2006.
21. Kathleen Hladky, "I Double-Dog Dare You in Jesus' Name! Claiming Christian Wealth and the American Prosperity Gospel," *Religion Compass*, vol. 6, no. 1, Jan. 12, 2012, http://onlinelibrary.wiley.com/doi/10.1111/j.1749-8171.2011.00325.x/pdf.
22. Elliott Wright, "Missionary in Oklahoma May Be United Methodist First from China," *Global Ministries News Archives*, Sept. 14, 2010.
23. W. Bradford Wilcox, "How Focused on the Family? Christian Conservatives, the Family and Sexuality," paper for Russell Sage Foundation, 2009, http://www.virginia.edu/sociology/News/HowFocusedontheFamily-wbw-gerson.pdf. Also, Ron Lesthaeghe and Lisa Niedert, "The Second Demographic Transition in the U.S.: Spatial Patterns and Correlates," Report 06-592, March 2006, University of Michigan Population Studies Center, http://www.psc.isr.umich.edu/pubs/pdf/rr06-592.pdf.
24. Interview with the author, Nov. 5, 2009.
25. Interview with the author, Dec. 2, 2011.
26. Cathleen Falsani, "On Evangelical Campuses, Rumblings of Gay Acceptance," Religious News Service, March 1, 2011.
27. "The Future of Evangelicals: A Conversation with Pastor Rick Warren," Pew Forum on Religion and Public Life, Nov. 13, 2009, http://www.pewforum.org/Christian/Evangelical-Protestant-Churches/The-Future-of-Evangelicals-A-Conversation-with-Pastor-Rick-Warren.aspx#2.

6. The Sorting Out

1. Interview with Maria Kefalas, coauthor of Patrick J. Carr and Maria J. Kefalas, *Hollowing Out the Middle: The Rural Brain Drain and What It Means for America*, Beacon, 2009, conducted Jan. 27, 2010.
2. Roberto Gallardo and Bill Bishop, "The B.A. Divide," *Daily Yonder*,

Oct. 18, 2010, http://www.dailyyonder.com/ba-divide/2010/10/17/ 2995.

3. William W. Falk, Larry L. Hunt, and Matthew O. Hunt, "Return Migrations of African-Americans to the South: Reclaiming a Land of Promise, Going Home, or Both?," *Rural Sociology*, vol. 69, no. 4, Dec. 2004, p. 490.

4. Centers for Disease Control, http://www.cdc.gov/obesity/data/index .html.

5. U.S. Department of Agriculture, http://maps.ers.usda.gov/FoodAtlas/ foodenv5.aspx.

6. Ibid.

7. "County Health Rankings: Mobilizing Action Toward Community Health," Robert Wood Johnson Foundation and University of Wisconsin Population Health Institute, http://www.countyhealth rankings.org/mississippi/coahoma.

8. Shaila K. Dewan, "Civil Rights Battlegrounds Enter World of Tourism," *New York Times*, Aug. 10, 2004.

9. Wendell Berry, "The Whole Horse," in *The New Agrarianism: Land, Culture and the Community of Life*, ed. Eric T. Freyfogle, Island Press, 2001, p. 63.

10. Andrew Lytle, "The Hind Tit," in 12 Southerners, *I'll Take My Stand: The South and the Agrarian Tradition*, Harper & Brothers, 1930, p. 205.

11. Freyfogle, *The New Agrarianism*, p. xiii.

12. Ibid.

13. Berry, "The Whole Horse," p. 64.

14. You can detect this tone of defensive superiority throughout *I'll Take My Stand*, and it pops up in surprising ways even today. About three-fourths of the way through Alexandra Pelosi's 2008 election documentary, *Right America, Feeling Wronged: Some Voices from the Campaign Trail*, the filmmaker (daughter of former speaker of the House Nancy Pelosi) stopped at a gas station in rural Mississippi to interview a white truck driver. If the filmmakers were looking for the typical White Southern Redneck, they had found their specimen. The truck driver was in the middle of making the usual racism-in-code objections to Barack Obama when two black men who had been sitting nearby suddenly interrupted the interview. They didn't object to the white truck driver's opinions; what burned them were

Pelosi's questions, and her status as a non-Southerner. "Like they don't say 'nigger' or 'coon' in New York! They [the filmmakers] gonna paint Mississippi like it's bad!" one of the men exclaimed as the camera swung around. "You should be ashamed of yourself, Miss Liberal!"

15. 12 Southerners, *I'll Take My Stand*, p. 14.

16. John Shelton Reed, *One South! An Ethnic Approach to Regional Culture*, Louisiana State University Press, 1982, p. 162.

17. Sabrina Tavernise, "Parenting by Gays More Common in the South, Census Shows," *New York Times*, January 16, 2011.

18. Isabel Wilkerson, *The Warmth of Other Suns: The Epic Story of America's Great Migration*, Random House, 2010.

7. Atlanta

1. Daniel Weinberg, "U.S. Neighborhood Income Inequality in the 2005–2009 Period," U.S. Census Bureau, American Community Survey Reports, p. 10 ff.

2. Frank, who was Jewish, was an Atlanta pencil factory manager accused of the rape and murder of a young employee, Mary Phagan; he was convicted and sentenced to death in what is now regarded as an unfair trial. When the governor commuted Frank's sentence to life, an angry mob kidnapped him from his cell and hanged him.

3. *The Complete Orations and Speeches of Henry W. Grady*, ed. Edwin Du Bois Shurter, Hinds, Noble & Eldredge, 1910, pp. 14–19.

4. W. J. Cash, *The Mind of the South*, Alfred A. Knopf, 1941, p. 176.

5. When the Boeing Corporation was faced with a strike by union workers at its Puget Sound factory, the company announced plans to move a production line to South Carolina, a nonunionized, "right-to-work" state. The move earned a rebuke from the National Labor Relations Board, which found that the move had been a direct retaliation against the union. Joe Atkins, "The Ghost of Henry Grady Hovers over the GOP's Drive to Undermine the NLRB," *Facing South*, posted May 17, 2011, http://www.southernstudies.org/2011/05/voices-the-ghost-of-henry-grady-hovers-over-the-gops-drive-to-undermine-the-nlrb.html.

6. Quoted in C. Vann Woodward, *Origins of the New South, 1877–1913*, Louisiana State University Press, 1951, p. 257.

7. "Birmingham Coal District Strike of 1908," in *Encyclopedia of Alabama*,

Auburn University, http://www.encyclopediaofalabama.org/face/Article.jsp?id=h-1478.

8. Southerners are still more likely to defend property with violence: one analysis of nonurban crime rates and attitudes toward violence of Southerners and non-Southerners showed that Southerners are roughly twice as likely as non-Southerners to "agree a great deal" with the idea that it is acceptable to kill an intruder in order to defend one's home. Richard E. Nisbett and Dov Cohen, *Culture of Honor: The Psychology of Violence in the South*, HarperCollins, 1996, p. 27. The way the Southern reverence for property values plays out in real life can be fascinating. In 1994, for example, the Florida legislature was considering a proposal to pay reparations to the survivors of the infamous Rosewood massacre of 1923, in which an entire black town in north-central Florida was burned to the ground by rampaging whites. Survivors and their descendants based their claim on the grounds that state officials had stood by and allowed the white mob to literally run riot, a clear violation of the civil rights of the black citizens of Rosewood. Conservatives in the legislature opposed the payments and the matter had reached a stalemate when lawyers for the Rosewood survivors switched tactics. Okay, they told the conservative holdouts, let's forget the civil rights argument here; there's still the fact that a whole lot of property was destroyed in this unfortunate . . . event, or whatever you'd like us to call it, and surely you can see that these people have a pretty good argument for compensation for all those houses and businesses that got burned down. The legislature promptly approved a payment of $1.85 million. (Anecdote courtesy of Rosewood plaintiffs' attorney Martha Barnett, interviewed on July 21, 2010.)

9. The riot was sparked by incendiary headlines in the *Atlanta Constitution*, among other newspapers, about four alleged assaults on white women downtown by black men. The assaults were never substantiated, but before the violence was over somewhere between two dozen and four dozen black men were killed at the hands of white mobs.

10. Kevin M. Kruse, *White Flight: Atlanta and the Making of Modern Conservatism*, Princeton University Press, 2005, p. 34.

11. Priscilla Painton, "Bond Keeps His Cool, Retains Popularity in Midst of Crisis," *Atlanta Journal-Constitution*, May 17, 1987.

12. Franklin's successor was Kasim Reed, who was elected in January 2010; he spent most of his first two years in office dealing with the city's underfunded pension program. It's too soon to evaluate his tenure, but as a Morehouse College alumnus, he is a member of the so-called Morehouse Mafia, which has long played a big role in city government.
13. Occasionally you will see statistics showing that the population of Atlanta is actually becoming increasingly white. This is true within the relatively small city limits, where it is due mainly to gentrification. This trend has important ramifications for city politics, but in terms of numbers it's dwarfed by the overall increase of blacks in the ten-county Atlanta metropolitan region.
14. William W. Falk, Larry L. Hunt, and Matthew O. Hunt, "Return Migrations of African-Americans to the South: Reclaiming a Land of Promise, Going Home, or Both?" *Rural Sociology*, vol. 69, no. 4, Dec. 2004, p. 490.
15. William Jelani Cobb, "Letter from Atlanta: The North and South of a City's Transformation," *Ebony*, Feb. 29, 2008.
16. "Homes, Not Handcuffs: The Criminalization of Homelessness in U.S. Cities," National Law Center on Homelessness and Poverty and the National Coalition for the Homeless, July 2009, http://nlchp.org/content/pubs/2009HomesNotHandcuffs1.pdf.
17. Melissa Turner, "Want a Job or a Contract? It's Who You Know," *Atlanta Journal-Constitution*, August 10, 2000.
18. Larry Keating, *Race, Class and Urban Expansion*, Temple University Press, 2001, p. 52.
19. Ibid., p. 200.
20. Interview with the author, Aug. 13, 2011.
21. Frederick Allen, "Crime Isn't Task Force's Real Worry," *Atlanta Journal-Constitution*, May 31, 1987, p. C1.
22. Based on 2010 U.S. Census figures analyzed by the University of Michigan Population Studies Center, http://www.psc.isr.umich.edu/dis/census/segregation2010.html. The Atlanta metro area ranks 59 on the 1-to-100 "dissimilarity index"—a tool used by demographers as a rough measurement of the extent of racial segregation. Chicago, Detroit, and Cleveland ranked 76.4, 75.3, and 74.1 respectively. A score of 0 would mean there were no neighborhoods where any particular ethnic group predominated; a score of 100 would theoretically apply to a place like, say, Gadsden, Alabama, in 1930.

23. Carol Morello, "Study: Income Does Not Explain Segregation Patterns in Housing," *Washington Post*, Aug. 2, 2011 http://www.washingtonpost.com/local/study-income-does-not-explain-segregation-patterns-in-housing/2011/08/01/gIQAJrLgoI_story.html.

24. Sue Sturgis, "Institute Index: U.S. Income Inequality Greatest in the South," *Facing South*, Institute for Southern Studies, Oct. 27, 2011. Figures based on analysis of data from a Congressional Budget Office report, "Trends in the Distribution of Household Income 1979 to 2007."

25. Statistics from Trust for Public Land, http://cloud.tpl.org/pubs/ccpe_Acreage_and_Employees_Data_2010.pdf. These figures do not represent very recent park development in Atlanta as a result of the BeltLine project, but even when this is factored in Atlanta has less parkland than any major city its size.

26. As an example, Larry Keating cites statistics from 1960, a year in which whites in Atlanta had access to twenty public football fields, while blacks had access to none. There were sixteen white recreation centers and only three for blacks; twelve white swimming pools, eight for blacks; twenty-two white baseball fields, three for blacks; 119 white tennis courts, eight for blacks; forty-two white parks, eight for blacks. Keating, *Race, Class and Urban Expansion*, p. 99.

27. Kruse, *White Flight*, p. 106.

28. Barbara J. Lipman, "A Heavy Load: The Combined Housing and Transportation Burdens of Working Families," Center for Housing Policy, 2006, p. 11.

29. The Housing + Transportation Affordability Index, a project of the Brookings Institution Urban Markets Initiative, http://htaindex.cnt.org/mapping_tool.php#region=Atlanta%2C%20GA&theme_menu=0&layer1=23&layer2=24.

30. Not all, though; a few are transplants who went native—including my friend Rick Allen, a New Yorker by birth who boasts of having been given the Jefferson Davis Medal by the Alfred Holt Colquitt chapter of the Daughters of the Confederacy, the UDC's highest civilian honor. He treasures the memory, he wrote, in part because of a certain number of native Southerners and True Believers who were in the audience that day, watching this apostasy "with their jaws agape and their dewlaps quivering."

8. Old Times There Are Not Forgotten

1. From the files of the Southern Claims Commission #12232, Office #74, Report #3, hearing held March 11, 1872, in Randolph County, Alabama. The SCC was a body convened by Congress to consider claims for reimbursement filed by Union loyalists in the South who had lost property to the U.S. government during the Civil War. My great-great-great-grandfather, Thomas Thompson, was one of those who filed a claim. The details above are gleaned from the stenographic records of his testimony, as well as that of two of his sons and two of his neighbors.

2. By my count—and I may be off by one or two—of the 103 members of Congress currently identified as being with the Tea Party, 55 are from the South—and out of the 160 members of Congress who are from the states of the Old Confederacy, 55 are aligned with the Tea Party. That's probably an understatement, because lots of Southern Republicans these days may not be explicitly signed up with the Tea Party, but their positions are fairly similar. In the vote to end the government shutdown of October 2013, Southern Republican whites voted overwhelmingly against the deal—73 against, 18 in favor, while the rest of the party was evenly split (69 in favor, 71 against).

3. Religious Landscape Survey, Pew Research Religion and Public Life Project, http://religions.pewforum.org/.

4. "A Look at Castle Doctrine and Stand Your Ground Laws by State," Lawyers Committee for Civil Rights Under Law, August 2013, http://www.lawyerscommittee.org/admin/public_policy/documents /files/Stand-Your-Ground-Castle-Doctrine-Map-LC-Logo8.13.13 .pdf.

5. See *Confederate Nationalism: Ideology and Identity in the Civil War South*, Drew Gilpin Faust, Louisiana State University Press, 1988.

6. "'The Central Event of Our Past': Still Murky," Andrew Delbanco, *New York Review of Books*, Feb. 9, 2012, p. 19.

INDEX

Page numbers beginning with 247 refer to notes.

Index

Index

Index

Hill, Samuel, 111, 124–25
Hispanic immigrants, 13, 17–18, 19–20,
  23, 26–30, 31, 38, 107, 130, 143,
  154, 198, 234–35
  see also Mexican immigrants and im-
    migration
history:
  identity and, 5–6, 7, 92, 232, 243–44
  integration of, 99–100
  Southerners' willful ignorance of,
    11–12, 38–39, 57–58, 65–69, 71–73,
    75–80, 163, 183–84, 227–28, 232,
    233, 240–41, 243
homosexuality, 138, 139, 143
Hope in the Cities, 102–3
Hose, Sam, 70, 105, 227, 243
housing:
  affordable, Atlanta's lack of, 180, 206,
    225–26
  racial covenants on, 116
Howard, Robert, 72
Hughes, Mose, 61
Hunter, Floyd, 187

identity:
  history and, 5–6, 7, 92, 232, 243–44
  race and, 81
Ifill, Sherrilyn, 77
I'll Take My Stand (12 Southerners), 144,
  145, 160, 255
immigrants, immigration, 17–40, 77, 234
  in antebellum South, 20–21, 28, 77,
    109, 122, 186
  in Atlanta, 179, 197–98
  as drain on public services, 27–28
  illegal, 19, 23–24, 27–28, 29, 237, 248
  legal, 30
  self-identification of, 17–18, 25
  as Southerners, 39–40
  stereotyping of, 17
  work-ethic of, 30–31
  see also specific nationalities

immigration laws, 26–27
immigration reform, 35–36
income inequality, 143–44, 200–203, 212
Indian immigrants, 19, 23, 39
individual rights:
  slavery and, 185–86
integration, 82–83, 116–18
Internet, genealogical research and, 64,
  84–85
interracial marriage and relationships, 9,
  13–14, 81–93, 235, 242

Jackson, Lynn McKinley, 78–80
Jackson, Maynard, 181, 193–94, 195–96,
  207
Jackson, Miss., 97–98
Jackson, Stonewall, 111
Jakes, T. D., 128
Jenkins, Dan, 60–61, 77–78
Jews, 1–2, 116
Jim Crow era, 9, 14, 22, 48, 71, 113, 163,
  179, 198, 211, 213, 235
Jindal, Bobby, 39
job loss, 142, 150
Johnson, Ceona, 104
Johnson, Lyndon, 117
Johnson, Robert, 147
Johnson City, Tenn., 76, 77
Justice Department, U.S., 95

Keating, Larry, 205, 207, 259
Keenan, Modest, 60, 62–63
Kelly, Ola Jean, 63–64
Kentucky, 114, 248
Kenyon, E. W., 128
Killen, Edgar Ray, 95
King, Martin Luther, Jr., 35, 101, 155,
  194, 226
Kingsport, Tenn., 76
Kout, Yacine, 17, 40, 41
Kovach, Bill, 76–77
Kruse, Kevin, 117–18, 214–15

Index

Index

Index

South, rural (*cont.*)
depopulation of, 21–22, 23, 119, 141–42, 143, 148–49, 152–55, 170–71
health care in, 151
schools in, 152–54
tourism in, 155–57
South, urban-suburban, 22, 124, 145
black remigration to, 174–77, 199–200, 215
pro-business doctrine in, 171–72
rural migration to, 142, 143
sprawl in, 171, 215
see also Atlanta, Ga.
South Africa, 39, 93, 96, 97
South Carolina, 15, 20, 21, 26, 30, 47, 109, 256
southern California, fundamentalism in, 119–20
Southern diaspora, 2, 119, 248
Southerners:
adaptability of, 11
antiauthoritarianism of, 186
blacks as, 3, 14, 20–21, 174
civility as expectation of, 211
code of silence observed by, 69, 71–73
cognitive dissonance of, 7, 75, 221–22
conflation of community and place in, 164–65, 168–71
conservatism of, 10–11, 221, 237
cultural similarities of Mexicans and, 33, 34–35
as "different," 1, 22, 38
in disentanglement from Confederate legacy, 241
dual identity of, 2, 241
exceptionalism of, 106, 107, 112, 163
government intervention opposed by, 9, 118, 120
idealized image of, 33, 49, 232
identity of, 2–3, 7–8, 37–40, 231, 232, 239, 241–44

immigrants as, 39–40
inferiority complex of, 180, 204, 255–56
insulation of, 15, 22, 38
Jews compared to, 1–2
property rights venerated by, 9, 117–18, 185–86, 216, 237, 257
race and, *see* race; racism
religion and, *see* religion
self-awareness as lacking in, 12–13, 49
slavery and, *see* slaves, slavery
stereotyping of, 1, 3, 11, 22
willful historical ignorance of, 11–12, 38–39, 57–58, 65–69, 71–73, 75–80, 163, 183–84, 227–28, 232, 233, 240–41, 243; *see also* Lost Cause myth
"Southern hospitality," 172–73, 210–11, 249
Southern Renaissance, 49
Southern Truth and Reconciliation (STAR), 100
Spelman College, 190, 211
Spiers, Elizabeth, 75
Standard Life Insurance Company, 190
Starkville, Miss., 219
states' rights, 12, 42, 46–47, 52–53, 236
Stephens, Alexander, 46–47
Supreme Court, U.S., 82, 115. 117, 190
Swaggart, Jimmy, 128

Talbot, Bill, 156, 157
Tea Party, 139, 236, 260
Tennessee, 15, 18, 75, 76
Texas, 15, 16, 42, 47, 99
textbooks:
Civil War as portrayed in, 42, 46–48
lynching and, 67–68
political correctness accusations and, 50–51
separate Southern editions of, 51–52, 65
Thackeray, William Makepeace, 46
Thomas, Patricia Moncure, 68–69, 87–92

About the Author

Tracy Thompson is a former *Washington Post* reporter and essayist who has written about subjects ranging from psychiatry to law to the Civil War. She is the author of *The Beast: A Reckoning with Depression* and *The Ghost in the House*. She lives just outside Washington, D.C., with her husband, their two daughters, one tabby cat, and an enthusiastic beagle named Max.